The Traffic in Women's Work

The Traffic in Women's Work

East European Migration and the Making of Europe

Anca Parvulescu

The University of Chicago Press
Chicago and London

Anca Parvulescu is associate professor at Washington University in St. Louis. She is the author of *Laughter: Notes on a Passion*.

The University of Chicago Press, Chicago 60637
The University of Chicago Press, Ltd., London

Printed in the United States of America

23 22 21 20 19 18 17 16 15 14 1 2 3 4 5

ISBN-13: 978-0-226-11824-6 (cloth)
ISBN-13: 978-0-226-11838-3 (paper)
ISBN-13: 978-0-226-11841-3 (e-book)
DOI: 10.7208/chicago/9780226118413.001.0001

Library of Congress Cataloging-in-Publication Data
Parvulescu, Anca, author.
The traffic in women's work : East European migration and the making of Europe / Anca Parvulescu.
pages cm
Includes bibliographical references and index.
ISBN 978-0-226-11824-6 (cloth : alk. paper)—ISBN 978-0-226-11838-3 (pbk. : alk. paper)—ISBN 978-0-226-11841-3 (e-book) 1. Women immigrants—Abuse of—European Union countries. 2. Women—Europe, Eastern—Social conditions. 3. Human trafficking—European Union countries. I. Title.
JV7595.P379 2014
305.4094—dc23

2013022930

♾ This paper meets the requirements of ANSI/NISO Z39.48–1992 (Permanence of Paper).

For my parents

Contents

Acknowledgments

I would like to thank the colleagues who, in various forms, have engaged with my project: Iver Bernstein, J. Dillon Brown, Colin Burnett, Adrienne Davis, Deborah Dinner, Steven Meyer, Linda Nicholson, Paula Rabinowitz, Carolyn Sargent, Jani Scandura, Wolfram Schmidgen, and Rebecca Wanzo. I would also like to thank the chairs of my two departments, Vincent Sherry and Joe Loewenstein, for their support over the last few years.

Julia Musha and Kate Fama helped me edit the manuscript. I am grateful to my undergraduate research assistant, Kristen Valaika, for her invaluable work. Undergraduate students enrolled in three versions of a course titled "The Traffic in Women and European Cinema" have offered the best experimental public forum I could have wished for.

The project benefited from support from the American Councils for International Education, the Center for the Humanities at Washington University, and the dean's office at Washington University.

Chapters 2 and 3 have been previously published as "European Kinship: Eastern European Women Go to Market" (*Critical Inquiry* 37, no. 2 [Winter 2011]: 187–213) and "Import/Export: Housework in an International Frame" (*PMLA* 127, no. 4 [October 2012]: 845–62).

Introduction

In the midst of an economic crisis that seemed to threaten the very existence of the European Union, Umberto Eco, the Italian writer and scholar, proposed the formation of an exchange program that would require not only students but also all workers to study in one European country other than that of their birth. Eco had a particular outcome in mind: "The university exchange program Erasmus is barely mentioned in the business sections of newspapers, yet Erasmus has created the first generation of young Europeans. I call it a sexual revolution: a young Catalan man meets a Flemish girl—they fall in love, they get married and they become European, as do their children. The Erasmus idea should be compulsory—not just for students, but also for taxi drivers, plumbers and other workers. By this, I mean they need to spend time in other countries within the European Union; they should integrate."[1] A study of contemporary fictional narratives of post-1989 European "integration," this book takes Eco's proposal at face value. Indeed, what is the relation between European integration and a workers' "exchange program" that seems to be bringing about a "sexual revolution"? Instead of focusing on the exemplary Europeanness of a Flemish/Catalan encounter, however, this book explores situations in which a fictive

East European woman, young or old, participates in a symbolic exchange program in West Europe. She does so as a worker, engaging in tasks historically performed by a wife. She might function as a domestic, a nanny, a caretaker, an entertainer, a sex worker, or, indeed, a wife. Although her work is for the most part not sexual in nature, it is often sexualized. Taking statements like Eco's as a starting point, the book aims to uncover the political economy of European culture in a post-1989 framework in order to ask questions about the meanings of transnational marriage and, especially, labor-based *marital-like* relations in the context of East/West European unification.

In Europe, 1989 is synonymous with the fall of the Berlin Wall and German reunification. The year also marks the beginning of what we have come to call the *New Europe*—a Europe reunited across its West/East Cold War divide. In the wake of the Maastricht Treaty (1992), the European Union has been premised on what are called the *four freedoms*: the free movement of goods, services, capital, and persons. This book starts from the premise that an important niche within the European exchange of persons is the gender-specific circulation of East European women in West Europe. Their mobility can be understood through the lens of a concept associated with Claude Lévi-Strauss: the traffic in women. This is not the traffic in women invoked by the media to refer to sex trafficking per se but a broad anthropological concept that describes the circulation of women between kinship groups, traditionally through marriage. Though anchored in its historical and theoretical configurations, the concept acquires new meanings and combinatory possibilities in the current moment. In this book, it explains the movement of women *as* women within Europe, locally and internationally, legally and illegally. The rhetoric of "the European family," often used by EU officials as well as by European media East and West to describe post-1989 unification, suggests that Europe is today figured as a symbolic structure of kinship. The argument of this book is that the traffic in women broadly understood is not a side effect of Europeanization but one of the *forms* that Europeanization takes. The fictional texts this book engages demonstrate that, in today's Europe, East European women, alongside women from the global South, are "exchanged" so that they can do a lot of the physical household work and the immaterial, caring labor traditionally performed by a wife within the institution of marriage.[2] Eco is right: marriage seems to be making Europe, but the institution of marriage needs to be historicized. Reproduction, broadly understood, is, indeed, at stake, but the meanings of contemporary reproduction require extensive qualification.

Pluralizing Europe

What does *Europe* stand for today? Europe is an elusive geographic reality, a peninsular-shaped continent with disputed borders, especially in the East. As a historical category, *Europe* is the outcome of a long list of cyclic processes of selective solidification and dissolution.[3] It is especially challenging to describe a historical Europe that would encompass its Western and Eastern regions alike. Finally, if one is tempted to think of a cultural or philosophical Europe, there is no "idea of Europe" that can gather all Europeans, East and West, under its aegis, although there have been myriad attempts to do so.

Rather than conclude that "Europe does not exist," let us nonetheless acknowledge the existence of many Europes, beginning with colonial Europe. This is the *Europe* that functioned as the name of the civilization behind a self-appointed colonial mission. An essential part of the education Robinson Crusoe gives Friday concerns Europe: "I described to him the country of Europe, particularly England, which I came from; how we lived, how we worshipped God, how we behaved to one another, and how we traded in ships to all parts of the world."[4] Friday's education is long and tedious and involves the reintegration of his culture's knowledge into a new, colonial horizon. The long-term goal of this education is to make "the country of Europe, particularly England," the new center of Friday's universe. To a large extent, Europe figured itself as Europe through the education of Friday. It is through this process that it defined its essential features as progress, individualism, Christianity, civility, private property, the state, and liberty; it is through this process that European modernity emerged and became consolidated. It follows that the postcolonial call is to "provincialize Europe," *England* being the name of one European particularism.[5]

In close conjunction to colonial Europe, there is the Europe that has served as a foil for the invention of "Eastern Europe."[6] The Cold War remapping of Europe is only one installment in the long history of "Eastern Europe." This Europe is part of a continent that goes by the name *Europe* but, not being Western, is therefore not European. As a result, the countries of East Europe have a history of needing to either *prove* their Europeanness or actively *produce* it. They cannot be too Balkan or too Slavic if they are to be European.[7] An example of this kind of positioning is the post-1989 resurrection of the concept of Central Europe, which made it possible for Poles, Czechs, and Hungarians (with many other East Europeans happy to join the bandwagon) to claim that they are not in fact East European. They anchor such claims in their Catholicism, the right kind of colonial history (Austro-Hungarian rather than Ottoman or Russian), and culture.[8] By contrast with the positive connotations of *Central*, *Eastern* is tainted with "Oriental" and thus with the "Oriental despotism" that has historically served as Europe's other.[9]

The contemporary counterpart to the history of producing "Eastern Europe" in its relation to Europe is the process of applying for EU admission and subsequent EU funding, a process that facilitates these countries' "*return* to Europe" (Vaclav Havel coined the slogan in 1990). Are you making enough progress? Are you modern enough? Civilized enough? Hardworking enough? Multicultural enough? Conditions for EU "admission" aside, the paternalistic undercurrent is suggestive: European parents scolding prodigal East European children.[10] One is reminded that the European civilizing mission has been premised on colonial generosity aimed at helping colonies catch up with the great civilization.[11] "Eastern Europe" thus slides into Transitland Europe—a quasi Europe forever in transit toward Europe.[12]

To continue the list of various Europes, many argue for the existence of a cosmopolitan Europe, taking us back to Kant, a rediscovered European hero. Colonial and postcolonial questions return here, especially with Kant. One cannot but be suspicious of a certain kind of cosmopolitan stance, which amounts to saying (in Jacques Derrida's words): "I am (we are) all the more national for being European, all the more European for being trans-European and international; no one is more cosmopolitan and authentically universal than the one, than this 'we,' who is speaking to 'you.'"[13] Derrida reminds us that nationalism and cosmopolitanism are not mutually exclusive: a structure of nationalist exceptionalism underwrites cosmopolitanism. The risk is that, today, "we Europeans" claim exceptionality on account of a European culture of cosmopolitanism. The temptation is to believe that Europeans have left their troubled (colonial) past behind, performed a purifying mea culpa, and emerged as trueborn cosmopolitans. This is perhaps the most insidious form of European nationalism.

The next Europe on the list should be provincial Europe. Colonial Europe overlaps with metropolitan Europe, Europe as metropolis. This is the metropolis Dipesh Chakrabarty has in mind when he calls for the provincialization of Europe, failing to note that some parts of Europe have always been provincial.[14] There is, of course, a famous French provincialism, a foil to Parisian cosmopolitanism (Balzac's "man from the provinces" coming to Paris and becoming recognizable as a parvenu, among other things, on account of his provincialism). But vast regions of East Europe have also historically functioned as the cultural provinces of Paris or Vienna. In a comedy of manners dramatized by local elites, they adopted language, trends, and institutions from the metropolis.[15] Through this history, the adjective *Eastern European* emerged with resonances of provincialism, backwardness. The figure of the Eastern European Jew, burdened with his nonassimilable East Europeanness, remains illustrative here.[16]

The question of an international stratification of provinces in relation to the European metropolis returns forcefully today, on the margins of a range of popular culture artifacts. For example, Isabelle Mergault's romantic comedy *You Are So Beautiful* (2005) depicts a young, educated Romanian woman living in Bucharest and eager for a chance to live with an elderly man on a French farm. The province called *Bucharest* comes across as less desirable than an isolated, decrepit French farm. Although in some of the ivory towers of Paris the adjective *provincial* implicitly refers to Normandy, Algiers, and Bucharest alike, we need to distinguish between these heterogeneous provinces. Today, in addition to the task of rethinking the relation between the provincialization of Normandy and that of Algiers, we also need to assess Europe's production of Bucharest's provincialism, in order to understand the process through which "the woman from Bucharest" becomes recognizable as a European parvenu. In its turn, having learned its European lesson, Bucharest (which advertises itself as "Little Paris") produces its own, national provinces, such that men and women from the Romanian provinces are provincialized twice, once in relation to Bucharest, and a second time in relation to Paris.

The list of various Europes goes on, but let us end with the Europe of EU institutions, the Europe that Umberto Eco invokes. EU institutions are actively working toward the creation of Europe. The European Commission, the European Parliament, and the European Court of Justice are this Europe's building blocks. The European Central Bank has, in the recent economic crisis, emerged as another crucial European institution. For the purpose of this book, most relevant is the Europe created in the folds of the EU Culture Programme. Next to Erasmus, perhaps most successful among its projects has been the European Capitals of Culture initiative.[17] But all EU culture projects work to socialize would-be Europeans in a common European culture and create European identity. The results have been mixed. EU programs create identity effects involving a range of affective attachments—desire, fantasy, promise; critique, rejection, depression; or indifference. Tanja Ostojić created her poster *Untitled/After Courbet (L'origine du monde)* (2004), an eloquent comment on East European women's relation to Europe, for a publicity event celebrating Austria's presidency of the European Union (see fig. 0.1).

Fig. 0.1. Tanja Ostojić, *Untitled/After Courbet (L'origine du monde)* (2004). Color photograph, 46 × 55 cm. Photograph by David Rych. Copyright/courtesy of Ostojić/Rych.

This book traces the contours of a Europe created by EU institutions, often through projects that are not explicitly on the European Union's agenda. Europe is a "traveling culture," to use James Clifford's phrase, a network of heterogeneous travel relations.[18] Among the forms of mobility and immobility that make Europe today, it often seems that Europe comes together most forcefully through EU immigration policies. Europeans who are otherwise indifferent to or ignorant of the European Union care about this Europe, which often goes by the name *Fortress Europe*. EU institutions focusing on the security, prosperity, and mobility of EU citizens also produce, more or less wittingly, a market for illegal border crossing, economic exploitation, and violence. Alongside non-European migrants and immigrants, East Europeans who are not EU citizens *and* some East Europeans who are EU citizens inhabit the ensuing precarity.

The argument of this book is that the project of pluralizing Europe also needs to account for the Europe brought together through the traffic in East European women. Faced with Ostojić's poster, one realizes that what is called *enlargement* or *integration* is a process deeply invested in East European women's bodies, sexuality, and labor. The effect of EU policies on the ground is a certain kind of Americanization. This is not the Americanization of the 1990s, the much-debated McDonaldization of Europe. It is a more insidious Americanization understood through the lens of the racial and ethnic stratification of "women's work." An Americanized Europe is a Europe in which racial, ethnic, and citizenship stratifications are mapped onto occupational stratifications. One becomes a domestic worker in Italy on account of being *from* Romania. It is the fact of *being from* East Europe that qualifies women for certain occupations. Writing about the United States, Evelyn Nakano Glenn charges that substantive citizenship requires a minimum of economic security without which people cannot exercise their rights and therefore enjoy only partial citizenship.[19] East European citizens "admitted" into Europe without full access to the EU labor market, or with access to a market in which their training and skills are not recognized, are partial European citizens. The Polish women who for years have cared for the elderly in Germany through a complicated structure that allowed them to circumvent EU labor regulations belong in this category.

Analyzing the social and political realities of post-1989 Europe, Étienne Balibar speaks about an emerging European apartheid. In dialogue with Balibar, I warn against an emerging process of Americanization.[20] The European narrative of transnational upward mobility—the East European fantasy that traveling West translates into upward mobility—is played out against the background of this Americanization. The narrative promises access to the accoutrements of EU citizenship for those who do not have it, and it assumes that partial EU citizens can one day become full EU citizens. Winston Churchill's 1946 invocation of the United States of Europe returns today with new irony. Europe is becoming a United States of Europe, but not in the sense Churchill imagined. Pierre Bourdieu and Loïc Wacquant's outrage at the application of American concepts and methodologies to European realities notwithstanding, Europe is becoming an object of study for Americanists—when seen through the lens of the racial and ethnic stratification of women's work.[21]

As a matter of cultural practice, one continues to read any given European text in a national context while also attending to the work of EU institutions and the pressures of the global. It is one thing to be the only "Eastern girl" (a euphemism for an East European sex worker) in a small town in Finland and another thing to be one of the thousands of sex workers trying to make a go of it in Rome. It is one thing for the Eastern girl to be from Hungary and yet another for her to be from Belarus. The particular national contexts of Finland and Italy, on the one hand, and Hungary and Belarus, on the other, need to be unpacked. The heterogeneity of "Eastern Europe" needs to be permanently foregrounded, or the region risks becoming a bloc once again. So does the heterogeneity of Western Europe, lest one be guilty of the essentializing tendencies Edward Said's critics have identified in *Orientalism*.[22] At the same time, the market for the Eastern girl in Finland and Italy alike is a Europe effect; we must discuss the two cases in a comparative framework. The traffic in women is one such framework.

Let me be clear from the outset: I am not a Euroskeptic. The European Union emerged in the aftermath of World War II. It thrived on the idea that a united West Europe could placate fascism. One has to acknowledge that widespread contemporary forms of "everyday fascism" are a lesser evil than pre-1945 fascism. One cannot afford to be a Euroskeptic. At the same time, one cannot afford not to be skeptical of certain post-1989 European developments. J. G. A. Pocock asks an important question: "Why is it being suggested that one cannot be a skeptic about Europe without being a fanatical opponent?"[23] If I am critical of Europe, it is not because I think that the European project has no positive dimensions. It certainly does, and those positive dimensions have their advocates. But some of the questions I raise are not often heard, and that is why I focus on them.

The Traffic in Women

In the media, the phrase *traffic in women* refers strictly to coerced sex trafficking.[24] This is not how I use it. This book traces a number of fictional narratives about the European traffic in women broadly understood, including, at the two extreme poles of the law, the traffic in women in marriage and the traffic in women in coerced sex work, as well as the middle ground of women circulating as domestic workers, nannies, personal attendants, and entertainers. In my use of the phrase *traffic in women*, I draw on a concept articulated by the French anthropologist Claude Lévi-Strauss in *Elementary Structures of Kinship* (1949) and *Structural Anthropology* (1958, 1973). Lévi-Strauss described the formation of culture through a tripartite exchange of goods and services, signs, and women. *Traffic in women* referred to the exchange of women. Beyond an economic and linguistic exchange, culture, Lévi-Strauss proposed (in an argument that resonates with Eco's understanding of European culture), is produced through the circulation of women between elementary or complex kinship groups, through marriage. Following the critique and rearticulation of Lévi-Strauss's concept by second-wave feminists, Gayle Rubin most prominently, I extend the purview of the traffic in women so that it can serve as a critical lens through which to conceptualize the legal and illegal circulation of women *as* women internationally, at a time when culture has gone global. This notion of traffic in women describes phenomena of gendered transnational exchange like transnational marriage (e-brides, e.g.) but also labor situations in which women travel transnationally to engage in work that used to fall under the purview of women's work, traditionally performed without pay by a housewife. To put it simply, the book juxtaposes Gayle Rubin's "The Traffic in Women,"[25] Barbara Ehrenreich and Arlie Russell Hochschild's *Global Woman*, and the contemporary debate on Europe.

The word *traffic* in the phrase *traffic in women* suggests movement, carrying, according to the *OED*, etymological resonances of "commercial transportation of merchandise or passengers." It in fact suggests excessive movement (*traffic* is inherently "heavy traffic"). These connotations are both productive and potentially misleading in the context of this book. The traffic in women has historically been a local affair, with women circulating, indeed *moving*, on local trajectories, between adjacent kinship groups.[26] In the global moment, mobility has become central to a range of economic, political, and cultural phenomena, with crucial effects for contemporary kinship. It has thus become possible and necessary to think about the traffic in women in an international frame and bring mobility to bear on its articulations.

Sex, kinship, and labor (key ingredients of the Lévi-Straussian concept) have acquired both European and global dimensions in the last decades, making it possible for women to be circulated, and to put themselves in circulation, transnationally. This last point is crucial, given that commentators of Lévi-Strauss often read the traffic in women as a structure that moves women around as pawns on a board, leaving no room for their agency. In my use of the concept, East European women are at the same time subjected to structures that engender the paths they travel (Europe) and agents who make creative decisions along those paths and imagine alternatives.

Coerced sex trafficking, the most violent and publicized form of women's transnational circulation (especially East European women's circulation), is a *niche* of the broad, labor-based, transnational traffic in women understood in a Lévi-Straussian sense.[27] This is sex and affective labor that trafficked women do not control, it does not provide them with an income (although it is highly profitable for traffickers), and it is performed in dehumanizing circumstances.[28] This is labor that belongs to the traditional category *women's work* but is performed in particular *conditions*. The much-debated distinction between coerced and noncoerced sex work (corresponding to narrow and broad understandings, respectively, of the traffic in women) becomes sharper in contexts in which sex workers' organizations mobilize against coerced trafficking while making it clear that sex work is legitimate, income-producing work. Sex workers attempt to save trafficked women not from moral turpitude, the underlying assumption behind many UN- and state-sponsored programs, but rather from dehumanizing, camp-like labor conditions. It is in this sense that we need to understand the not-so-surprising fact that women who escape situations of coerced sex trafficking often return to sex work. When they do not, they try to get married or turn to other jobs on the continuum of women's work, like nursing.[29] In other words, they escape situations of coerced sex trafficking in order to participate in the more agentive and less violent sectors of the broad traffic in women. I discuss coerced sex trafficking in chapter 3, in order to place women's work in a biopolitical framework, with sex trafficking as the limit at which the biopolitical underpinnings of the contemporary traffic in women broadly understood become graspable.

The work of Michel Foucault reminds us that contemporary politics is invested in *life*—a concept that emerges in modernity as the coproduction of modern biology (whose unit of analysis is organic structure) and a new economics (which reinvents labor): "The organic becomes the living and the living is that which produces, grows and reproduces."[30] Labor, health, sexuality, family, death—and, indeed, migration[31]—become the domain of the politics of life: biopolitics. This book returns to a broad, biopolitical notion of reproduction, one invested equally in biology and political economy, as an entry point into the workings of contemporary biopolitics as seen through the lens of the traffic in women. Reproduction is today in the process of being radically reconfigured through new reproductive and regenerative technologies (on the biological side) and new, post-Fordist economic realities (on the political economy side). The two faces of reproduction have also acquired a transnational dimension in the last decades. On the biological side, we speak of globalized markets for adoption, egg donation, surrogacy, stem cell tissues, and clinical trials. On the economic side, we speak of a global market for domestic work, child and elder care, and sex work. East European women work in all these markets, which are interconnected, with different branches often overlapping.

To make use of reproduction (or, for that matter, the traffic in women or women's work) as a category of analysis is not to advocate for it, certainly not to endorse its familialist assumptions. Lee Edelman has argued passionately against "reproductive futurity," where reproduction is the horizon of a redemptive future revolving around the ideologically charged figure of the child.[32] I align my project with the spirit of Edelman's critique, which has become the spirit of a queer critique of reproduction. But Edelman works with a narrow understanding of reproduction as procreative heteronormativity, to which he opposes the queer death drive, a negativity that resists any social vision and future. Marxist and materialist feminist theories of reproduction, on the other hand, remind us that we all, Edelman's death-driven queer man included, engage in reproductive work and behaviors. For Marx, reproduction assures, first of all, that we all show up for work every day, and that we produce the next generation of workers, children. By limiting his analysis to the latter, Edelman offers a limited critique of reproduction. The risk is that, when the queer man rejects reproduction *tout court*, women from around the world continue to carry its burden—and not because they are mired in the ideology of the child. Edelman's Scrooge, like the protagonist of J. M. Coetzee's *Slow Man* (2005), might hire an East European nurse to care for him in his old age or in sickness. As long as he continues to live, even within the horizon of the death drive, the queer man reproduces himself from day to day, from one second to the next. To not pay attention to the political economy of reproduction is a luxury that queer theory cannot afford.

There has been a lot of talk about reproduction in Europe in the last decades. For the most part, the debate has been about Europeans' low birth rates, population aging, and perceived challenges associated with high reproduction rates in European immigrant communities (Foucault would have recognized the biopolitical debate par excellence, a mixture of concerns about the reproduction of the population and racism). Conservative commentators worry about the inability to replace the European population with descendants of "real" (read: white) Europeans. One such alarmist statistic tells us that in the Ruhr region of Germany, for example, more than half of people under thirty are of immigrant origin. This worry is best understood through a traffic-in-women framework. In today's Europe, the work of reproduction—biological and social—is in the process of being displaced on non-European and East European women. Its tasks are in the process of being denationalized, fragmented, and commercialized and are performed by women from outside the family and often from outside the nation.[33] It is this phenomenon that conservative commentators deplore on the biological side (genetic reproduction) but tacitly endorse on the social side (child and elder care, domestic work) with symptomatic exceptions on the biological side (organ donation, surrogacy, adoption).

Reproduction used to fall under the purview of what in 1975 Louis Althusser called *ideological state apparatuses* (ISAs).[34] ISAs used to be *state* institutions like the church or the school system that, alongside the family, reproduced the capitalist relations of production. Today, such institutions remain under the purview of various states but are also increasingly Europeanized and globalized. As European welfare states are entering an era of austerity, with cuts in the budgets of various educational ISAs, the tasks of reproduction are displaced onto new media, on the one hand, and returned to the family, on the other. Research shows that the influence of the old ISAs in the socialization of the young is lessening as they increasingly learn information and skills from their digital media encounters.[35] This book is concerned with the second assumption: that the traffic in women produces a new extended family (nannies, domestics, and care workers are figured as "one of the family") within which the old tasks of reproduction are performed. Ostojić's poster drives home the fact that the traffic in East European women is instrumental in the reproduction of Europeans, the next generation of laborers (and the next generation of the unemployed), whether women work as mothers, surrogates, egg donors, nurses, nannies, domestic workers, or sex workers. They are *l'origine du monde*. It will come as no surprise that the poster was considered a scandal and was removed from public space in Austria.[36]

Reproduction, Althusser argued, assures a complicit submission to the order of things. Through the work of reproduction, an East European nanny working in a West European household helps reproduce the relations of production of contemporary global capitalism, inevitably becoming complicit with them. She also helps reproduce the relations of reproduction and their attendant stratifications. In other words, she reproduces her own situation. At the same time—and this might well be the opening Althusser did not envision when he doubted the possibility of anti-ideological intervention on the part of a teacher working within the educational ISA—she is likely to perform her labors of reproduction with a twist.[37] Seen from the point of view of reproduction, the contemporary extended family is a site of European and international class tensions and class struggle.

It will be asked, What is new here? If the European Union is a relatively recent reality, globalization is not.[38] The transatlantic slave trade was a global phenomenon; women slaves performed biological and social reproductive labor. To consider what is new, let us revisit Defoe's *Robinson Crusoe*. At the end of the novel, having returned to Europe, Crusoe decides to visit "his colony" again. Once he assesses its needs, he sends a package: "Besides other supplies, I sent seven women, being such as I found proper for service, or for wives to such as would take them. As to the Englishmen, I promised to send them some women from England, with a good cargo of necessaries, if they would apply themselves to planting. . . . I sent them, also, from the Brazils, five cows, three of them being big with calf, some sheep, and some hogs, which when I came again were considerably increased."[39] Women circulate transnationally in the colonial context of the eighteenth century, alongside cows and other supplies and necessaries. Their role is to *increase—reproduce*, in both senses of the word. But in Defoe's novel, although women are scarce in the newly established colony, Crusoe thinks that he needs to send the Englishmen on the island English women.[40] The women he sends from Brazil are good for service, including marriage—"to such as would take them." Native women do not enter the equation. My argument is that today these distinctions are unnecessary because women's services are increasingly translatable globally. Were Crusoe to send a package to a hypothetical island today, he could send the Englishmen Thai, Filipina, or Ukrainian wives, but the men in question would not necessarily need wives since the category *wife* has been disassembled and the different tasks of a wife have been fragmented and commercialized such that they can be outsourced to Thai, Filipina, or Ukrainian women. The latter's reproductive services (biological and social) are marked ethnically and racially, but they are trusted to translate (not without difficulty) globally. Classification is deployed to mitigate the difficulty as women's reproductive capacities are marketed according to specific categories (some women are good mothers, others make excellent domestics, and others are splendid sex partners).[41]

The international division of labor that neoliberalism inherited from colonialism is in this way further divided along lines of gender and sexuality. Men and women (mostly women) on one side of the line function as "the women" for the men and women on the other side of the line. Ursula Biemann contends that we are faced with "a sexual economy in which it has become thinkable to reorganize women geographically on a global scale."[42] This book considers the traffic in women in relation to the European version of this reorganization, focusing on a group of women called *Eastern European* and their adventures in a Europe shaped by its noncoincidence with the European Union. Although they have moved transnationally before, since 1989 East European women have been on the move in unprecedented numbers, doing a range of jobs *as* women. Most importantly, they pursue transnational jobs in the contemporary care industry.[43] Europe, their main destination, is at the same time fascinated by the women who have emerged from what is figured as a postsocialist slumber and puts them to work as cleaning ladies, nannies, entertainers, etc. This is one—but only one—face of a widespread global phenomenon. Through a restricted but comparativist study of narratives that trace the traffic of East European women in Europe, the chapters that follow strive to contribute to a large body of literature that analyzes the political economy of women's global mobility.

It is crucial to acknowledge that East European women are not at the bottom of the European hierarchy of female migrants. Writing about the differential tariffs on housework in today's Europe, Bridget Anderson speaks of "a recognized hierarchy among both employers and workers, with Filipinas generally at the top and black Africans at the bottom," a hierarchy "most clearly manifested in pay."[44] Anderson emphasizes that this ranking is racialized but that it is not based on skin color. Albanians, Ukrainians, and Romanians working in Greece in the late 1990s (when Greece was considered by East Europeans to be an affluent European state) were, like black African women, low in the hierarchy. It is the economic position at the bottom of this hierarchy that is racialized and, with it, the women who come to occupy it, regardless of their skin pigmentation. The hierarchical ladder of coerced sex work is racialized in similar ways, with Nigerian and Romanian women sharing the bottom of the pay hierarchy.[45] How, then, does racialization work here? Where do we position the "Eastern European" within a much-denied European racial field?[46] In what ways do our racial binaries (white/black, Christian/Muslim, European/non-European) render her visible or invisible? How might we go about triangulating or multiplying such relationalities?

Rosi Braidotti writes: "People from the Balkans, or the South-Western regions of Europe, in so far as they are not yet 'good Europeans,' they are also not quite as 'white' as others."[47] I maintain that Olga, the protagonist of *Import/Export*, the film discussed in chapter 2, a blonde Ukrainian nurse who works as a cleaning lady in Austria, is not quite white. We need to learn to position Olga within Europe's racialized hierarchies, even if in her case what Stuart Hall calls *class-occupational stratification* does not overlap with familiar patterns of racial stratification.[48] While the class-occupational structural position she occupies is racialized, she can also pass as white and might encounter forms of "positive racialization."[49] The concept of racialization, with its emphasis on process, allows for the fact that not all East Europeans are racialized in all situations and that those who are racialized are not always racialized negatively. Racialization works with the assumption that certain occupational positions, religious markers, and issues and debates (immigration, criminality) have become imbued with racial meanings that are variable, often contradictory, and differentially applied.[50] This argument does not allow East European women to disavow the privileges that come with the possibility of passing. They often find various labor opportunities in the care industry precisely through their "white" (i.e., not quite white but close enough) credentials. They often capitalize on these credentials, claiming superiority over those who cannot pass ("We are not Africa" is a well-known East European refrain).

Fatima El-Tayeb, for example, does not include East Europeans in her account of race in contemporary Europe, on account of their assumed invisibility and ability to pass.[51] Likewise, David Theo Goldberg mentions East European forms of racism, but fails to consider the figure of the "Eastern European" within an otherwise complex articulation of what he calls *racial Europeanization*.[52] While skin color provides a form of visibility that triggers particular forms of racism, for the most part racial Europeanization targets East Europeans on the basis of markers that are not limited to color. We still need to learn to recognize and read the "stratification insignia" (Hall's term) that overdetermine East European women's European and global mobility. They include racialized physical characteristics like hair, teeth, body type, and clothing styles as well as education, religion, and "values." Language skills straddle the distinction, stratifying according to both accent and communicative skills (more on this in chapter 2).

While a game of comparisons often places other women and men in worse positions, this book works off the assumption that it is necessary to think about the particulars of East European women's racialization. The long-term task, only partially taken up here, is not only not to fall into the trap of "white hysteria" but also to describe the processes through which an East European woman can be racialized.[53] This is, in Goldberg's vocabulary, "raceless racialization," its racelessness a function of the fact that race as a scientific category has been left behind by most Europeans. Racialization, on the other hand, is fiercely at work in Europe today. Robert Miles introduced the term *racialization* in 1982 to describe the situation of migrant workers in Britain in the twentieth century.[54] It was inclusive of "white" workers coming from racialized European populations (Italian, Irish), the same populations that today racialize "white" migrants coming from East Europe.

In recent years, racialization has been taken up by a range of scholars of comparative critical race theory. The racialization of East Europeans has received little attention. We know that in the nineteenth century Europeans were divided into racial types (Celts, Slavs, Latins, etc.). It is also well-known that European migration to the United States at the end of the nineteenth century fell into distinct racial categories, with "real whites" coming from Northwest Europe. While the term *Caucasian* has been used in the United States in the second half of the twentieth century to arguably whiten East European and Jewish immigrants, no similar whitening has occurred in West Europe, which returns not a white/black binary but rather a number of place-determined, fluid racialized hierarchies.[55] In contemporary Europe, the task is to assess how heterogeneous terms like *Arab*, *Chinese*, or *Romanian* become, in given situations, racial terms.

Film

This book makes its arguments on the margins of a number of recent European films. Among the forms of engagement that cinema has claimed in the last decades, it has participated in and partially produced a critical debate on the traffic in women.[56] I agree with the film historian Thomas Elsaesser when he claims that art cinema—through the film festival circuit—has come to function as an alternative public sphere: "Film festivals have in effect created one of the most interesting public spheres available in the cultural field today: more lively and dynamic than the gallery-art and museum world, more articulate and militant than the pop music, rock concert and DJ-world, more international than the theatre, performance and dance world, more political and engaged than the world of literature and the academy."[57] This is a cinematic public sphere, a relational being-with of filmmakers, cinematic texts, and various heterogeneous publics. This book starts from the premise that art cinema creates a lively, dynamic, and engaged transnational public sphere for the debate on the traffic in women.

Elsaesser's statement needs to be complemented by an assessment of the role of television, which has its own public sphere, and digital media, perhaps the most influential media today. Neither, however, is both European and global in quite the same way art cinema is.[58] Film festivals emerged in the postwar period as part of a project of producing Europe (*rejuvenation* was the keyword used).[59] Since 1989, the film festival has become the key force in the European film industry, in East and West Europe. If there is a European cultural product that crosses the former East/West divide, it is cinema. Many European films on the festival circuit are coproductions; many have EU funding. The images discussed in this book not only dramatize movement in their very medium and thematize it within their narratives but also move themselves on restricted global and European paths. This predicament—and the tensions at its heart—render art cinema, including its modes of production and circulation, "useful," a productive archive for a project on the movement of women in contemporary Europe.[60]

To say that cinema is a public sphere is to say that it assumes a relational, plural spectator. A certain "we" is watching the film. The viewing "we," Miriam Hansen has argued, is a function of a necessarily intersubjective, inclusive, open, common historical horizon.[61] This horizon is only partially dependent on the empirical space of the movie theater as it is very much in the air as a common plane of experience (immigration as a public debate, e.g.). When it comes to cinema, a film addresses a public (*solicits* is Hansen's verb) that it in fact creates. In order to sustain the attention of audience members, a film shapes itself against a historical and an aesthetic horizon (through the use of certain media, genres, institutions of circulation, and affective investments). The close, multileveled analysis of film that the chapters of this book perform can reveal this horizon. What a film puts in front of its viewers cannot be completely new and is most likely mediated by the circulation of other texts (locally and globally). Films tell us a lot about what is *assumed* to be known (everyday perceptions of East European women, e.g.), often through small, unscripted gestures. This is the documentary dimension of feature films. At the same time, although any cinematic horizon has its historical contours, its dialogic, relational character renders it unpredictable. This means that cinema is also a site of creativity and experimentation. This is its activist, sometimes utopian, dimension.

Images in recent European art films linger on situations that dramatize various kinds of care deficit, in which a fictional East European woman, whose story is often a "found" one, fills in gaps produced by recent readjustments in benefits offered by states (such as care for the elderly) and in the functioning of modern families (dual-career families or single-parent families). What these films make visible, once subjected to patient close reading, is the fact that the East European woman in question is paid to *touch* her employers. In chapter 2, as I discuss Ulrich Seidl's *Import/Export*, I foreground the female protagonist's awareness of the nature of her work: she is hired as a cleaner but engages in a number of caring tasks, literally touching the patients in a geriatric ward. Lukas Moodysson's *Lilja 4-Ever* (2000), one of the films discussed in chapter 4, suggests that the sex industry is a niche of the care industry, too. The sixteen-year-old protagonist, who is coerced into sex work in Sweden, begins her career as a sex slave in response to a destitute, sad Swedish man's desire to be touched. The film does not excuse the man's participation in the violence perpetrated against Lilja; it only points to the man's need for touch (what we used to call *human touch*), which leads to a violent sex act. The films under scrutiny here belong to a cinema of tactility, which, in its politicized form, takes it on itself to thematize the workings of the contemporary care industry. These films frame a range of heterogeneous touches—sexualized, laboring, caressing, accidental, violent, solidary, consoling, utopian. Cinema is a medium that can make these touches visible; cinema itself can be said to be part of the care industry, momentarily touching often alienated viewers in search of a sense of community and political purpose.

This book also offers a possible answer to the much-debated question of what valence the humanities have in the current moment. In times of economic crisis and austerity, are they, perhaps, less needed or even dispensable? While this book is itself not based on empirical research, it is an exercise in interdisciplinarity, and, as such, it is in dialogue with research in the social sciences. But my hope is that the humanities scholar *as* a humanities scholar can and should intervene in ongoing debates like the one on Europe.[62] Today, an analysis of the circulation of economic goods cannot be separated from a discussion of human mobility. In its turn, human mobility cannot be understood in the absence of a sustained account of the mobility of cultural texts. A project on the traffic in women anchored in an analysis of cultural texts is invested in a study not only of representation but also of the coconstitutive nature of the three forms of mobility.

Overview

Drawing on the resources and interdisciplinary liberties of the essay form, I read closely one or two films in each chapter, in dialogue with a large interdisciplinary body of secondary material. Each chapter has a theoretical stake in a question I find urgent for the debate on the European traffic in women: transnational marriage (chapter 1), housework and its relation to immaterial and affective labor (chapter 2), reproduction and the female *homo sacer* (chapter 3), passports and identification documents (chapter 4), and hospitality (chapter 5).

Chapter 1 is a reading of Cristian Mungiu's *Occident* (2002). The film dramatizes the dilemmas of two Romanian women faced with the prospects of marriage and contemplating their local and European options. Starting from a reading of the film, the chapter traces the second-wave feminist debate on the traffic in women, a debate that builds on the work of Marx and Lévi-Strauss and includes figures like Gayle Rubin, Luce Irigaray, and Judith Butler. It proposes that the notion of kinship developed by Lévi-Strauss and critiqued by second-wave feminists resonates critically with contemporary discourses that describe the European Union as a family. Culture, according to Lévi-Strauss, is made through the exchange of goods and services, signs, and women. Mungiu's film suggests that, in an effort to become part of European culture, and in the absence of an abundance of goods, services, and signs, East European countries participate in an exchange in women.

Chapter 2 brings together the book's argument about the category *women's work* in the context of post-Fordism. The narrative basis for the chapter is offered by Ulrich Seidl's *Import/Export* (2007), a film that documents the labor of a Ukrainian nurse who is employed in Austria as a cleaning lady in a middle-class home and a geriatric ward. The chapter revisits the second-wave feminist debate on housework, emphasizing the place of women's work in a Fordist economy. It juxtaposes with this history the analysis of contemporary work offered by Italian autonomist neo-Marxists, who often take the figure of the housewife as exemplary of the post-Fordist worker. What happens, the chapter asks, if we consider the Ukrainian cleaning lady as a new housewife figure and take her work to be exemplary of post-Fordist labor? The chapter ends by pointing to the existence of a European linguistic hierarchy, arguing that the calculated failure of translation is an important ingredient in the traffic in women.

Chapter 3 picks up the discussion of coerced sex trafficking started in the introduction, to theorize its place within the broad, labor-based traffic in women. The chapter builds its argument through a reading of Giuseppe Tornatore's *The Unknown Woman* (2006), which it develops into a critique of Giorgio Agamben's work on the *homo sacer*. The woman in Tornatore's film does coerced sex work that the film places on a continuum with other reproductive work: domestic work, child care, and pregnancy. The chapter brings the feminist literature on reproductive technologies, surrogacy, and regenerative labor to bear on Agamben's notion of biopolitics, in order to analyze the production of the sex-trafficking camp at the intersection of a number of overlapping and competing sovereignties.

Chapter 4 considers the role that various passport options available to East European women inside and outside the European Union play in the traffic in women. Two films provide its narrative basis: Lukas Moodysson's *Lilja 4-Ever* (2000) and Jean-Luc and Pierre Dardenne's *Lorna's Silence* (2008). In both films, various papers mediate the traffic in women—in one case, for the purposes of coerced sex, and, in the other, for the purposes of coerced marriage. The chapter traces a brief history of the passport in Europe, arguing that the rhetoric of Europe as a borderless haven is productively misleading. Passports are less visible in contemporary Europe, but the two films under scrutiny bring them back forcefully to frame them as labor documents and mediators of the traffic in women.

Bringing the book to a close, chapter 5 returns to the theoretical framework developed in chapter 1 in order to consider its utopian underpinnings. How do we get out of the traffic in women? The narrative impetus for the argument is offered by Andrea Štaka's *Das Fräulein* (2007). The viewer of

Štaka's film is lead to believe that her protagonist will follow into the footsteps of female characters in the other films discussed in the book and become either a waitress or a sex worker. Instead, she initiates a gift economy. She offers both sex and labor gratuitously. The chapter revisits Mauss and Lévi-Strauss's work on the gift in order to describe the conditions under which such an economy becomes discernible. At the same time, it probes the promise of another form of gift—hospitality—often considered to be the utopian solution to the free movement of *persons*. The chapter unpacks the gendered nature of hospitality, pointing to the risks inherent in a utopia of hospitality. Returning to the early twentieth-century origins of the feminist critique of the traffic in women, the book concludes with a discussion of free love as an imagined exit from a traffic-in-women culture.

1 European Kinship

East European Women Go to Market

An episode in Cristian Mungiu's *Occident* (2002) presents us with a scene in a matrimonial agency in Romania: A worried mother is searching for a husband for her twenty-four-year-old daughter, Mihaela. The conversation in the waiting room informs us that she has brought the necessary bribe because the agency offers good choices: "They have doctors and Americans." Once inside, she is asked what nationality she is looking for. She would prefer "one of ours" but is told that the agency deals only in international marriages. Europe, America, and Asia are on the menu. The mother prefers Europe. The agent shows her a slide with a number of photographs (see fig. 1.1). "Don't you have anything younger?" the mother pleads. The agent rolls his eyes and pulls out another slide. With a suggestive, almost scientific gesture, he points to a photograph: a distinguished gentleman, from Saudi Arabia. "He's ugly," argues the mother. She takes the initiative and gestures toward another face. A sailor, from Cyprus. The mother shows her disappointment: "Don't you have a doctor?" The agent is irritated; we are not at the market, he protests, the men are human beings, and there is no bargaining. The mother is asked to pay the fee and leave a picture and her daughter's details. The agent will get back to her. The mother complies and adds a poem to the package: the bride-to-be is a poet.

Fig. 1.1. A Romanian mother hopes to find a West European husband for her daughter. Frame from Cristian Mungiu's *Occident* (2002).

A series of amusing encounters follow, through which Mihaela (played by Tania Popa, a Romanian actress originally from Moldova) meets caricatured older, working-class, uneducated European men. "I write poems," she says in French to a man who smiles encouragingly but to whom Baudelaire's name sounds only vaguely familiar. "Money is not important to me," she says in English to a man who gesticulates back that he does not have it anyway. "I like to travel . . . not to cook, wash," she adds for another one. Mihaela is clearly not interested in her European suitors, not only because they are utterly uninteresting, but also because she is in love with a young Romanian man, Lucian, who has just been left by his Romanian fiancée, Sorina, for an overweight, middle-aged Belgian businessman.

Mihaela's mother is persistent and soon finds her a good match, a well-situated Italian. He runs a publishing house and has read and liked Mihaela's poems. This last detail catches Mihaela's attention. There is no photograph, but on the phone he passes all the tests; he apparently is young and tall and even has hair. "If he publishes my poems, I'm going with him," Mihaela declares. The Italian is invited to visit. The house is cleaned, local wall art is replaced by sketches of classical Roman gods, furniture is moved around, pasta is cooked. Finally, the big moment comes. The father opens the door and freezes. "Ciao, sono Luigi," says a young black man. The Romanian family is in disarray. "Nu corespunde" (lit., "He does not correspond"), the father declares. Yet all the prerequisites are there, and the daughter wants to marry. The black Italian is a European impossibility the family did not anticipate. The film's three alternative endings (in the tradition of *Run Lola Run*) play with variations on whether the two Romanian women, Mihaela and Sorina, take the European road to marriage, emigrate without marrying, or settle for the local husband.

What these scenes in *Occident* offer us are snapshots of a new Europe.[1] Since 1989, East European women have become hot objects of European exchange, packaged in a variety of wrappings, whether as domestic servants, nurses, nannies, prostitutes, or wives. Mungiu's film challenges the perception that the European Union facilitates East European mobility, including the mobility of East European women. Reversing the terms, it prompts reflection on the ways in which the formation and sedimentation of "Europe" across its East/West post–Cold War divide is made possible by the circulation of East European women. In order to begin to understand this Europe, this chapter revisits the second-wave feminist argument about the traffic in women and draws out its implications for the European Union.

The Marriage Market

More than thirty five years have passed since Gayle Rubin published "The Traffic in Women: Notes on the 'Political Economy' of Sex."[2] Reprinted in various anthologies, the essay has become a feminist classic, having maintained its urgency, and having been repeatedly used as a springboard for the reconsideration of its arguments in light of new configurations of traffic, economy, the political, or sex. I propose that, alongside Luce Irigaray's articulation of the argument for the French side of second-wave feminism,[3] Rubin's essay can offer an entry point into the transnational traffic in women in the current European moment. I retrace the archaeology of the debate here before I return to *Occident*. This will be a somewhat convoluted journey, one, however, that will offer a framework within which to understand the Europe that *Occident* dramatizes.

The precedent for Rubin's essay, and an enduring reference point in the conceptual combination known as *traffic in women*, is a short article carrying the same title by Emma Goldman from 1910. Goldman writes: "It is merely a question of degree whether she [woman] sells herself to one man, in or out of marriage, or to many men. Whether our reformers admit it or not, the economic and social inferiority of woman is responsible for prostitution."[4] *Traffic in women* is the phrase Goldman uses to describe the circulation of women between men, *in general*. Rather than referring to exceptional cases of human trafficking, it describes an economic continuum on which both prostitution and marriage are situated. For Goldman, the difference between prostitution and marriage is one of degree, a question of how many men participate in the transaction. The scandal here is to propose that marriage, the respectable form of women's circulation, is a variation on the economic theme of prostitution. In the modern world, this is a scandal for men, who would prefer to have this truth veiled, and it is also a scandal for women, who would prefer to think that they enter (and stay in) marriages by virtue of a love choice. Goldman, however, insists that love and marriage belong to two separate registers. In another essay, she declares: "Marriage is often an economic arrangement purely, furnishing the woman with a life-long insurance policy."[5] In 1910, as today, it was radical to hold that love is largely irrelevant to an analysis of marriage, serving only to obscure the fact that the system of circulation both in prostitution and in marriage is an *economy* and that it should be scrutinized as such. While Goldman's statements need to be historicized to allow for the changes brought about by a century of feminism, her arguments about the broad economic continuum between marriage and sex work remain in force. Laura Kipnis's recent *Against Love*, a book that calls for an understanding of contemporary marital relationships as sexual and affective work, can be read as an attempt to update these arguments for the turn into the twenty-first century, with similar polemical energy.[6]

In 1975, Rubin acknowledged her debt to Goldman as she developed her own notion of traffic in women understood on the continuum between prostitution and so-called normal forms of exchange, marriage in particular. Her essay describes "a set of arrangements," which she calls "the sex/gender system," through which sex is translated into gender, the performance of a set of social relations. Her project is to come to a better understanding of the conditions that produce women's position in society. In the course of her analysis, she shows not only that marriage is always arranged but also that marital arrangements serve as a foundation for other forms of societal exchange. Where does one begin such a project? Rubin proposes that we read closely the overlap between Claude Lévi-Strauss's and Freud's descriptions of the social apparatus and women's place in it. This, however, only after she puts aside her hope in Marx.

Capitalism, the Marxist argument goes, is in the business of extracting unpaid labor from the laborer, which it transforms into surplus value. Rather than being directly correlated to value, wages are set in light of what is needed to reproduce the conditions of production: commodities such as food, clothing, housing, etc. Wages are meant to cover these costs and help reproduce the conditions under which the laborer does more work—from day to day and from one generation of workers to the next. Rubin and other materialist feminists of her generation interrupt Marx at this point to emphasize that such commodities come in an unprocessed form, that they require labor in order to reproduce the laborer. In an argument we will revisit in chapter 2, they point out that the food is cooked, the clothes washed, the house cleaned, budding future laborers looked after, family life managed administratively and emotionally, etc. This is *housework*, more recently rethought under the names *family work* and *care work*. Traditionally, this has been the labor of women: *women's work*. Women are indispensable to the reproduction of labor, hence to the production of surplus value, hence to capitalist economy. In fact, it can be argued that women's unpaid labor within the household is the first (indirect) source of the surplus value on which capitalism thrives.[7]

How, then, Rubin continues, does one explain the fact that in many noncapitalist economic regimens women have occupied similar roles within the familial household? Her argument is that the economy under scrutiny is a function of a wider cultural heritage, a deeper history.[8] In *The Origin of the Family, Private Property, and the State*, Friedrich Engels went a step further than Marx in his analysis of a second type of production, that of human beings themselves. Engels dissociated the reproduction of the conditions of production from the reproduction of human beings and located the latter firmly within the institution of the family. His insight is to have proposed that it is only through a focus on the family that we can hope to make visible the network of relations within which women live, including economic relations. The first "class" to be economically oppressed are women within kinship structures; their oppression remains at the basis of other forms of economic exploitation. Rubin finds Engels invaluable for having produced a major methodological shift toward an analysis of kinship, but she proposes that he has not pursued the implications of his insight, or not sufficiently. This is where she turns to Lévi-Strauss and his magisterial *Elementary Structures of Kinship*.

The fabric of a society, Lévi-Strauss has famously argued, is formed by a series of cyclic, obligatory, and reciprocal exchanges among kinship groups. Society is in fact nothing other than this network of exchanges. Lévi-Strauss draws on Marcel Mauss, who claimed, against political philosophers like Thomas Hobbes, that there has never been a state of nature because any society we know of has had a market form, with its networks of exchange functioning as a rudimentary social contract. The various exchanges that these markets facilitate are, in Mauss's own words from his 1924 *Essay on the Gift*, "banquets, rituals, military services, women, children, dances, festivals, and fairs."[9] This network of exchange is a social contract *avant la lettre* and is something like an anthropological first principle.

In an attempt to move from the disjunctive logic of Mauss's list to a more systematic description of societal exchange, Lévi-Strauss sifts through the "inessentials" on this list to argue that there are three levels of communication in any given society, corresponding to the circulation of three sets of interrelated objects: "The rules of kinship and marriage serve to insure the circulation of women between groups, just as economic rules serve to insure the circulation of goods and services, and linguistic rules the circulation of messages."[10] The three categories of societal exchange are goods and services, signs, and women. The relation among the three goes beyond analogy as Lévi-Strauss makes it clear that women in fact *are* goods, that they *are* signs. He concludes that the circulation of women in marriage is the arch form of exchange. In the beginning there is the exchange of women. The incest taboo is posited as the structure's limit because, according to Lévi-Strauss, by its means a whole clear-cut network of relations is formed; a woman a man cannot marry is necessarily a woman he must offer to another man.[11]

The question that interests Rubin is how to *read* this system of exchange. Most importantly, how immutable is it? If one agrees that the exchange and circulation of women constitute the very fabric of culture, is it possible and desirable to fight culture? At stake, Lévi-Strauss charges, is the very security of the collective, its principle of organization: "It is not an exaggeration, then, to say that exogamy is the archetype of all other manifestations based upon reciprocity, and that it provides the fundamental and immutable rule measuring the existence of the group as a group." Moreover, the exchange of women yields a network of reciprocal relations among brothers-in-law: "The brother-in-law is ally, collaborator and friend."[12] The brother-in-law is at the basis of what Mauss celebrates under the rubric of solidarity—a solidarity of brothers, collaborators, and friends. The exchange in women is what founds not only community but also solidarity, the very foundation of politics. In a long tradition from Aristotle to Carl Schmitt, politics is a game played among brothers and friends and brothers qua friends.[13] If this is the case, the feminist predicament is profoundly paradoxical since it implies a project of articulating a politics against politics.

For her part, Rubin concludes that, while the traffic in women has a lot of explicative power ("our sex/gender system is still organized by the principles outlined by Lévi-Strauss"), structuralist kinship is itself a myth, a fiction of origins, and a very powerful one at that, as it has added an apparently incontestable scientific wrapping to its many, already seductive folds.[14] Rubin reminds us that the language of "mere" observation abounds. Mauss wrote about *The Gift*: "We have no wish to put forward this study as a model to be followed. It only sets out bare indications."[15] Lévi-Strauss spoke of the goal of his project in terms of it aspiring to be "real, simplifying and explanatory."[16] How, then, does one interrupt a myth that presents itself as "bare indications" and "real, simplifying and explanatory"? Rubin insists that we need to read symptomatically; she describes her own reading practice as "freely interpretative, moving from the explicit content of a text to its presuppositions and implications."[17] We also need to read exegetically, at the same time acknowledging the undeniable force of Lévi-Strauss's work (it is scripture-like) and calling for interpretation. After all, exegesis often unnoticeably slides into blasphemy.

This reading practice produces a few "mutations" in our understanding of Lévi-Strauss's argument.[18] In Rubin's wake, two points need revisiting. One is the context in which, in describing the analogy between words, goods and services, and women, Lévi-Strauss allows that women occupy a paradoxical object position: "Words do not speak, while women do; as producers of signs, women can never be reduced to the status of symbols or tokens."[19] Since kinship is a symbolic structure and ultimately a linguistic structure, the conflict over the very meaning (and immutability) of kinship is fought in language. Moreover, the reproduction of the myth at the individual level occurs in language, through the reiterative socialization of new generations on their way, as Rubin puts it, toward the missionary position. Women speak, and the language they produce circulates, often on unpredictable trajectories. As producers of signs, they can rewrite the signs they themselves are. Women are producers of literature in the broadest sense, and literature is the space in which relation, including that of an exchange between author and reader, has been challengingly rethought, such that literary signs do not necessarily travel on a traffic-in-women model.

The second point is the juncture where Lévi-Strauss emphasizes that kinship is a symbolic structure and thus "an arbitrary system of representations" but insists that the system is gendered in a unidirectional way: "Could we not conceive of a symmetrical structure, equally simple, where the sexes could be reversed [i.e., a traffic in men]? . . . This is certainly a theoretical possibility. But it is immediately eliminated on empirical grounds. In human society, it is the men who exchange the women, and not vice versa."[20] Lévi-Strauss would later renounce this formulation in favor of what he acknowledges here only as a "theoretical possibility." Allowing that traffic can be a two-way street, he would come to say that "groups consisting of both men and women exchange among themselves kinship relations."[21] Responding to his insistent critics on another occasion, he would eventually exclaim: "How many times will I have to repeat that it makes no difference to the theory whether it is men who exchange women or the opposite?"[22] In other words, while acknowledging that the initial statement in *Elementary Structures of Kinship* was an infelicitous formulation, Lévi-Strauss maintains that the theoretical apparatus of the book stands even if we agree that today both men and women participate, as exchangers, in the circulation of kinship relations. This is where political economy needs to return, to explain why, even though today anybody can play the wife, our instituted modes of exchange remain gendered, effectively producing wives who, empirically speaking, most often are women.

Before we turn to political economy, however, we need to follow a last twist in the Rubin-inspired debate on kinship. Judith Butler revisited this conversation in *Antigone's Claim* in an attempt to update Rubin's argument and offer a queer theory of kinship for the contemporary world, accounting for the fact that today it would seem that men and women exchange kinship relations in nontraditional ways. Her entry point into the conversation is the figure of Antigone, whom she places on a philosophical continuum between Hegel and Lacan's reading of Lévi-Strauss. Butler agrees with Rubin that Lévi-Straussian moments like the one quoted above are symptomatic of theories of kinship and their own investment in the immutability of what they purport to merely describe. She asks: "And to the extent that the symbolic reiterates a 'structural' necessity of kinship, does it relay or perform the curse of kinship itself? In other words, does the structuralist law report on the curse that is upon kinship or does it deliver that curse?"[23] Butler brings into the conversation Lacan's formulations on the symbolic, which the latter developed through an explicit engagement with Lévi-Strauss. In this theoretical configuration, kinship structures, insofar as they are linguistic structures, underwrite the symbolic. Oedipus and the incest taboo offer us linguistic positions that render culture intelligible. Butler's engagement with Lacan takes the feminist predicament Rubin identified to yet another level of paradox as kinship becomes the presupposition of intelligibility, which for Butler also implies livability since only intelligible lives (and loves) are deemed livable. The question becomes, Is feminism struggling not only against society's fundamental and immutable rule but also against the very premise of cultural intelligibility?

In the philosophical tradition that Butler traces, Antigone's name is synonymous with the act of defiance whereby she buries her brother, Polynices, despite her uncle's edict that he is to remain unburied. Against Hegel, for whom she represents kinship at the moment when it is superseded by the state, Butler proposes that Antigone does not act in the name of kinship because her act has only one application. While for Lacan Antigone's brother is "pure Being," a structural/linguistic position within kinship, a position anyone can occupy, Butler insists that this particular brother is irreplaceable; he is Polynices, in all his radical singularity. She argues that, rather than act as a guardian of the law of kinship, Antigone acts in the name of love, which, given the placement of the incest taboo at the heart of kinship, cannot be assimilated to a symbolic order and thus remains incommunicable. She proposes that Antigone's act constitutes a transgression of kinship "that gives kinship its prohibitive and normative dimension but also exposes its vulnerability."[24] Butler focuses on prohibition here to draw attention to the dialectic of prohibition and transgression. If prohibitions trigger their own transgression, they also reveal the vulnerability of the law being transgressed.

As with Rubin, the question becomes, What do we do with this inheritance? If Lévi-Strauss and Lacan seem to be our destiny, how do we face what appears to be a structuralist curse? Butler's solution to the conundrum of immutability (whose symptom is figured as the necessity of Antigone's death) is to insist, against "the Lacanians," that the symbolic is not inseparable from the social and that change is possible in the field of the social: "Antigone represents neither kinship nor its radical outside but becomes the occasion for a reading of a structurally constrained notion of kinship in terms of its social iterability, the aberrant temporality of the norm."[25] Kinship is a function of its iterability in a social world, and, as we know from all Butler's work, iterability allows for perversity and aberration. Butler's way of dealing with the structuralist curse is to foreground its being an *in heritance* and to propose Antigone as a figure of the heir. Antigone is what comes *after* Oedipus; she is post-Oedipal and poststructuralist, as it were.

In the essay she wrote to elaborate on the notion of kinship at work in *Antigone's Claim*—"Is Kinship Always Already Heterosexual?"—Butler describes and analyzes the transformation of kinship studies while criticizing the lack of any apparent parallel progress in psychoanalysis.[26] She maintains that structuralist notions of kinship developed by Lévi-Strauss and his commentators have become anachronistic in the contemporary world of transnational migration and reproductive technologies. She invokes a predicament in which kinship, defined as "a set of practices that institute relationships of various kinds which negotiate the reproduction of life and the demands of death" and "address fundamental forms of human dependency and support, generational ties, illness, dying, and death (to name a few)," is inseparable from community and friendship and knows a multiplicity of nontraditional sites, in addition to Oedipal reproduction and heterosexuality.[27] The implication of her argument is that, while Lévi-Strauss might be useful to our understanding of premodern and not-quite-modern societies, in our world kinship works differently.[28]

Butler describes her project's historical situation in the following terms:

> I ask this as well during a time in which children, because of divorce and remarriage, because of migration, exile and refugee status, because of global displacements of various kinds, move from one family to another, move from a family to no family, move from no family to a family, or in which they live, psychically, at the crossroads of the family, or in multiply layered family situations, in which they may well have more than one woman who operates as the mother, more than one man who operates as the father, or no mother or no father, with half-brothers who are also friends—this is a time in which kinship has become fragile, porous, and expansive. It is also a time in which straight and gay families are sometimes blended, or in which gay families emerge in nuclear and nonnuclear forms.[29]

The irony in Butler's formulation is that the family seems to have proliferated and multiplied. But the fact that there is a family for every taste and need means not that the institution is in crisis, only that it can elastically adjust to pressures. Indeed, this is perhaps most visible in global situations of migration and displacement. When it comes to the effects of globalization on children, the privileges associated with the Western normative family (heteronormative or homonormative) are unevenly distributed globally, but not necessarily with queering effects. Nilita Vachani's documentary *When Mother Comes Home for Christmas* (1996) offers a counterpoint to Butler: children left behind by women who commute across the world for work relate to their absent mother, who remains a presence through the regular checks and letters she sends home, even if she comes home for Christmas once every seven years. Other women might function as mother figures in their lives, but these children put their hopes of economic survival in their mother.

Alternatively, one could claim that transnational adoption functions as a limit case here, as David Eng has shown, in that it is, potentially, an instance of alternative transnational kinship rearrangements. But the political economy of transnational adoption, which many critics describe as a traffic in children, is hard to reconcile with the poststructuralist ideal of kinship whereby, in Eng's words, a child "might grow up to exist in a world where the psychic structure of two—indeed, three, four, five, or perhaps no—mothers of various races could be psychically accommodated."[30] This is the point where it becomes clear that kinship remains a much-needed category of analysis, opening up questions of migration, race, and nation. It also becomes evident that, in addition to engaging in what Rey Chow calls *subject work*, today we need to uncover a political economy of kinship in a transnational frame.[31]

Butler and Eng work within a Foucauldian framework that assumes a historical shift away from kinship and toward sexuality. Glossing Foucault, Michael Warner describes this shift: "People reckon family and descent through households, affinity, and blood rather than through the symbolic exchange of ritual marriage. Some early modern features of marriage, like publishing the banns, have vanished; others, like the fertility ritual of flinging rice, survive only in vestigial form. Still others, like giving away the bride, probably retain greater significance than anyone would like to admit. But as the world-orienting horizons of kinship and exogamy have receded, the state as mediator has loomed up in their place."[32] Foucault's argument is that sometime in the eighteenth century the "regime of alliance" (governed by kinship) was supplemented by a "regime of sexuality" (governed by the state). Foucault charges that at this time sexuality is *superimposed* (his word) on alliance. With the reduction of the extended family to the nuclear bourgeois family, alliance does not disappear; without displacing the regime of alliance, sexuality eclipses its importance. Often covered up in a language of sexuality, alliance is thus reconfigured in relation to the new apparatus of sexuality.[33] In Foucault's often-cited formulation: "The family is the interchange of sexuality and alliance: it conveys [*transporte*] the law and the juridical dimension in the deployment of sexuality, and it conveys [*transporte*] the economics of pleasure and the intensity of sensations in the regime of alliance." Sexuality and alliance remain in a state of "interpenetration" (*épinglage*, the pinning up of two parts).[34] Although Foucault argues that reproduction loses its centrality in the regime of sexuality, the family, as the interplay of sexuality and alliance, as well as the larger biopolitical project of "controlling populations," which links women's bodies to the social body ("whose regulated fecundity it was supposed to ensure," he adds parenthetically), return us to an ever broader notion of reproduction. What is clear is that for Foucault the regime of sexuality is thoroughly *saturated* (his word) with alliance. The latter is no longer premised on blood but anchored in sexuality (sexuality "props up [*sout*(*ient*)] the old deployment of alliance").[35]

Thus, when we speak of sexuality, we are not outside kinship but rather in its midst. It is through the *interpenetration* of alliance and sexuality that Foucault explains the universalization of the incest taboo in anthropology, Lévi-Strauss in particular: the incest taboo assures that the deployment of sexuality remains dependent on alliance. Statist forms of racism likewise find their rationale in the ruins of alliance. Law enters the stage; the state (and transnational institutions) becomes an important actor in the "coupling" of the two regimes. Once we bring the nation back in relation to the state, kinship returns as a category necessary to any analysis of sexuality and the state. Like Foucault, Rubin, whose work is often read as a progressive narrative, moving from "The Traffic in Women" to "Thinking Sex," insists repeatedly that the latter does not displace the former in importance: to "think sex" does not mean that the traffic in women is left behind.[36] The critical task is to assess the haunting influence of the traffic in women in a world in which, on account of its anchoring in alliance, it *appears* to be anachronistic.

What does this debate tell us? While the political project of imagining post-Oedipal forms of kinship is laudable and in the best tradition of radical feminism, Butler's postkinship framework cannot account for the fact that the traffic in women seems to have gone global but otherwise goes on undisturbed. Alongside the institution of the brother-in-law and homosocial exchange, Butler leaves the traffic in women behind as out-of-date. We would, of course, want to forget the traffic in women, but what if, as a myth, the traffic in women does not forget us? Can we afford not to see it, for example, in the scene in *Occident* with which I began this chapter? This scene dramatizes the traffic in women in relation to an imagined European structure of kinship, challenging us to rethink what critical use, in the tradition of Rubin, we can still make of the concept.

The Marriage Market (French Versions)

Two years after the publication of Rubin's "The Traffic in Women," on the other side of second-wave feminism, Luce Irigaray published *This Sex Which Is Not One*, which included two suggestive chapter titles: "Women on the Market" and "Commodities among Themselves." Looking back at 1970s Western feminism, it is striking to note the overlap between Rubin and Irigaray, an overlap that today appears as an invitation to reconsider what for a long time seemed to be two incompatible faces of second-wave feminism.[37] The traffic in women is a point where the two feminisms almost seem to agree on a common radical project. There is a bit more work to do, then, before we return to *Occident*.

Irigaray begins with a matter-of-fact statement: "The society we know, our own culture, is based upon the exchange of women. Without the exchange of women, we are told [*dit-on*], we would fall back into anarchy (?) of the natural world, the randomness (?) of the animal kingdom. The passage into the social order, into the symbolic order, into order as such, is assured by the fact that men, or groups of men, circulate women among themselves, according to a rule known as the incest taboo."[38] Irigaray mimics the language of Lévi-Strauss. She does not seem to question the first apparent truth here: society as we know it is based on the exchange of women.[39] When it comes to where we would be *without* this exchange, however, mimicry doubles as incredulity: "we are told" (by whom? in the name of what interest?) that without the exchange of women "we" would regress into two related forms of monstrosity: anarchy and animality. Irigaray's question marks punctuate the irony that, as Lévi-Strauss knows, neither of these are unproblematically presocial in any strict sense.

What is clear for Irigaray, as for Rubin, is that the exchange of women "is an economic issue, perhaps even subtends economy as such?" Irigaray turns to Marx to do the work of exegetical reading that Rubin does with Lévi-Strauss, to conclude that in capitalism men "exchange their women-commodities among themselves." Irigaray reads Marx's *Capital* by way of "going back through analogy," the analogy between women and commodities, to focus on Marx's use of prosopopoeia, whereby in his account commodities are dressed and undressed, step forth, stand on their heads, and, indeed, speak.[40] Irigaray's "women-commodities" name the more than analogy already at work in Marx's description of how commodities—those "enigmatic" things—acquire value. There is no going back to women *or* commodities' use value because they are always already caught in an exchange in which they have value only insofar as they are compared to other women or commodities as objects of a potential exchange.

Irigaray draws attention to Lévi-Strauss's explanation of the exchange of women as having its basis in their scarcity: "The deep polygamous tendency, which exists among all men, always makes the number of available women seem insufficient. Let us add that, even if there were as many women as men, these women would not be all equally desirable . . . and that, by definition . . . , the most desirable women must form a minority."[41] Men are by definition polygamous, and, faced with this "fact," there simply are not enough women to satisfy their desire. Women are a minority in the face of men's insatiable desire. Moreover, men desire many women, and not just any women, but only desirable women. Desirability is posited as a property of the object (women's bodies), which in its turn is desirable by virtue of being desired by men. It is clear to Irigaray that economy has a libidinal core.[42] The desire that moves it is infinitely polygamous, as each man desires to capitalize more women than the others. It follows that women are strangely equal insofar as they are separated from each other by the "general equivalent" ("the sublime standard," Irigaray calls it) that functions as the measuring stick according to which they are compared.[43] Women's separateness guarantees that they cannot exchange themselves among themselves. Structurally, the argument goes, women cannot desire each other because desire as such flows within an economy in which women are strictly/structurally objects of desire (we will return to this in chapter 5).

Irigaray reaches a point where the question of immutability returns: "For, without the exploitation of women, what would become of the social order? What modifications would it undergo if women left behind their condition as commodities—subject to being produced, consumed, valorized, circulated, and so on, by men alone—and took part in elaborating and carrying out exchanges? Not by reproducing, by copying, the 'phallocratic' models that have the force of law today, but by socializing in a different way the relation to nature, matter, the body, language, and desire." And: "*But what if these 'commodities' refused to go to 'market'?* What if they maintained 'another' kind of commerce, among themselves?" It is not an easy thing to do, this refusal. Irigaray anticipates the response: "Utopia? Perhaps. Unless this mode of exchange has undermined the order of commerce from the beginning . . . a certain economy of abundance."[44] Her vision is not a utopia if one strategically posits sexual difference and thus the fact that the male commerce in women has been paralleled by another kind of commerce.

Where does one look for traces of this other commerce in the folds of a culture predicated on its nonexistence? The last chapter of *This Sex Which Is Not One*, "When Our Lips Speak Together," is Irigaray's literary experiment, an attempt to stage a different kind of commerce. Here, an unidentified *I* speaks to an unidentified *you*. *I* and *you* are a two that cannot be separated into ones. There is a continuous exchange, but no transaction, no contract, no traffic in women. The sense of touch offers Irigaray a way to envision this other commerce. In her experiment, *I touch you* carries the possibility of being at the same time transitive and reflexive (*se toucher toi*). One touches the other and oneself at the same time: "I am touching you, that's quite enough to let me know that you are my body." Touch is also the only sense that can function as a guarantor of existence: "I/you touch you/me, that's quite enough for us to feel alive." There is no organ of touch to channel the sensation on striated paths; touching is experienced by the surface of the skin as a whole: "You are there—like my skin." This is a form of circulation that does not distinguish between subject and subject and between subject and object: "Exchange? Everything is exchanged, yet there are no transactions. Between us, there are no proprietors, no purchasers, no determinable objects, no prices. Our bodies are nourished by our mutual pleasure.

Our abundance is inexhaustible: it knows neither want nor plenty. Since we give each other (our) all, with nothing held back, nothing hoarded, our exchanges are without terms, without end. How can I say it? The language we know is so limited." Yet Irigaray insists that one needs to struggle to wrest the intensity of this *feeling* from language. The other commerce has been there all along. Even if there are no words for it, one can *feel* it: "Let's hurry and invent our own phrases."[45] Her hope is that we will be able to say "I love you" on the model of "I touch you," eventually bringing love—*this* notion of love—to bear on this conversation.

Irigaray's *you* opens into a relationship with a reader. One of the most compelling dialogues has been that between Irigaray and Italian feminists, the Milan Bookstore Collective in particular.[46] The bookstore (the Milan bookstore opened in 1975) is a "practice of relationships among women," circulating signs, desire, and commodities.[47] Importantly, the Milanese women refuse the equality offered them through the traffic in women. The practice of what they call *the symbolic mother* assumes that one woman can *learn* from another, with whom she has an asymmetrical, unequal relationship. The Milanese women refuse the proper name, publishing their book collectively. They also refuse property, offering the space of the bookstore to all who enter it. Beyond any calls for emancipation or rights, the bookstore is a "theoretical practice" that effectively rewrites the traffic in women.[48] Irigaray's utopia is read by the Milanese women as a very concrete starting point of practice.

Irigaray's *you* finds an oblique echo in Jacques Derrida. Ultimately, the *I love you* that Irigaray is after would have to contaminate the notion of friendship that functions as the foundation of politics. Derrida takes up the issue, making sure we remember that "the figure of the friend, so regularly coming back on stage with the features of the *brother* . . . seems spontaneously to belong to a *familial, fraternalist* and thus *androcentric* configuration of politics." Before being properly political, the politics of friendship is always already haunted by kinship. It is important to emphasize, however, that one is not born a brother: "Do you not think, dear friend, that the brother is always a brother of alliance, a *brother in law* or an adoptive brother, a *foster brother*?"[49] In his book on touch, Derrida elaborates on the brother, drawing attention to the fact that "the word [*fraternity*] privileges some 'virility.' Even if he is an orphan, a brother is a son and therefore a man. In order to include the sister or woman or daughter, one has to change words—generously—and then change the word 'generosity' while one is at it."[50] For Derrida, too, it is clear that this is "our" inheritance, a testament that Europeans inherit from their Greek forefathers. In that, however, it is also an opportunity: "The testament is the Bible of hermeneutics."[51] Reading the testamentary inheritance in an attempt to denaturalize the figure of the brother and especially Carl Schmitt's pretense that his placement of the friend/enemy distinction at the heart of the political is a mere "diagnosis," Derrida finds in the same tradition the graft for a "friendship without friendship," beyond friendship qua brotherhood, an an-economic friendship based on an asymmetrical, unequal, but also nonreciprocal and nonprofitable relation with an other—a gift. The relation is imagined by Derrida as a mixture of friendship and love in the middle voice—*aimance* he calls it, borrowing from the literary field. This loving friendship allows for a woman friend, such that a woman can be a partner in relation rather than a conduit to it. For Derrida, this means moving beyond the exemplary figure of the prostitute (Georges Bataille's Edwarda) to a new figure of the sister, not only not a variation on brother, but also not the sister of a sisterhood. We are beyond the traffic in women at this stage in the argument because we are beyond familiar, familial notions of community. The sister is the "ally, collaborator and friend"—the new comrade, if you will.

European Exchange

For Lévi-Strauss, kinship remains linked to the family, but it is largely a symbolic system. It is, in his words, a "system of attitudes" resulting in a range of affects. What it does is "'pump' women out of their consanguineous families to redistribute them in affinal groups."[52] Affinity opens the gate for the term *kinship* to describe affective relations among a variety of groups. Solidarity and fraternity are anchored in affinal rather than natural kinship. Peter Wade glosses this insight when he writes: "The destabilization of nature highlights the different possible meanings of nature and the variety of modes of naturalization and this, in turn, opens up kinship studies in various ways that connect them usefully to studies of race, ethnicity and nationality."[53] Indeed, we know that the nation is imagined as a community of affines, a brotherhood or fraternity brought together by the affective mix called *patriotism*. The nation is an affective economy; in Benedict Anderson's words, it is a "deep, horizontal comradeship . . . a fraternity."[54] The nation is predicated on the *possibility* of an exchange among the brothers of the imagined fraternity. What theorists of nationalism (or of diaspora) do not pursue is the implication that the brothers whose connections form the fabric of the nation are brothers-in-law, brothers by virtue of an ever more diffuse and largely imaginary exchange. Wade emphasizes that this is racialized kinship, where affinity is underwritten by tacit racial assumptions.

It needs to be acknowledged that kinship comes with the risk of reinforcing the concept's familialist foundations. Camille Robcis has shown how structuralist arguments inspired by Lévi-Strauss and Lacan have been used in France for conservative purposes in family law.[55] Yet I concur with Janet Carsten when she writes: "Rather than simply assuming that the connection between family and nation is a metaphorical one, I think it is worth scrutinizing the 'blurred boundaries' between kinship, the nation, and religion more carefully. . . . [T]he power of the hackneyed metaphor of the nation as family rests partly with its very familiarity. As a 'metaphor we live by,' it structures our experience of nationhood. But under extreme conditions, this metaphor can become a living actuality. And this slippage is a vital component of the force of kinship in the political realm."[56] In the European Union (which is not a nation but is a nationalism), kinship becomes a living actuality, for example, when immigration policy is reduced to "family reunification." This book's wager is that to fail to read kinship in this reality is a greater risk than the always present worry of (heterosexual) familialism.

Today a film like *Occident* challenges us to ask how a transnational entity like Europe might function as a complex structure of kinship. In order to begin to answer this question, we need to enter the terrain of European studies and its modes of discourse.

The rhetoric of the European Union often draws on the archaic language of the family. The 2007 EU "enlargement" was announced under the banner "Romania and Bulgaria Join the European Family." The first Romanian European commissioner, Leonard Orban, described the moment thus: "The fifth round of enlargement is now complete with Romania and Bulgaria's accession to the EU. This is an historic moment, both for the EU and for the new member states. Most Romanians believe that EU accession represents the moment when their country has returned to the European family."[57] "Welcome to the European Family" was the aegis under which Croatia joined the European Union in 2013.

The idea that Europe is a family has a long genealogy. In 1849, Victor Hugo gave an address at the first International Peace Congress in Paris in which he spoke of the day when "all you nations of the continent, without losing distinctive qualities or your individual glories, will bind yourself tightly together into a single superior entity, and you will come to constitute a European fraternity."[58] Hugo's idea would find resonances in the last decades of the twentieth century. In 1997, François Guizot's *History of Civilization in Europe* found that Europe's only feature is diversity but that no one can deny the existence of a "family likeness, which it is impossible to mistake," recognizable across European difference.[59] Anthony Smith has likewise described Europe as a "*family* of cultures."[60] In the context of his musing on the benefits of the Erasmus program, Umberto Eco speaks of the "fratricidal wars" that have long plagued Europe.[61] In contradistinction, Turkey's EU candidacy is described as a possible "forced marriage."[62] Within European debates on immigration, a language of generation is deployed to describe the long temporality of European acculturation (we speak of first-generation immigrants, second-generation, etc.). Needless to say, generations are familial categories.

Furthermore, whether with recourse to a familial rhetoric or not, the European Union imagines itself as a community. The European market was instituted in 1957 under the name of the European Economic Community. The 1992 Treaty of Maastricht refined the name into the European Union and performed an unprecedented transnational double move: it created European citizenship and the conditions for the euro. As a market, the European Union is a system of exchanges. The most visible objects of exchange are economic in nature—goods and services. But the European Union also circulates signs within a structure imagined as a public sphere. Significantly, Jürgen Habermas has revisited his theory of the public sphere in light of the perceived urgency to think the European Union as a public sphere.[63] At the most basic level, the European Union circulates languages and translations. It is the job of European media, like Euronews or Eurozine, to facilitate linguistic exchange. Although they have not achieved the status of pan-European sources of information and continue to be sifted through national and global networks, these media are instrumental in at least building the *illusion* of a common European public space.

An important dimension of Europe's network of circulation is education. The Erasmus program is a highly successful *exchange* program, circulating students on their way to becoming European citizens. European tourism is in close proximity to educational programs. Europe sponsors a number of cultural events that mobilize large numbers of bodies to move across its "erased borders." Adding to the success of the European Capitals of Culture initiative, in 2007 the European Parliament started the European Film Prize (LUX), which facilitates the subtitling of the winning film into all European languages and makes it available in all member states. In 2009, the EU Prize for Literature was inaugurated to "promote the circulation of literature within Europe and encourage greater interest in non-national literary works."[64] These programs are conducted under the large umbrella of culture, and their explicit goal is the circulation of the signs that form culture. We can slowly begin to make our way back to *Occident* by asking how the beneficiaries of the European Union's eastward expansion fare in this exchange.

The essence of the kinship structure described by Mauss or Lévi-Strauss is that the relations it entails are reciprocal (I throw a party for you; you throw a party for me). But, in the economic landscape of the East European 1990s, one could hear a recurrent complaint: "We have nothing to sell."[65] The countries of East Europe had few desirable commodities for the consumer heavens of glitzy West Europe. As for the public sphere, there has not been much of an exchange in signs either, as European intellectual exchange is most often a one-way street. With the exception of a few émigrés from the Cold War era, who for a long time tended to reproduce Cold War narratives in neoliberal garb, few East European voices are part of a genuine intellectual exchange across the East/West European divide.[66] In many ways, the current situation continues a Cold War pattern of West European intellectuals whispering into East European ears the secret to their emancipation.

But if East European goods and services, on the one hand, and signs, on the other, have been scarce as objects of European exchange, what the countries of East Europe did have in the wake of 1989 were women. They have often been described as *good women,* embodiments of a nostalgic past untainted by feminism in which women presumably knew and enjoyed staying in their place. Ursula Biemann's video essay *Writing Desire* (2000) describes the fantasy an East European woman is thought to approximate: "she is beautiful and feminine / she is loving and traditional / she is humble and devoted / she likes to listen to mellow music / the smile is her rhetorical gesture / she believes in a lasting marriage / and a happy home / she is a copy of the First World's past" (see fig. 1.2).

The irony is that, when they decide to go to market, East European women *can* sell this fantasy on the European market. Having passed through the "real-existing socialist" experiment, East European women are thought to have come out as traditional women who cook, clean, and smile. Matrimonial agencies promise they will be grateful. They are often referred to as *model-looking,* a euphemism that describes the fact that their bodies do not (yet) carry traces of what Europeans dread under the name *McDonaldization.* Within the global market of women, they can also pass as white and can reproduce white children in a Europe worried about the birth rate among its "native" population. They are trusted to raise these children dutifully, disseminating the motherly love that is argued to have become scant in the Western world in the wake of second-wave feminism.[67] As Arlie Russell Hochschild would put it, East Europe is a fresh reservoir of love.[68] If neoliberal discourse attempts to save these women by modernizing them, many West European men nostalgically desire their backwardness.

Fig. 1.2. Ursula Biemann frames the technologies that produce East European backwardness. Video still from Ursula Biemann's *Writing Desire* (2000).

It should go without saying that East European women are not the traditional brides-in-waiting that Internet descriptions market. In *Occident*, Mihaela insists that she does not cook, wash, etc. After all, traditional women do not marry foreigners through matrimonial agencies. These potential brides are active and knowledgeable with regard to marketing techniques and do what they deem necessary to sell themselves. They know how to use new media and new technologies. On their way to market, East European women manufacture their backwardness; they present themselves as prefeminist ideal wives in order to have a chance to attract attention on a very busy market. But a lot of aesthetic labor (in some ways similar to that done by the models to which they are likened) goes into the production of organic femininity. Like Bollywood divas, East European women wear their hyperfemininity as a form of drag. They visibly overdo it, producing a free-floating surplus of sexuality. Indeed, one could say that these women are career oriented, except that (for now at least) marriage to a Western man is the only career available to them.

Since one cannot live on credit forever, not responding to the economic gifts coming from the wealthier members of the European Union, lest one lose *face* (Mauss's word for status and honor), East European countries export women. In return, they get not other women but goods, services, and plenty of signs. Any marriage comes with gifts, Lévi-Strauss argued.

This is an oblique, fragile, and unequal form of reciprocity, an ironic comment on Lévi-Strauss's warning that there will always be those who try to acquire more wives, aesthetically or economically more appealing. Unequal exchange is a sign of what Derrida critiques in the notion of generosity, which translates into political prestige for the party offering more than can be reciprocated. It is the privilege of the Big Man—and First World nations.

When it comes to transnational European marriage, as a rule East European women marrying on the European market marry down, according to what sociologists call the *marriage gradient*. This is the principle according to which men usually marry down economically and socially while women marry up. In other words, for women, marital romance is usually an upward-mobility narrative. However, East European women who take the European road to marriage marry both up and down. They marry down because they marry the undesirable men of Western Europe. They marry the men Western women for one reason or another do not want, the odds and ends of the national marriage market. At the same time they marry up because Europe performs a gendered redistribution of class across the West/East divide. An East European woman marries up simply by virtue of marrying a Western man, even one who would not be a match for her locally.

On the Western end of exchange, what is imported through women is affective labor. East European nannies, maids, and nurses care for their employers in West European nations. Wives do the same kind of labor, except they are not paid and do not benefit from labor protections. It is a much better economic deal for a German working-class man to marry a Romanian woman than to hire a domestic servant to take care of his house, a nurse to attend to his elders, and a prostitute to have sex with occasionally. The Romanian wife brings it all in one package. The fact that there is emotional attachment in the mix only reinforces the point.[69] It is affect and sex-affective labor that is circulated. The labor involved in affective labor, as Michael Hardt and others have argued, has as its stakes the production of a relationship, in this case a marital relationship. There are serious limits to the parallel in the contemporary world, but one would have to ask, with Goldman, how this situation is both similar to and different from prostitution. One way to answer this question is to acknowledge that prostitution is a form of affective labor, too.[70] The prostitute does a lot of work—affective work—before and during sex. Most importantly, she works to produce a relationship with her clients; she uses her skills to construct an image that sells; she cultivates certain aspects of her affective personality to create bonds that endure over time; she works to produce the illusion or reality of shared interests and good conversation. And she makes it all appear easy and pleasurable. Kipnis has shown that contemporary domestic relationships, marriage in particular, require precisely *this* kind of labor.[71]

But, if, as Hardt maintains, immaterial affective labor has become generalized through the informational economy and women's work (on a continuum from sex work to marriage) is a model for this larger trend, one still feels the need to distinguish among acutely gendered labor situations in which "the division between economy and culture begins to break down."[72] In the imaginary case offered above, the Romanian woman in the German household is both at work and at home, participating around the clock in both production and reproduction, creating life and community, in a precarious labor situation with no labor rights, no protection, and no guarantee of remuneration. This is immaterial, affective labor, but it also needs to be rethought through the lens of the traffic in women as women's work in a European and global frame.

Arlie Russell Hochschild speaks of *emotional imperialism*, which extracts emotional resources from poor countries.[73] This is emotional caring work (which does not preclude physical work) that supplements the labor of those Western women who have become suspicious of their traditional roles as caretakers and have moved on to claim their right to full citizenship by participating in the paid labor market. Since the generic worker in the contemporary capitalist economy is expected to work around the clock and is assumed to be without baggage like family or children, the labors of care and family work have been largely commercialized. Rather than redistributing it among the men and women of wealthy nations, the second shift has been outsourced to economically less fortunate women. An Italian female academic who hires a Romanian nanny to care for her children while she is writing or teaching thus occupies the structural position of exchanger while at the same time reinforcing the gendered structure of exchange.[74] This is not to say that the Italian woman (and, by extension, feminism) is to *blame* for this situation, although she is complicit with it. As we will see in chapter 2, the feminist project has been to denaturalize women's work as the destiny of women and redistribute its tasks within the Western family and across the social body. The project was conceived as long-term. Somewhere along the way, globalization, post-Fordism, emerging austerity, and the presumption of postfeminism have created the conditions for the outsourcing of a substantial chunk of women's work to non-European and East European women.

The European Union has since its inception encouraged the mobility of labor. What is new in the recent predicament is the large number of women who, although European, travel *to* Europe for work and marriage. Despite the focus on the aggressiveness of the *Polish plumber* (the figure that for a while was used to refer to East European migrant workers), what circulates is a feminized labor force. This is not an issue for debate in the mainstream European publics because it is often invisible labor—housework. But, even when this labor is visible, the issue still does not become relevant enough for European debate. Habermas argues that one of the functions of the public sphere is to filter public discourse.[75] It is unlikely that the traffic in women in all its ramifications will be on the EU agenda in the near future. After all, no family washes its dirty linen in public. *Occident* is here, however, to draw our attention to the existence of publics in which a debate on the traffic in women can be traced.

The Desire for Occident

Occident makes it clear that for a Romanian the European is not a foreigner in the same way a Saudi man is.[76] There are affinities among Romanians and Belgians or Italians, though they too were once structurally impossible matches. Mihaela's parents, very much of the generation that lived the "real-existing socialism" experiment in isolation (a famous Romanian actor, Dorel Vișan, plays Mihaela's father), are willing to and proactive in securing a European marriage for her.[77] They do what they can to foreground an essentialized sense of trans-European affinity. Europe is a function of a set of languages (a lot is made of Romanian and Italian being Romance languages, sister languages), traditions (see the sketches of Roman profiles on the walls of the Romanian apartment), and culture (pasta, music, etc.). There is an assumed layer of shared civility as mannered behavior, exploited for comic effect, but also doing important ideological work. Europe is also the performance of exclusion on tacit racial, ethnic, and religious grounds, as evidenced in *Occident* by the black Italian, and as the debates about Turkey's EU candidacy demonstrate. Although he is both an Italian and a European citizen, Luigi is not European, which is why he does not correspond (friends as brothers correspond in that they are a symmetrical match for each other, they answer to each other). He thus cannot participate in the European traffic in women. For Mihaela's father, who would need to accept him as a partner in exchange, he is African. And Africa is not even on the global map offered by the Romanian matrimonial agency, before Mihaela's options are narrowed to the familiar European marriage. This is not to say that Mihaela's family is white in the larger European framework. It is because he is anxious about his own racial status that the Romanian father is so vehement in his refusal of Luigi. Intuiting that racialization works differently at home and in the West European metropole, he anticipates that in order for his daughter to be European she needs to form alliances with white Europeans.[78]

Mihaela's parents put pressure on her to marry (she is twenty four, and they fear that she is getting old), but they do not force her. Nor is there an immediate economic pressure, as she has a relatively comfortable life with her parents. But stories circulate about a certain Emilia who married abroad and now lives comfortably doing nothing as a housewife and about a life of glamour in Occident, with daily trips to McDonald's. These rumors produce their own pressure; they create desire, and thus migration leads to further migration. Mihaela too can do what these other women have done, proving her worth as a woman. Besides, she wants a better life, and she wants to publish her poems (one wonders who reads Romanian poetry in Italy). She is not a victim; a European marriage is what she wants. This is also what she has been brought to want both by the long history of the Cold War, with its glimmers of a forbidden heaven in the West, and by the post-1989 predicament, with its deferred promises of democratic consumerism. Mihaela is a subject, in both senses of the word, which is not in contradiction with the fact that, at a structural, systemic level (that of European kinship), she is also an object of traffic.

What is the situation of Romanian men in this predicament? In *Occident*, Lucian comes across as the representative of an injured masculinity. He is a researcher, but he has a job in advertising, walking around the city as a mascot. ("Commodities have a soul, too," he is told. His job is to give soul to a beer bottle.) It is clear that the future has nothing bright in store for him. In his personal life, he is confronted with oppressive poverty, a form of precarity lived in some of its most acute forms by various East European masculinities. At the very beginning of the film, Lucian and his fiancée, Sorina, find their things in the middle of the street as they have just been evicted from their apartment. The viewer is unsure whether this is good or bad because the building in which they lived (the literal ruins of "real-existing socialism") hardly looks livable (see fig. 1.3). An oppressive grayness (the East European staple color) defines the mood of the place. Their only hope is an old aunt who owns an apartment in another decrepit building. The aunt would have to die to make space for the new generation, yet she does not because she is waiting for her son, who has disappeared in Germany. As Lucian and Sorina discuss their future, he is literally knocked down, hit by a bottle, and throughout the film he does not seem to be able to overcome his headache,

Fig. 1.3. The ruins of the communist project. Frame from Cristian Mungiu's *Occident* (2002).

the immediate source of his confusion. Lucian tries to enact various outdated scripts of masculinity, all of which fall flat, triggering the laughter of the film's audience.

Sorina has reached the point at which it seems like the only solution to her problems is emigration. For reasons that are not completely clear, Lucian resists. "This is our home," he reminds her timidly. It is not an argument anymore. "Why should I go," he asks a friend, "to clean toilets there?"[79] Besides, he thinks that it is his duty to care for his dying aunt. But he finds himself in the paradoxical position in which he cannot compete for his own fiancée. The "best women" have become "export material."[80] The result is a clear sense of emasculation. This loss of masculinity is not necessarily something to be deplored as Romanian culture has an important macho dimension in need of a more balanced gender dynamic. But, if change is to have lasting effects, it should perhaps not be the outcome of transnational humiliation.[81]

Occident provides ironic commentary on the golden age of "real-existing socialism." In a central scene in the film, Lucian and Mihaela struggle to remember an old song from their childhood. They are surprised when the tune and the words come back to them, as if from another life. It is a pioneers' song about the year 2000, the projection for the millennial coming of communism. Mihaela and Sorina's generation had the glorious mission of bringing the dream to fruition in the year 2000. But the century of communism has become obsolete, and it has abandoned its children. They now have a choice between giving life to global capitalism locally or exporting their labor power to the new promised land of Occident. "Is this how you imagined the year 2000?" Lucian asks.[82]

The Traffic in Women as a Category of Analysis

This chapter has argued that the *traffic in women* continues to have explanatory power when it comes to contemporary kinship structures, however altered and diffuse. It helps explain the networks of exchange within the European Union, which it makes visible as an anthropological structure, and can function as a starting point for a critique of the underlying political economy. But, if *Occident* offers a genuine *j'accuse* of European kinship, the impact it could have is diminished not only by the fact that most East Europeans (including Romanians) have not seen it but also by Mungiu's interviews, in which he often denies the political implications of his work. In the Romanian political landscape, the European Union could only be embraced. Only the nationalist Right and, more recently, a number of opportunistic politicians have been critical of "integration," and any skepticism risks the embarrassment of this association. The same neoconservative predicament has made *feminism* an insult word, and Mungiu would not want to be thus labeled. As a result, he insists that he makes comedies, and, indeed, during screenings of *Occident* the movie theater is filled with laughter. But we have come to know that there is laughter and laughter, and the long, hysteric bursts that punctuate the film's marriage market scenes offer their own logic of critique.

It is as if the cinematic public sphere comes to remind us that critique—if possible, without its paranoid dimensions—is the proper business of European intellectuals in East and West Europe. The European Union is still in the making, and, for a while at least (how long?), it remains a promise that we might want to pursue.[83] Europe is an opening, an opportunity to play with kinship such that the black Italian is not a structural impossibility and East Europe is not the handmaiden of Europe. In the meantime, an arranged marriage between Luigi and Mihaela does seem a good idea if it is understood as a comradeship/*aimance* between South and East on European territory—but only insofar as the two work against the mediation of Europe, which has historically predetermined their relation, rendering their solidarity impossible, for the sake of Europe.

So far, Mihaela's story seems to confirm the European traffic in women in the global European moment. Mihaela is sad as she leaves, saying good-bye to the man she loves, who in his turn is mourning the loss of his love object bound for Europe. "We do what we have to do," she tells him. Her parents retire and return to the village from which "real-existing socialism" took them. The experiment is over, they have just exported their offspring, and there is nothing else left to do. Their life in the city (they are first-generation urbanites) has become historical refuse. The young Romanian man has been quiet all along and is left in a sad, deserted industrial landscape. He can go back to his beers with his friends and talk infinitely about the ones who left and the ones who are preparing to leave (an estimated three of twenty million Romanians work abroad). This is a relatively good situation, given that, in films like Lukas Moodysson's *Lilja 4-Ever* and Jean-Pierre and Luc Dardenne's *Lorna's Silence*, the focus of chapter 4, the figure of the ambitious East European young man seems to have no choice but to endorse the European traffic in women.

As *Occident* ends, there is no reason for the viewer not to go on, speculating about what will happen to Mihaela in Occident. I see two scenarios but will propose only one: Mihaela writes day and night, slowly moving away from the poems of her youth, to test possibilities for relation at the (if possible, unromanticized) limits of literature, broadly understood. Sooner or later she meets a version of a symbolic mother (it could be a man), who invites her to join a contemporary variation on the feminist bookstore. In time, they disseminate a new writing and its accompanying practices in a Europe in which the narratives of women's exchange and the Europe created in their folds slowly become unrecognizable. Mihaela has a lot of work to do. But I have high hopes for her.

2 Import/Export

Housework in an International Frame

Traditionally done by women under the auspices of the family, "women's work" has been outsourced over the last two decades to women from outside the family and often from outside the nation. This chapter will rethink housework in an international and European frame and consider its affinities with other forms of labor engendered by late capitalism. Ulrich Seidl's *Import/Export* (2007) dramatizes the European housework predicament and serves as my entry point into the housework debate. The film exposes viewers to the embodied knowledge of nonprofessional actors, who lend documentary immediacy to fictional scenes, characters, and dialogue. A close reading of the film expands our understanding of the contemporary, transnational continuum of women's work, pointing to the post-1989 emergence of an international private sphere. Arguments about foreign language learning and translation are central to the film's project, as is the use of visual gesture in a context in which language often fails or feels inadequate. I will take a brief excursion through Seidl's film before turning to the second-wave feminist debate on housework and identifying its points of convergence with autonomist neo-Marxism, one of the most influential theories of post-Fordist labor.

Released on the cusp of the European economic crisis that began in 2008, *Import/Export* put "the four freedoms" invoked by EU officials in their rightful economic framework, rethinking the free movement of persons as the gendered import/export of labor. In the film's title sequence, the red space of *import* almost unnoticeably slides into the white of *export*. Whether a person is the object of import or export is relative to one's location in Europe. Location, however, is highly unstable ground in late capitalism, when the position of importer of cheap labor is fragile and one can always become an exporter of one's own labor power. In the film, a young Ukrainian woman (Olga) and a young Austrian man (Paul) are, for different reasons, simultaneously "export material" in their countries of origin and "import material" in each other's countries. The film deals with import/export in two specific countries, Ukraine and Austria, but it takes these locations as emblematic of the continent's two poles, "Western Europe," which often goes by the name of *Europe*, and "Eastern Europe." Although only half the film is devoted to Olga, I will focus on her. I will argue that she embodies a new figure of the housewife, one that foregrounds the place of housework within the contemporary traffic in women.

Two Europes

Olga is played by Ekateryna Rak, a nonprofessional Ukrainian actress selected by Seidl through a casting call. Seidl described his casting choices in an interview: "I thought it would be better to get somebody who doesn't know the language and has never been to the West. So we did a casting call in Ukraine, with the requirements that there would be no actresses from Kiev, only women from the sticks who had never been in front of a camera."[1] At the beginning of the film, the viewer witnesses Ekateryna Rak–turned–Olga attempting to supplement her salary as a nurse by working in the Ukrainian branch of the global cybersex industry. The viewer becomes privy to a series of scenes that show Ukrainian women posing for Internet voyeurs, who order them to strip, dance, and orgasm. The women do it mechanically, sometimes chatting among themselves. A handheld following shot motivated by Olga's movement passes by room after room in which young Ukrainian women fake technology-mediated pleasure for global Internet consumers. Sex and its attendant affective performances become hot postsocialist commodities. The scene spotlights the widening abyss between post-1989 idealism (1989 is our "last revolution") and the materialities of the crudest, most unregulated form of market capitalism that has followed it. Everything is for sale.

Fig. 2.1. Ukrainian cybersex workers learn German. Frame from Ulrich Seidl's *Import/Export* (2007).

In the context of the cybersex sequence, Olga is given a German language lesson. What kind of foreign language skills does work in cybersex require? Olga does not need to say much in front of the webcam, but the little she does say is essential to the success of the economic transaction. Even if she does not speak ("I do not want to see your face," one customer shouts at her), she needs to understand what she is asked to do. Listening skills take center stage. The composition of the language-lesson shot is reminiscent of a Toulouse-Lautrec painting (see fig. 2.1). We are accustomed to seeing dancers dancing, but, like Toulouse-Lautrec, Seidl plays with the viewer's expectations. Here, sex workers are learning foreign languages. It is a casual, quiet, intimate scene. Framed by the walls of a narrow hallway in a decrepit postindustrial Soviet building, Olga and her friend are taking a cigarette break. They use the opportunity to practice their German. The camera is obdurately static in this scene, focusing the viewer's attention on minute gestural shifts.[2] Struck by the incongruity of a language lesson conducted in the industry's livery, Olga bursts out laughing, only to be admonished that work is no laughing matter. She eventually has to give up the job not only because she is stiff, clumsy, and embarrassed and cannot quite perform its visual tasks but also because she cannot translate its minimalist communicative transactions. She would need to learn what Habermas would call *core European languages* (German, French, English) to be able to successfully sell postsocialist sexuality on the European market.[3]

Olga's Ukraine is metonymically represented by a bankrupt postsocialist medical system (a stand-in for the East European state in a perpetual state of transition toward European and Euroatlantic institutions) and the cybersex industry (a stand-in for market capitalism). The film takes this Ukraine as the background to Olga's European travels. The bottom line in the film's initial situation: Olga cannot make a living in Ukraine. The West European labor market is no haven, but certain gender-specific jobs present themselves as opportunities.[4] When one day a mysterious letter arrives, presumably from a friend asking Olga to join her in Austria, Olga packs her things in the middle of the night and places her infant son on her mother's bed. The nonprofessional actors in Seidl's film improvised all dialogue, and, in this particular scene, mother and daughter choose to say nothing. Silence is an eloquent cinematic gesture. The mother knew all along that Olga was export material; it was only a question of when her time to leave would come. The silence between mother and daughter is thick with unspeakable, contradictory, yet structurally congruent affective attachments to past and future promises, socialist *and* capitalist. It goes without saying that Olga's mother will care for her infant son. Such is the beginning of Olga's narrative of transnational motherhood.

Once Olga is in Austria, the slowness of Seidl's camera becomes a mimetic repetition of the temporal tediousness of her tasks. In a long, painful scene, Seidl has her Austrian female employer teach Olga how to brush the teeth of a decorative stuffed dog's head on the wall, satirizing the Austrian lower middle class turned European bourgeoisie with their petty pleasures and decorative objects. In other scenes, we see Olga dust and scrub floors. We see her retire to her room, a laundry room with an Ikea bed in one corner. We see her pack and leave, carrying suitcases and bags, after she is fired. We see her move to another job, as a cleaning lady in a geriatric ward. In this new job, she is reprimanded for combing a patient's hair. She is not a nurse, an Austrian nurse reminds her; she is a cleaning lady. Olga had been a certified nurse in Ukraine, but Seidl's film makes sure its viewer understands that a new European division of labor is in force to keep Olga in her place as a cleaning lady.

When Olga enters the West European labor market, she simultaneously enters a new sex market. She attracts the attention of two men in the geriatric ward. "Are you from Serbia?" a young male nurse inquires. The film does not pause to mark the irony. In today's Europe, the only question asked about a "white" cleaning lady is *where* in East Europe she comes from.[5] One of the patients in the geriatric ward, Erich, also takes an interest in Olga. He goes so far as to propose to her: "You can stay with me. . . . I'll pay you, you'll live with me. . . . I'll have a pretty woman again. . . . And if you're good, I'll even marry you." Olga laughs. "It's a great chance for you to stay in Austria as an Austrian," the man retorts. Olga stops laughing. One of her East

European friends (played by Seidl's own cleaning lady) tells her about the advantages and risks of a "paper husband." Marriage would land Olga the job of personal attendant, a detail presented by the film with matter-of-fact, almost Rabelaisian grotesque realism.[6]

Having positioned Olga on the market for men's sexual attention, Seidl's film ends with a wrestling match between Olga and a female Austrian nurse. This conclusion follows a party in the geriatric ward given for the entertainment of the patients. A young male nurse asks Olga to dance. Later, as she leaves the party, a female nurse attacks her. Filmed in a medium long shot that captures the violent yet intimate imbrication of two half-naked female bodies, the scene foregrounds the growing tension between East and West European women. "A young, blonde pretty thing like you always finds a man," Olga was told earlier in the film. Both nursing jobs and marriageable West European men seem to have become scarce commodities, and women—Westerners, Easterners, and women from the global South—fight for them. The year is 2007. Only forty years have passed since Julia Kristeva hailed "European women" as the collective agent of a future European feminism. What happened?

Housework

Seidl's film documents the continuum of labor on which a woman like Olga moves—from unpaid care work for her family, to nursing and cybersex in Ukraine, to cleaning, elder care, and potential marriage in Austria. Prostitution is always in the air as a possibility. These are jobs on the continuum of women's work, variations on the role of the traditional housewife. I want to assess what it means for Olga to engage in this labor while the former Western housewife often toils in other sectors of the labor market. Housework has once again become a prism through which to understand the workings of political economy, this time in an international and European frame. Barbara Ehrenreich memorably described the rallying of second-wave feminists around the rejection of housework: "When, somewhere, a man dropped a sock with the calm expectation that his wife would retrieve it, it was a sock heard around the world."[7] When today a man drops a sock with the calm expectation that various Olgas will retrieve it, it is in fact a sock heard around the world. Seidl's film attempts to capture the rippling echoes that the quiet landing of such a sock produces in the cinematic public sphere and, possibly, outside it as well. What, then, is housework?

Having for a long time looked at the Marxist tradition for an understanding of the economic dimension of oppression, second-wave feminists emphasized the limits of its application to the economics of women's oppression. Their premise was that *women* constitutes an economic category in relation to the capitalist mode of production. *Housework* was the keyword around which this insight developed. Whether women participate in the paid labor force or not, for the most part they are responsible for the labor of reproduction. "This incessant reproduction, this perpetuation of the worker, is the absolutely necessary condition for capitalist production," Marx had written.[8] Women's labor in the familial household is instrumental to the maintenance and reproduction of what Engels called *immediate life*, the labor power on which the reproduction of capital depends.[9] This work involves cooking, cleaning, the care and education of children, and sometimes sex.[10] If women went on strike for a meaningful amount of time, there would be no reproduction and, therefore, no production.[11] "Wages for housework" seemed the logical conclusion—not primarily for the wages but because only waged labor was recognized as labor. "To say that we want money for housework is the first step toward refusing to do it," Silvia Federici wrote.[12]

Second-wave feminists provided a thick description of the labor involved in housework. They took pleasure in listing the dreaded tasks: "Here's my list of dirty chores: buying groceries, carting them home and putting them away; cooking meals and washing dishes and pots; doing the laundry; digging out the place when things get out of control; washing floors. The list could go on but the sheer necessities are bad enough. All of us have to do these jobs, *or get someone else to do them for us*."[13] They spotlighted the work's monotony. Onerousness. Pervasiveness. Repetitiveness. Circularity. Futility. The endless routine. The isolation. The smells. The emotional toll: "Neuroses, suicides, desexualization: occupational diseases of the housewife."[14]

Commenting on the medium's disinclination to represent work, domestic or otherwise, Chantal Akerman's film *Jeanne Dielman, 23 Quai du Commerce, 1080 Bruxelles* (1975) portrayed the dreaded routine. A fictional housewife, Jeanne, is filmed by a frontal camera that remains fixed, suggesting that no action worth following is taking place. Jeanne cooks, dusts, tidies up, serves dinner to her son, and has sex with a few male visitors. Everything unfolds in extended duration, at the same pace, and at the same level of enthusiasm (see fig. 2.2). What film critics call *temps mort* becomes the stuff of cinema for Akerman. Viewers are forced to live the ensuing slowness, repetitiveness, and boredom as a function of spectatorship. Hard at work on the tasks of spectatorship, they learn "on their own skin" (if they do not already know) how it *feels* to move from kitchen to bedroom and back to the

Fig. 2.2. Three instances of housework.
Frames from Chantal Akerman's *Jeanne Dielman* (1975).

kitchen and then back to the bedroom, each time turning the light on and off, seemingly a million times.

Having offered a diagnosis, second-wave feminists imagined solutions to the problem of housework. One was the commune; housework should be done collectively, by men as well as women. More widespread was the demand for the socialization of housework, which often went hand in hand with the industrialization of housework. This meant that housework should be done professionally, by the state (in the case of socialization) or by private businesses (in the case of industrialization), employing people from outside the family, trained for these purposes, who would be paid accordingly. Ellen Malos added an important qualification to this demand: "A struggle for *both* socialized housework *and* shared tasks of personal maintenance across sex lines in the home . . . sharing of necessary housework with men (and children) is important too, since not all housework can be taken outside the home."[15] It is often forgotten that central to the struggle for the socialization of reproductive housework, at least in its early stages, was the mobilization for the right to "universal, twenty-four-hour child care." While abortion was meant to liberate women from the burden of biological reproduction, child care would liberate them from the labors of social reproduction.[16]

Second-wave feminists imagined that the socialization of housework would undermine the sexual division of labor. Their goal was to slowly render irrelevant the economic category *women*. It was an argument dependent on place: the place of women's labor, inside or outside the home. If they so desired, women should enter the paid labor market and work outside the home—or at least outside their own homes. The risk remained that they would continue to do women's work, extending the parameters of the sexual division of labor. Vivien Leone put it succinctly: "When you do it for free, you're a wife; when you do it for money, you're a maid."[17] Wendy Edmond argued: "A lot of the work that I did at my job in a shop was housework. . . . [S]omehow I hadn't stopped being a housewife."[18] In an article titled "The Home in the Hospital," the Power of Women Collective insisted: "The hospital worker is a waged houseworker. . . . [H]ospital work is socialised, industrialised housework."[19] Juliet Mitchell extrapolated: "At present women perform unskilled, uncreative service jobs that can be regarded as 'extensions' of their expressive familial role."[20]

In response to this realization, the performance artist Mierle Laderman Ukeles staged events in which she cleaned private and public spaces, in an effort to bridge the private and public dimensions of housework, unwaged and waged (see fig. 2.3). For Ukeles, housework proper and its "extensions" came to be captured by the phrase *maintenance work*.[21] The project assumed

Fig. 2.3. Housework outside the house. Mierle Laderman Ukeles, *Hartford Wash: Washing, Tracks, Maintenance* (1973).

that, once staged as "care art," maintenance work and the sexual division of labor on which it rests would lose their naturalness.[22] Housework would come to be valued and enjoyed as creative labor, and, thus, its implacable synonymy with habit made famous by Proust's words "Habit! That skillful but very slow housekeeper" would in time become obsolete.[23]

The feminist arguments of the 1970s need rearticulation in light of post-1989 globalizing political and economic developments that, among other things, brought Olga to Vienna.[24] The sexual division of labor is very much in force. It has remained in force in the Western family, where women continue to be responsible for most of the housework since the much-desired redistribution of housework between the members of the family has not occurred.[25] But the sexual division of labor has also been further extended in the last decades—on both old and new patterns of class, racial, and ethnic stratification.[26] Today there is an international and European sexual division of labor; women do women's work, the old chores of housework, transnationally, on a traffic-in-women pattern. The statelessness implicit in the old familial private sphere is often literalized.[27] What we are describing on the margins of Seidl's film is a process whereby the private sphere has been rearticulated around the figure of the stateless foreigner and, often in the case of the European Union, the second-class citizen. The statelessness of the children on this scene is separated along parentage lines between those who do not yet enjoy full citizenship rights but can aspire to them and those (whether present or absent) who are likely to inherit their parents' disenfranchised status (those second- and third-generation "immigrants").

For the most part, as was often the case in the past, there are "wages for housework." They are not, however, the wages that second-wave feminists imagined. They are meager, passport-determined wages (we will return to passports in chapter 4). They certainly are not a "breadwinner's wages," enough to support Olga's daily maintenance costs in Austria and her long-distance reproductive costs in Ukraine.[28] "All of us have to do these jobs, *or get someone else to do them for us*," Mainardi's formulation, resonates somewhat differently today, when *or* often marks the rule rather than the exception—at least, for "us" (an ever-growing constituency of West European and American citizens).[29] Instead of coming to be valued as creative and enjoyable work, housework has been returned to its historical degradation, even as its tasks have multiplied.[30] Women do housework outside their own homes and care for children other than their own. If the commune has receded from the horizon of historical possibility, the socialization-cum-industrialization of housework seems to have been accomplished, with a perverse twist.[31]

In *Import/Export*, the woman in the middle-class Austrian household does not do the housework. There is no man in the house, a way for Seidl to reaffirm the enduring assumption that the question of housework is dramatized strictly "between women." One assumes that the Austrian family could hire a company to do the work. Or it can hire Olga—a self-employed East European woman working *as* a woman.[32] Blending elements from Viennese actionism, Italian neorealism, and feminist filmmaking (Akerman) as well as the postcolonial tradition of Ousmane Sembène's *Black Girl* (1966), Seidl's film provides a thick description of Olga's labor.[33] That labor remains tedious, onerous, circular, repetitive, futile. It is physically strenuous. It is taxing psychologically. Olga forever dusts a range of objects, familiar—to her and the viewer—from the global market of cultural images. Once in the West, she does not acquire such objects, contrary to what the global fantasy of mobility promises. But she gets to touch them as she dusts, in an affective milieu of isolation and alienation. "Is this France?" the young Senegalese woman in Sembène's film repeated in 1966 as she moved about the apartment in which she was effectively imprisoned. "Is this Austria?" Olga echoes in 2007. This is not to say that Senegalese women are no longer engaged in this work. They are, but Olga has joined them in their occupational ghettoization. East European women and African women are in competition for the same jobs.

Why, we need to ask, is the figure of the East European domestic worker, in Seidl's film and elsewhere, highly sexualized? Olga replaces the West European wife in some of her roles in the house, which leads to confusion as to where one draws the line on the continuum of care. Reading Freud, Kathleen McHugh reminds us that the Wolfman's repressed image of Grusha, the maid, scrubbing the floor is a cover for his memory of parental coitus, a memory in which the mother is in the same position. We do not know much about Grusha, but her name bears witness to the history of East European women's association with cleaning in metropolitan Vienna. (Grusha is a diminutive for Agrafena, the Russian variation on Agrippina.) McHugh writes: "The inferred but unmentioned figure in this cleaning scene is the prostitute. She, like the maid and governess, supplements the services provided (without pay) by the wife."[34] The bourgeois wife is a nonmaid and a nonprostitute. The triangulation sullies the image of the maid: on her knees, she deals in physical dirt, scrubbing floors; but the position is also associated with the moral dirtiness of the prostitute. The maid becomes a quasi prostitute dwelling at the very heart of the *domus*, as "one of the family." In Seidl's film, the bourgeois mistress of the house is anxious on two counts: Olga is threatening her mothering,[35] and she is a potential prostitute figure for the (absent) man of the house.[36] The viewer witnesses a series of gestures of what Seidl continues to call *everyday fascism*, as the Austrian employer looks through Olga's things before dismissing her. She smells Olga's lipstick in disgust. She inspects her clothes, which look to her like the clothes of a prostitute. She concludes that Olga is too "dirty" and has to leave. The film trusts its viewer with the racial decoding of cleanliness and dirt. The act of spectatorship forces the viewer to "recognize" racialized characteristics in Olga's appearance and behavior.[37]

Olga is the new housewife. As such, she offers an entry point into a new traffic in women. In the 1970s, Catherine Hall did the invaluable work of historicizing the housewife: "Being a housewife, then, is a condition which is socially defined and its definition changes at different historical moments. When we talk about a housewife now we mean a woman whose work is to maintain and organize a household and look after her husband and children—we think of washing, cooking, cleaning and the full-time care of preschool children."[38] Today we witness a new stage in the history of the housewife. To say that Olga is a housewife is to argue that the category theorized and historicized by second-wave feminism needs to be rethought as a structural, nonessential, fragmented, often transnational economic position that anyone can occupy. Not only do Western men often find wives who make good housewives transnationally, but also, when the job is fragmented and outsourced, it is outsourced transnationally.[39] West European parents do not ship their children to Ukraine (a provocative thought experiment proposed by Nancy Folbre),[40] although they have started to ship their elderly to various parts of the world.[41] The tasks of housework are still performed in the Western household, but by a housewife who inhabits it temporarily, as an employee, having commuted across Europe and sometimes across the globe.

Judith Rollins writes: "The domestic is . . . an extension of, surrogate for, the woman of the house."[42] In the typical twenty-first-century middle-class Western family, there still is a wife in the household, but, when she can afford a surrogate, she is not necessarily a housewife. She often works outside the home. She might even love her work since it might be, as Freud imagined, "freely chosen" to respond to "existing inclinations."[43] However, the Western woman may also hate or be indifferent to her work but needs to make ends meet as part of a dual-career couple or as a single mother. Or she may be caught in a vicious circle in which she has to work if she is to be recognized as a modern woman. It is also possible that she does not work but needs "help" anyway—in order to approximate the imperatives of round-the-clock intensive parenting, for example. The heavy demands on the Western woman's time and the fact that housework has not been redistributed among the members of the family produce the *care deficit* that Olga fills.

Olga continues to provide care for her family in Ukraine, her infant son in particular. This is long-distance care, mediated by a phone (see fig. 2.4). It has become a familiar image across contemporary media: mothers talking to their children, often infants, on the phone. Through the sound of her voice, Olga attempts to provide the minimum of care, her concern otherwise manifesting itself in a monthly check. In Ukraine, where, despite the history of "real-existing socialism" and its attendant "state feminism," care has remained a function of kin, the cleaning, cooking, and changing of diapers is done by a grandmother turned mother figure.

Fig. 2.4. Olga calls her son. Frame from Ulrich Seidl's *Import/Export* (2007).

Olga's long-distance mothering is captured by a distant camera. The medium shot relies on the expressivity of Olga's voice, as she sings lullabies to her infant son on the phone, but denies access to the intimacy of her face. The scene may well move the viewer, but it refuses his or her attempt to emotionally short-circuit the long-term intellectual task of understanding what motherhood might mean in a long-distance situation in which care and love are mediated by old and new media (voice and, increasingly, video calls).[44] If it is clear that Olga has to, as we say, work at it when, earlier in the film, she has her son on her lap and unsuccessfully attempts to pacify him, long-distance phone care for a child who might not remember his mother's face has to be recognized as work as well.

Arlie Russell Hochschild has argued that we are witnessing the emergence of a new form of imperialism, whereby emotions—care, love—become distributable resources. We know we can displace and redirect our love, project it on a number of objects. Love, then, can potentially be extracted from poor countries and exported to neocolonial sites. Seidl's film suggests that we might have reached a novel stage in the history of this idea. Olga's female Austrian employer knows about the risks of outsourcing care. It is as if she has read Hochschild and Ehrenreich's *Global Woman*. What she wants from Olga is strictly physical labor. She gives her very detailed instructions. She fires Olga for playing with her children. She does not allow Olga to care. The predicament is repeated on the "public" side of the equation. In the geriatric ward, Olga is urged to stick to her job as a cleaning lady. She is not allowed to touch the patients. Or talk to them. Or comb their hair. The fantasy that East Europe is a new reservoir of love seems to have reached its point

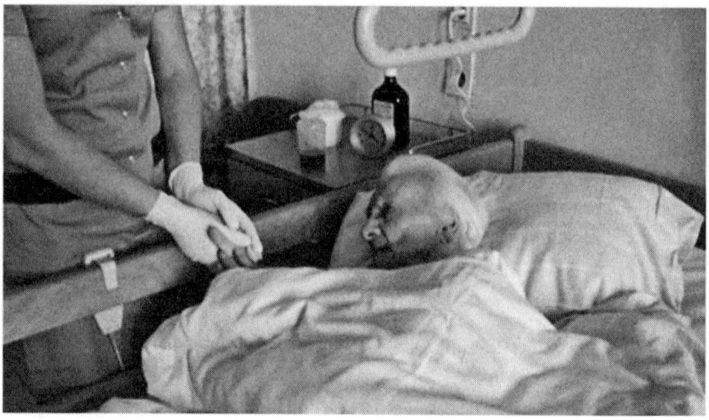

Fig. 2.5. Olga is hired as a cleaning lady but offers unremunerated care. Frame from Ulrich Seidl's *Import/Export* (2007).

of backlash. Love and human touch are not supposed to be on the list of imports from East Europe. *Import/Export* seems to suggest that they come as inevitable by-products, as a function of the surplus humanity that Seidl attributes to "Eastern Europe."[45]

In the context of the 1970s housework debate, Caroline Freeman wrote: "We must aim to draw a wedge between the physical tasks of housework and the emotional servicing wives and mothers are expected to do *as women*."[46] If only we could. Reproduction is a broad category; its physical and emotional tasks are interrelated and not easily separable. The labor involved in mothering is a test case here. Hypothetically, the Austrian mother could provide emotional, loving care to her children, like talking, laughing, caressing, singing, and occasional playing, while Olga could cook the children's food, wash their clothes, walk them to school, and clean their messes. On the one hand, we would have quality time, and, on the other, the dirty work.[47] On the one hand, spiritual work, and, on the other, menial work.[48] The problem is not only that the Austrian mother does not actually perform the spiritual tasks of parenting but also that the dirty work itself is infused with care: Olga touches the patients in the geriatric ward through her cleaning gloves (see fig. 2.5).[49]

The sequence that culminates in this image is filmed at first from a distance by a shaky handheld camera, then by a calmer camera that allows for more proximity but still hesitates and holds back. Finally, the camera stops to frame a planimetric, frontal shot of Olga's head as it slowly tilts down to reveal a photographic pose of her gloved hands touching a patient. The camera's transition from distance to closeness repeats Olga's own evolution in acknowledging that her work as a cleaner involves both menial and spiritual tasks. Seidl's episodic framing of touch points toward a cinema of tactility that, in its politicized forms, dramatizes the dilemmas of the contemporary care industry. This capacity explains why cinema serves as a vehicle for the study of transnational housework. Film can linger indefinitely on scenes in which apparently nothing happens. At the visual level, Seidl's image slowly foregrounds a touch, a gesture of care. This image could be supplemented by Mona Hatoum's assisted ready-made *Untitled* (*Wheelchair*) (1998–1999), which makes visible the subtle and quiet violence inherent in such touches: Hatoum replaces the handles of the wheelchair with knife blades.[50]

Immaterial Labor and Women's Work

It has been noted that post-Fordist labor patterns structurally resemble work traditionally considered women's work. Italian autonomist Marxists have been at the forefront of the theorization of immaterial labor as the new mode of labor and the harbinger, in Maurizio Lazzarato words, "of a 'silent revolution' taking place within the anthropological realities of work and within the reconfiguration of its meanings." The latest form of capitalism, increasingly referred to as *cognitive capitalism*, seeks to "involve even the worker's personality and subjectivity within the production of value."[51] The worker's soul (language, creativity, affect) has been put to work, Franco Berardi argues. Instead of being controlled in a disciplinary, factory based regime, the new worker is asked to participate cheerfully in the life of the company. The worker's desire is invested in work because, in the absence of alternatives, the most interesting part of life is work. Whether one works for a company or not, in the new economy one is always quasi-self-employed, an entrepreneur managing one's own labor power and its transformation into value in an ever-changing market. The location of labor is no longer the factory; dislocated, work happens everywhere, often at home. This means that the Marxist credo "He [the worker] is at home when he is not working, and when he is working he is not at home," does no longer stand; the worker is always at work and thus never at home—even at home.[52] The temporality of work shifts as well, for it becomes increasingly impossible to distinguish between work time and leisure time. As a consequence, the Marxist categories of production and reproduction become virtually indistinguishable. Labor necessitates the creation of social and communicational relationships, such that work is done collectively, in teams, and communication broadly understood is often the measure of entrepreneurial success. This is not just the labor situation of highly skilled workers; it is a general condition. Lazzarato lists the qualifications of the new work: "Precariousness, hyperexploitation, mobility, and hierarchy."[53]

At times reluctantly acknowledged, and at times enthusiastically celebrated, the feminist debate on housework is an important precedent for the autonomist theorization of post-Fordist labor.[54] The feminist critique of Marxism revealed the value extracted from housework as physical, relational, and affective labor. In the second-wave feminist debate, housework took place inside and outside the home, at all times. Life and work were indistinguishable. There was no separation between work and leisure. Work involved some fun, and the worker's desire was certainly entangled in her work. Second-wave feminists considered divorce an always present occupational hazard, driving home arguments about labor precariousness. They also argued for the right to refuse work. The solution to the problem of housework was "to take back our time, which happens to be our lives."[55] While family work has been paradigmatic to the theorization of women's work, several writers have extended that analysis into work that takes place outside the home. Thus, Hochschild proposed that the work of the stewardess and of other female service providers involved the commercialization of sociality and affect.[56] Rollins argued that, in addition to its physical tasks, domestic work involved the creation of a complex form of sociality between employer and domestic, the latter needing to be "an amiable and pleasant person."[57] Sex work has only recently been theorized as a form of affective labor, but sex workers' organizations have long argued that it involves the commercialization of certain forms of sociality, affect, and language, as the cybersex scene in Seidl's film also suggests. It should be clear that many arguments of Italian neo-Marxism are present in the second-wave feminist literature, inside and outside Italy.[58]

How do these arguments relate to Olga? If we agree that she is the new housewife and that the post-Fordist worker is a variation on the figure of the housewife, what would it mean to take her labor as a model for the theorization of labor? First, following the feminist instead of the autonomist line of reasoning, we might need to retool reproduction for our post-Fordist times. An overly strict distinction between Fordist and post-Fordist economies risks relegating Olga's dusting to anachronistic modes of production and reproduction, to some pre–information economy, a rudiment of a bygone era, when, in fact, the new economy thrives on the contradictions that make up the fabric of her labor universe, including the cohabitation of the archaic and the postmodern (see cybersex). In an international framework, Fordist and post-Fordist become geographic categories. Some economies are post-Fordist because they outsource Fordist productive labor and its attendant forms of reproductive labor to other parts of the world. The distinction between Fordist/post-Fordist rehearses and amplifies the international division of labor that neoliberalism inherited from colonialism.[59] That distinction renders certain kinds of reproductive work once again invisible, internationally. Although this is not their intention, when autonomist Marxists note the collapse of the categories of production and reproduction, the spiritual tasks of reproduction metonymically stand in for reproduction as such. It is the "soul" of the housewife that they see in the post-Fordist worker. The phrase *immaterial labor* is meant to include various forms of physical labor, but it leaves out many aspects of Olga's working life.

In having Olga work in a middle-class Austrian home and a geriatric ward, *Import/Export* couples the two sites in ingenious ways. Aside from the question of care, and in an oblique relation to it, there is the question of waste management. This might be the bottom line of material labor. "I did not come to America to do this," a woman declares in Anayansi Prado's documentary *Maid in America* (2005) as she cleans a toilet in a middle-class American home. It is a reminder that toilets, human waste, and their odors are recurrent motifs in narratives of transnational mobility. What makes the viewer uncomfortable with the scene is the fact that toilets are supposed to be private. Dominique Laporte argues that in France toilets became private at the time when the king imposed the duty of waste removal and cleaning on individuals: "We witness the *domestication* of waste, as a result of which the subject sees the object assigned to its 'true' place; that is to say, to his home, *in domus*. If waste ensconced itself in the home, and consequently in the private sphere . . . , it must certainly have played a role in the emergence of the family and familial intimacy. . . . What happens in my home, in my family, my dirty laundry, and all the rest is no affair of yours. This little heap in front of my door is my business; it is mine to tend."[60] Laporte does not tell us that "it is mine to tend" is just a way of speaking as the master of the house delegates the tending to others in his household. When the housewife is without "help," it is her job to remove waste. The issue is managed in silence, in the home, as each family's private business. Today, given that Olga is often responsible for this job, in the middle-class Austrian home and the geriatric ward alike, the private has gone international. Olga's two jobs no longer cross the private-public distinction that second-wave feminists critiqued. They belong to a reconfigured, international private sphere, the space where cognitive capitalism quietly takes care of its dirty laundry.

Paolo Virno argues that post-Fordist economy is centered on information and communication, that "*language itself has been put to work . . . has become wage labor*." For Virno this is very much the case for immigrants, "for whom

Fig. 2.6. East European cleaning ladies listen to instructions. Frame from Ulrich Seidl's *Import/Export* (2007).

the struggle over wages is never separable from confrontations and frictions with language, forms of life, ethical models."[61] Olga reminds us that information and culture flow not in language but in specific languages, in a global and European linguistic hierarchy that parallels a citizenship hierarchy. Olga is perpetually lectured on the how-to of cleaning, not because she does not know how to do it, but because lecturing is a technology of power through which hierarchies—domestic and international—reproduce themselves. Her limited and accented knowledge of "European languages" places her on the "feminine" side of the international division of labor. The lecturing that she endures is always delivered in articulate, quasi-scientific, unaccented German. The content of the lecture is not important because such homilies send only one message: you are constitutively unable to achieve this level of language proficiency. Olga and her East European coworkers pose for a shot that captures their skeptical listening as an exercise in endurance (see fig. 2.6). If one can speak of the dignity of labor (an autonomist leitmotif) in Seidl's film, that dignity would be located in the boredom of these faces.

Olga has knowledge, not only because she is trained as a nurse in Ukraine, but also because she works, as a function of what Marx called the *general intellect*. The term has received renewed attention recently, serving as an anchor for the autonomist celebration of the affirmative potential of immaterial labor. The lecturing scenes in *Import/Export* dramatize the realization that, if Olga is to continue to clean European toilets and provide unacknowledged, unremunerated care labor on the side, the translation of her knowledge into productive communicative information needs to fail. As the viewer follows the minute movements of her face, it becomes clear that

Olga is constantly interpreting and translating information.[62] Lecturers are present, however, to make her knowledge appear inadequate. After all, they make a living out of the staged failed translation of her knowledge.

Seidl filmed *Import/Export* in winter. White snow offers a visual continuity between Austria and Ukraine. On account of the winter landscape, a few times in the film the viewer is unsure whether a given scene happens in Austria or Ukraine. If there is a continuous Europe in *Import/Export*, it is a mood induced by this disturbing white snow. Stylistic choices are restrained as the film oscillates between static, planimetric camera shots and shaky, handheld shots. One could say that Seidl is taking austerity measures, *avant la lettre*. The austere episodic continuity of the film constructs an affinity between Olga and the protagonist of the second half of the film, Paul, a young, unemployed Austrian man exported to Ukraine. Olga and Paul belong to the same precarious generation of European youths. But Seidl's film tells us something important about the uneven distribution of vulnerability and labor precariousness between the sexes gone transnational. His protagonists never meet; they never occupy the same space, the same boat, the same precariat. They travel on tracks that resonate with each other (*rhyme* is the word used by Mattias Frey) but never intersect.[63] The material realities of two parallel Europes pressured Seidl to look for a form that would do them justice (import/export). He does not tell us that Paul remains sutured to the Austrian welfare state and a potential "income of citizenship," made possible, at least in part, by the surplus extracted from Olga's labor.[64] Their adventures are structurally parallel, but Olga and Paul are segregated by the international sexual division of labor as well as by the new, racial, ethnic, and citizenship-based European stratifications—the new wall, if you will.

The Female *Homo Sacer*

The Traffic in Coerced Reproduction

3

As Giuseppe Tornatore's *The Unknown Woman* (*La sconosciuta*, 2006) begins, the viewer is sutured to the role of spectator in an intriguing performance. Three young attractive women in underwear and high heels stand in the middle of an improvised stage, their backs turned. The light is dim and mysterious and spotlights parts of the bodies in front of us for theatrical, eroticized effect. We are in a decadent space; it could be an old palace if it were not for the sound of a passing train. Minimalist furnishings and a white lamp against the background of a wall filled with paintings complete a gothic-bohemian setting. An unusual performance is under way; it could be a lingerie runway show, a beauty pageant, a modeling contest, or a strip show. "Turn around," an unidentified voice orders brusquely. As the women mechanically turn to face the camera and the viewer sees their fixed, forced facial expressions, it becomes clear that none of the above scenarios apply (see fig. 3.1*a*).

If this is a competitive casting call, the women's movements betray that they are not invested in winning it. Their synchronized walk is professional but mechanical, blasé. They walk out and are replaced by three other women in underwear and spiked high heels, with the same fixed facial expressions. As the camera comes closer for a midshot, the viewer realizes that the women are all wearing

Fig. 3.1. An eye watches an intriguing performance.
Two frames from Giuseppe Tornatore's *The Unknown Woman* (2006).

the same white mask. Whatever the stakes of the performance, it involves bodies with inexpressive faces attached to them. The sovereign voice asks a woman identified as Georgia, distinguished from the others by her platinum blonde hair and white underwear, to stay, and the other two women to leave. The voice then orders her to strip, which she does, with matter-of-fact gestures. She marches to the center of the stage for a pose. "Turn around slowly," orders the voice. The reverse shot reveals an eye—not the eye of the ordering voice—watching the performance through a hole in the wall with paintings (fig. 3.1*b*).

It is clear that, although this alert eye has been watching all along, the performance is no ordinary peep show. This is not a lustful eye; the naked woman in spiked high heels is not an erotic object. "She'll do fine," a whisper attached to the eye concludes. The ordering voice—attributed, in the next cut, to a man standing in profile behind a curtain who has orchestrated the performance for the benefit of the buying eye—familiarly dismisses the woman. She puts her underwear back on and, as she turns to leave, takes her mask off for a face-to-face encounter with the viewer, interrupting and interrogating his or her fascination with the scene. The film has just cast her as the titular "unknown woman." She will remain unknown throughout the film, *la sconosciuta*, a reflection of the fact that the job she is chosen to perform remains, for most viewers and the European public sphere at large, unknown.

The nature of the opening performance is revealed toward the end of the film. These are women coerced into sex and reproductive work in Italy by an organization under the control of a man known as Muffa. The English subtitles refer to him as Mold. The eye behind the wall (which could be the eye of a man or a woman) is there to choose a woman who can carry a pregnancy to term. It is not clear what the criteria for the choice are, other than an intuition of reproductive health and the whiteness signaled by Georgia's platinum blonde hair. Georgia, who is Ukrainian and whose real name is Irina but whose "Italian name" is Irena, becomes pregnant. She continues her sex work until the fourth month of pregnancy, when she is isolated in a room. Mold is present at her delivery and promptly whisks the baby away, to be sold to an Italian couple. In interviews, Tornatore claims that the scene condenses a number of real accounts of infants being sold on the market.[1] In Tornatore's film, Irena has had nine such pregnancies in twelve years.

The film works with the conventions of the thriller to exaggerate and hypervisualize its points, teasing the viewer to uncover the enigma at its heart. While the camera that has just produced the spectacle related above seems to be complicit with the buying eye and objectify the female bodies on stage, I argue that the film's visual politics cannot be grasped through feminist critiques of fetishistic scopophilia. Tornatore filmed the casting scene in a theater and composed it in an overly theatrical manner. Its images function as a provocation for the viewer, who slowly begins to grasp the fact that female nudity can be detached from erotic fantasy to become a platform for reproductive calculations. Although in his own commentary on the film Tornatore insists that he made a genre film—and not a film of social critique or a feminist film—I propose that it is from within the genre of the thriller, itself loaded with the history of the Cold War and its figurations of "Eastern Europe," that *The Unknown Woman* is doing its critical work.

The film's opening scene critically frames the fact that Georgia constitutes what Giorgio Agamben would call *bare life*: life stripped of its human qualifications, depersonalized, and depoliticized. This life is also, I would add, deeroticized so that it can be commercialized as a particular kind of commodity—reproduction. The paradigmatic figure of bare life, Agamben charges, is the *homo sacer*, sacred in the tradition of Roman law in the sense that he is outside the *polis* and exposed to nonpunishable violence; anyone can harm or kill him. The refugee and the torture victim are today considered exemplary instantiations of the *homo sacer*. In this chapter, I argue that Tornatore's film offers a prism through which to both understand and complicate Agamben's notion of bare life in the contemporary political landscape. I juxtapose *The Unknown Woman* with a large body of literature on reproductive technologies and their effects on contemporary kinship.[2] In my reading, the film spotlights the female *homo sacer* at the center of the contemporary biopolitical stage, where she dwells in a particular kind of camp.

Agamben's camp can be understood on three models. The first is the extermination camp, which distributes death. For the most part this is a historical camp; Auschwitz is its metonym. The second is the refugee camp, which distributes survival. This is a camp produced by Fortress Europe in an attempt to secure its borders. In it, the European state (working in tandem with EU institutions) asserts its sovereignty by walling itself off from the undesirables of the world. The barbed wire of the refugee camp stands in for the "wall around the West."[3] The inhabitants of the refugee camp are hostages of a disciplinary regime; stripped of their rights and political status, they wait. I am proposing that we consider a third camp, the sex-trafficking camp, which distributes reproduction. This camp is situated within the territory of various European states, in the corners of various urban centers (increasingly divided along racial and ethnic lines, following a pattern of Americanization), yet it is abandoned by the states to which it theoretically belongs. As in the other two camps, life here is exposed to violence and death, but it is also protected because this camp houses a thriving enclave economy, exploiting a most valuable resource: women's reproductive potential.

This chapter works toward two interrelated goals: to briefly identify Agamben's philosophical project and bring the traffic in women to bear on his understanding of the biopolitical horizon of modernity and, at the same time, on the margins of *The Unknown Woman*, to offer a critique of some of his assumptions regarding the biopolitics of sex and gender. As we have seen in chapters 1 and 2, in the context of this book *reproduction* has Marxist and materialist feminist overtones, referring both to biological reproduction (the reproduction of human beings) and to social reproduction (housework and family work). If chapters 1 and 2 offered an analysis of social reproduction, this chapter focuses on a fictional limit case of biological reproduction in an international frame, in an attempt to place reproduction as such, biological and social, on a biopolitical continuum. The woman trafficked illegally into coerced sex work and the woman trafficked legally as a domestic worker inhabit this continuum but are located differentially on it in relation to the law and therefore to heterogeneous forms of violence. The biopolitical continuum of life includes human bodies, body parts and tissues, and bodily functions (sex, affect, labor). Agamben's notion of the camp (and the critical debate around it), complemented by a discussion of the biopolitics of sex and gender and a critique of his notion of sovereignty, can serve as a way out of moralizing, sex-panicked responses to coerced forms of sex trafficking, articulated both by human rights advocates and by the media. A focus on the biopolitical dimensions of sex trafficking helps us bracket the justified moral outrage and allows us to place coerced forms of sex trafficking on the continuum of "women's work." In turn, this placement should allow us to intensify our calls for European labor rights and protections.

Today we are faced with national and global markets that offer a range of reproductive products, biological and social, combined in creative ways: eggs, surrogacy, regenerative tissues, reproductive technologies, nanny services, domestic work, food and laundry services, sex. As we have seen, some East European women work as nannies, domestic workers, wives, etc. Others supplement their income through the commercialization of their reproductive and regenerative functions (eggs and oocytes). Others are drawn into coerced sex work. It is crucial to underscore that these transactions operate within interlocking economies, following the same geopolitical routes.[4]

As I write this, many voices propose that we take our theoretical investigations "beyond biopolitics." This chapter aligns itself with recent efforts to assess what critical purchase the notion of biopolitics has today—not beyond biopolitics as such but perhaps beyond Agamben, which also means *with* Agamben.[5]

Detective Work

Tornatore's protagonist, Irena, is played by the Russian actress Ksenia Rappoport. She is the only unknown name among the cast; all the other actors in *The Unknown Woman* are recognizable to the film's Italian and European audiences.[6] Tornatore declared in an interview: "In the end I selected nine actresses from Ukraine, Russia, Moldavia, Romania, et cetera. These nine actresses in Rome made some key screen tests. After shooting the screen tests immediately I knew that Xenia was the right actress for my movie. Even her name was very magical, because the name Xenia in Greek means 'unknown' or 'foreign.'"[7] Tornatore cast an "Eastern woman" in the role of Irena. She could have come from various countries in the East (the "et cetera" at the end of the list of East European countries is indicative of an endemic lack of patience with the region's particularisms). Similarly to Seidl, *Ukraine* is a placeholder for *Eastern Europe*. A native informant quality attaches to the actress who plays the role of the East European woman. She is trusted to know about "Eastern Europe" and can give voice (or face) to its realities. Tornatore wanted Rappoport to speak in her accented Italian, which he thought the film needed in order to reach the desired level of expressivity. An enigma clings to the East European woman, actress and protagonist alike, such that she necessarily remains unknown to the end—*xenia*, "the foreign guest."

Having made its extradiegetic casting choices, *The Unknown Woman* starts abruptly with the intradiegetic casting scene recounted at the beginning of this chapter. On account on her performance, one East European woman has been selected to carry a pregnancy to term. The next cut changes settings. We are now in an urban environment (Trieste), the preferred landscape of the thriller genre. A few years have passed since the casting scene. Platinum blonde has given way to brunette, and Irena is wearing a quasi-respectable trench coat. She looks older, her face chronically sad and preoccupied. The viewer sees her inquire about domestic work in a beautiful palazzo. The interview with the porter is brief. "Where are you from?" is the only question asked, the one-word answer enough for the porter to throw back the racially inflected response that "people like you" are not trusted by his tenants. People "like you" are a function of accented language: people who speak Italian with the thick accent required by the filmmaker and who pronounce *Ukrayina* all too convincingly. Irena offers the porter 20, then 30 percent of her earnings. The porter's lament ("People these days [immigrants, foreigners] . . .") is followed by a cut to his accepting the deal. His smirk suggests his hope that this economic arrangement might be complemented by sexual favors. While Irena is "white enough" in some contexts (she can give birth to a white child), she is not in others (the labor market). The interview with the porter is a linguistic and visual encounter that produces a racialized subject, in this case, the Ukrainian Irena.[8] Responsible for the racialization is the porter and, in the eyes of the viewer, the film itself, which, in order to represent Irena's foreignness in the eyes of the porter, necessarily produces it, with a wink to the viewer.

Foregrounding the reproductive continuum of women's work, *The Unknown Woman* has Irena move from coerced sex work to cleaning to child care. In the tradition of Italian neorealism, the film documents the minutiae of her labor scrubbing floors, the luxurious building's stairs in particular. The camera lingers on the stairs' ornate curved architecture as if anticipat-

Fig. 3.2. Transnational nannies line up for an interview with a female Italian employer. Frame from Giuseppe Tornatore's *The Unknown Woman* (2006).

ing the descent of a glamorous young woman. Instead, as the camera follows the curves of the stairs, it finds Irena, a beautiful but fallen woman, stooped in her scrubbing posture. The dizzying feeling produced by the stairs anticipates the film's descent into Irena's experience. The building's middle-class inhabitants occasionally pass by, their verticality emphasizing Irena's lowly position in the European order of things.

Following another racialized casting call through which she is chosen for the job of nanny, Irena moves up in the occupational hierarchy. A long line of women, migrants from around the world, apply for the job, their presence a challenge to locate Irena within a very complex field of racial positions (see fig. 3.2). Her selection might well be a case of positive racialization (in this case, she is chosen because she is "white enough"), but racialization nonetheless. Once she is selected for the job, the viewer witnesses her performance of another set of tasks in the Italian bourgeois household: tidying up, cooking, doing laundry, and caring for the family's only child, Thea. Irena's facial choreography is tightly controlled and ever watchful, suggesting a complex and, for the viewer, obdurately unreadable emotional life.

From the moment Irena enters the Italian palazzo, the viewer witnesses her scheming toward a project he or she cannot grasp. The thriller framework of the film, complete with a mesmerizing Ennio Morricone score, induces the viewer's own racialized apprehension of Irena (what is the stranger woman up to?), inviting him or her to play detective. A scene in the supermarket in which Irena is suspected of having stolen something confirms the feeling of distrust. As an outcome of this suspense-creating game, the viewer is tempted to speculate that Irena is trying to insinuate herself into the intimate life of a respectable Italian family, to become "one of the family" in a sense that exceeds her jobs as housekeeper and nanny. Whatever it is she is planning—and for most of the film the viewer cannot tell—it cannot be good.

Formally, Tornatore's film alternates scenes of Irena's life as a maid and nanny with brief and abrupt flashbacks to her past life as a sex worker in conditions of bondage (in most scenes, Irena is tied). Especially painful are the scenes in which Mold breaks her in through violent rape, to transform her, psychologically, into a docile sex worker. In these images from the past, Irena is under Mold's sovereign control; he controls her mobility, her labor, and her reproductive rights. All flashbacks involve Mold (played by a metamorphosed persona of the famous Italian actor Michele Placido), who comes across as perversely, obscenely caring. The continuity between Irena's past and her present is guaranteed by the viewer's genre-determined suspicion that the traumatic past will sooner or later return to haunt the present. The gap between the past and the present is further bridged by Rappoport's acting. The latter plays very different, credible roles across her past and present selves, but her acting *style* assures a strong sense of continuity. Gradually, the viewer is led to question whether Irena's two lives are as disjunctive as the quick cuts (another marker of the thriller) make them seem. It slowly becomes clear that Irena believes that the little girl she is caring for, Thea, is her own daughter, the daughter she conceived, as one of the flashbacks reveals, with the one man she loved. Mold killed her lover and sold the newborn into adoption.

Irena has a vexed relationship with Thea's adoptive mother, Valeria. In a crucial scene, the viewer sees her admiring the Italian upper-middle-class woman's body. "You have a nice body. . . . You have the body of a young girl," she declares. "You wouldn't say you've had a child," Irena continues, knowing that Thea is adopted. Guilt makes its way into the face of the Italian woman. She has not deformed her body through pregnancy, either by choice or by necessity (the film does not linger), but she is marked by the situation in which she has not given birth to her child. Tornatore's film suggests that Valeria's feelings of guilt also explain her current love affair. It is for the sake of possible romance that the Italian adoptive mother needs an adolescent body. After the violent death of her lover, Irena closed that chapter of her life, which may have been a fantasy all along (the viewer can never be sure that the light-filled, dream-like flashbacks of Irena and her lover are not just that, dreams). The scene suggests her envy of Valeria's youthful body at the same time as it shows Irena caring for it (see fig. 3.3). It is a powerful image that challenges the viewer to grasp the middle-class Italian woman's youth

Fig. 3.3. Irena admires Valeria's body.
Frame from Giuseppe Tornatore's *The Unknown Woman* (2006).

in relation to the subproletarian Ukrainian woman's precocious aging. As the film progresses, the viewer realizes that the former indirectly vampirizes the latter's bodily resources.

The Italian family in *The Unknown Woman* is dysfunctional: Thea's parents are separated; her mother is having an affair. Thea's mother seems to have given up the familial project. She nonetheless has an (adopted) child, so she hires other women to care for her. Laura Mamo claims that the international adoption market is an effect of an ideology that she calls *compulsory motherhood*, which today afflicts Western heterosexual and lesbian women alike.[9] Women like our fictional Valeria feel pressured into motherhood, even in situations in which they are infertile or cannot afford or dislike the parenting time. Women like our fictional Irena step into the resulting structural gap to do the reproductive work—as surrogate mothers and nannies.

For Irena, given her sex-trafficking past, the question that haunts the narrative is, Can someone like me hope to have a future? Irena rents an expensive, beautiful apartment across the street from her employer but does not set up house; she literally camps in it. The bourgeois everyday is not doable. She furiously but ultimately unsuccessfully takes care of a few plants. It seems that the only way she can reenter the law is as a criminal. The thriller framework of the film induces the viewer to criminalize her throughout the film, too. Legal studies have found that one of the reasons international antitrafficking laws are ineffective is that most often the women coerced into sex work, who are usually not "perfect victims" (and thus not ideal protagonists for the innocent-on-the-run thriller subgenre),[10] are criminalized as sex workers, as illegal immigrants, or under other charges.[11] Working with similar assumptions, Tornatore's film induces the viewer's sustained suspicion of Irena. Events transpire to confirm this suspicion: Irena pushes Thea's first nanny down the stairs so that she can take her job; she eventually kills Mold. She is certainly not a perfect victim—and, in fact, not a victim at all (we will return to this).

But, even when women like Irena do not engage in any criminal activity, they are often part of the large population of deportable aliens. Deportability—a threat that traffickers use to keep women "in their place"—is also used by the law to criminalize women's presence at the site of trafficking. In *The Unknown Woman*, Irena emphasizes repeatedly that she has an Italian ID card, but that ID card, too, belongs to Mold. In order to reenter the law, even as a criminal, she has to confess and retroactively produce a narrative of victimization. Irena has suffered the violence she describes, but it is only at the point of confession, in a legal context, that her experience takes a narrative form. Ending on this legal note aligns the film with other visual narratives of victimization that raise awareness, in a human rights context, about sex trafficking in an effort to secure legal protection for the women involved.[12]

At the same time, there is something productively excessive about Tornatore's use of the thriller genre. (It is this excessiveness that sets *The Unknown Woman* apart from Hollywood sex-trafficking thrillers, like Pierre Morel's *Taken* [2008]). In its insistence on being a hyperthriller, the film can be said to be framing the legal apparatus that demands and to a certain extent produces Irena's confession and narrative of victimization. The secret of the genre film is that its structure is predetermined, from the beginning. Tornatore's comments on the project of *The Unknown Woman* aside, the film drives home an awareness that today the thriller is part and parcel of the legal apparatus of sex trafficking. The law *demands* a thriller.

The Biopolitical Condition

Agamben published *Homo Sacer* in 1995.[13] The series to which it belongs is an exercise in political philosophy, produced under the urgent demand to rethink the political in the wake of 1989 and the imminent globalization of the world.[14] Since Agamben's work, especially *Homo Sacer*, is familiar to many readers, I will only review a few junctures in his work that are central to the argument of this chapter.

It is well-known that his project finds its impetus in what Agamben considers a "strangely unclear" point in Michel Foucault's work.[15] His starting point is the distinction between what the Greeks called *zoē*, the simple act of living, and what they called *bio*, politically specific forms of living. Foucault had shown how the "threshold into modernity" is the point where *zoē* becomes the stake of power and politics become biopolitics, the management of populations.[16] What Foucault missed, according to Agamben's reading, is the connection between the biopolitical thread in his work (located on a horizontal axis) and his preoccupation with the workings of sovereignty (located on a vertical, theological—or postsecular—axis). The integration of biopolitics and sovereignty becomes for Agamben the organizing principle of the Western discourse on power. Agamben proposes that we reread the history of political philosophy retracing the archaeology of this principle. The promising suspicion here is that the history of *zoē* constitutes the underside—and at the same time the "most precious center"—of sovereignty. It is important to emphasize, however, that *zoē* as such is not recoverable beyond what Agamben calls "the threshold of indistinction" between life and law. This is why *Homo Sacer* has as a protagonist not *zoē* but *la nuda vita*, translated into English as *bare life* or *naked life*, a notion that Agamben borrows from Walter Benjamin to refer to "the bearer of the link between violence and law."[17] Bare life is not *zoē*; it is politicized life, but politicized in the very particular manner of its abandonment to, rather than protection from, violence and, eventually, death.

Agamben's other major premonition is that there appears to exist a "secret complicity between the sacredness of life and the power of law."[18] Reminding us that the sacred is to be found both at the most exalted and at the most abject ends of culture, Agamben proposes the notion of *sacred life* as the third term of the relation between bare life and sovereign power.[19] The figure of the *homo sacer* is structurally congruent to bare life in its being a form of exception. The *homo sacer* is defined by the possibility of his being killed but not sacrificed; he is a creature outside both human law (which sanctions killing) and divine law (which presides over sacrifice). But there is, according to Agamben, more to this connection than "mere analogy." If the sacred is *the* originary exclusion from the juridical order, bare life and sacred life become indistinguishable in their relation to sovereignty.[20] *Homo sacer* comes to name the relation of inclusion/exclusion of bare life in the sovereign ban. If the *homo sacer* is an exile of sorts, he is exiled from the *polis* not into some form of *oikos* (the private household) but outside the very distinction between *polis* and *oikos* and thus apparently outside the political *tout court* while nevertheless remaining included by way of its very exclusion.

Agamben's argument is that bare life, being what sovereignty originally banned, has accompanied the history of sovereignty all along, like a river.[21] The relationship is the organizing structure of political philosophy, Agamben charges, against Carl Schmitt, who proposed the same role for the friend/enemy distinction.[22] The sovereign decision "traces and from time to time renews" the threshold on which bare life and sovereignty meet.[23] In Agamben's restaging of Foucault, what modernity brings is not biopolitics as such, since power seems to have always had bare life as its proper matter, but rather a condition that we might want to call *biopolitics without reserve*—an all-encompassing investment in all aspects of life.

Starting from this reevaluation of biopolitics, Agamben proposes a new paradigm of modernity—the camp. The camp is to space what the *homo sacer* is to the sacred. It is the spatial "materialization of the state of exception," a form of "captured outside."[24] It thus becomes for Agamben "the hidden paradigm of the political space of modernity, whose metamorphoses and disguises we will have to learn to recognize."[25] This is what he does in the last section of *Homo Sacer*, developing a practice of deciphering the contours of the camp in its different disguises (inhabitants of the camp are figures like the bandit, the *Muselmann*, the overcomatose).[26] In subsequent work, Agamben theorized the refugee camp, often referred to euphemistically as an *accommodation center*, as the contemporary exemplary camp.[27] His structuralist provocation is that we are "facing a camp virtually every time such a structure is created, regardless of the nature of the crimes committed in it and regardless of the denomination and specific topography it might have."[28] As a structure, the camp has a "dislocating localization."[29] It has a chameleonic nature, and we must learn to recognize its updated, heterogeneous formations. This chapter responds to Agamben's provocation, wagering that a focus on the sex-trafficking camp, rather than on either the extermination camp or the refugee camp, yields an alternative figure of the contemporary *homo sacer*.

This is where I return to Tornatore's *The Unknown Woman*. The film dramatizes the production of bare life in the camp that shelters coerced sex trafficking. Once one understands the fact that sex work is work (not just work, but work nonetheless), it becomes possible to understand coerced sex work as one form of coerced work in general and coerced reproductive work in particular. The ensuing critical task is to unpack the meanings of the adjective *coerced* when applied to contemporary labor practices. It is well-known that Marx referred to waged labor as such as *coerced* and *forced* on account of its alienating effects. For Marx, work in the service of capitalism is coerced because the worker never feels "at home" in his or her work. He concluded: "[The worker's] labor is therefore not voluntary, but coerced; it is *forced labor*."[30] While there are still reasons to theorize waged labor as forced against contemporary labor discourses that encourage us to feel at home in our never-ending work (as we have seen in the previous chapter), in this context the word *coerced* acquires its meanings as a supplement to Marx's notion of alienation. Coerced work, including coerced sex work, is forced because it is not only alienating but also unwaged, dehumanizing, and violent—it takes place in camp-like conditions. Additionally, in the context of contemporary migration, one is not only not at home in one's work but also not at home in one's home since home itself eludes one's horizon of possibility and, often, desire.

The phrase *modern-day slavery* is often used to describe contemporary forms of coerced traffic in women.[31] It is a risky phrase because slavery, associated in the Western imagination with the transatlantic slave trade, has a clear historical framework. It too is modern, but modern-day slavery belongs to a contemporaneity in which the historical circumstances of the transatlantic trade are not reproducible. When placed in the long history of modernity as seen through "the colonial turn," however, the comparison between early modern and contemporary forms of slavery becomes necessary. In the early modern period, the transatlantic slave trade provided muscular plantation labor as well as household-based reproductive labor, including sex—in other words, women's work. The word *chattel*, inherited from this history, resonates in the world of contemporary sex trafficking. The slave market is a place where women's teeth, breasts, and genitals are evaluated (according to labor and reproductive criteria) before a price is agreed on. The scene with which I began this chapter can be read in a reproductive chattel sense. One of the most well-known paintings of an American slave market, *The Last Sale of Slaves* (1871), by Thomas Satterwhite Noble, depicts the sale of a young African American woman holding an infant. She is offered up for sale on account not only of the labor she can provide but also of her reproductive potential.

Yet critics like Kamala Kempadoo resist the analogy between slavery, understood in terms of property relations (slaves as human chattel), and coerced forms of traffic in women, preferring to speak of debt bondage, indentureship, forced labor, and "slavery-like practices."[32] This resistance is part of an attempt to broaden what counts as trafficking to include not only sex trafficking but also other forms of coerced labor. Julia O'Connell Davidson gives voice to such a concern: "The package of violations covered by the UN Protocol definition of 'trafficking' (violence, confinement, coercion, deception and exploitation) can and do [*sic*] occur within legally regulated as well as irregular systems of migration and employment, and within legal as well as illegal systems of migration into private households."[33] We are less likely to include migration and employment-based coercive practices under the banner of modern-day slavery. Yet there is no clear line to be drawn between legal and illegal modes of the trafficking of women either into employment (domestic work, e.g.) or the private household (e-brides, e.g.). How, then, can the word *slavery* cover this range of labor phenomena?

With such warnings in mind, we would do well to return to the work of Orlando Patterson for an example of rigorous comparative work on slavery. His study *Slavery and Social Death* (1982) traces the history and ramifications of slavery as a global institution, cyclically reproduced throughout history and in all parts of the world. Patterson proposes a shift in the definition of slavery away from property (chattel) and toward a consideration of coercion as a function of a specific relation to natality. He thus defines slavery as "*the permanent, violent domination of natally alienated and generally dishonored persons*."[34] Natal alienation is the condition of the slave as a nonperson who cannot make claims of birth, either to his or her ancestors and tradition or to his or her offspring. Natal alienation, coupled with everyday dishonor as well as actual or virtual violence, desocializes and depersonalizes the slave and produces what Patterson calls *social death*. It is this definition of slavery that resonates with Agamben's work on bare life, with the debates on coerced forms of traffic in women, and with *The Unknown Woman*. Indeed, critics like Achille Mbembe and Ewa Ziarek have persuasively linked Agamben's notion of bare life to slavery, in order to bring the history of colonialism and its attendant racisms to bear on the figure of the *homo sacer*.[35] For Mbembe, the slave as bare life suffers a "triple loss: loss of a 'home,' loss of rights over his or her body, and loss of political status."[36] This chapter rethinks this tripartite loss in the context of coerced forms of traffic in East European women and their racializing practices, taking Tornatore's film as a starting point.

Demystifying the Unknown Woman

What does *The Unknown Woman* tell us about Agamben and the biopolitical condition more generally? What does it tell us about the traffic in women and its East European instantiation in particular? What does it tell us about the relation between coerced sex trafficking and coerced reproduction and between coerced sex work and paid domestic work or child care? One cannot require a film to answer all these questions. Nevertheless, given that these are the concerns that make up the fabric of the ongoing critical conversation and that the film (if not necessarily the filmmaker) participates in this conversation, I will point to eight arguments that it prompts, gestures toward, or makes possible.

1. ***Irena's life as a coerced sex worker is productive.*** Irena works. The contemporary camp cannot be understood on the model of Auschwitz because it is not inherently an extermination camp. Inmates in Nazi camps worked, but, as Hannah Arendt argues, from an economic point of view this work could have been done more productively under different circumstances. Arendt speaks of "uselessness" and "anti-utility."[37] By comparison, the life exploited in a sex-trafficking camp is productive. When the female *homo sacer* inhabiting such a camp is put to (physical and affective) work, her labor yields a profit. It is only when Irena threatens to stop working that she can be killed. The manner in which she is exposed to violence is, to use Mbembe's words, that of being "kept alive in a *state of injury*."[38] *The Unknown Woman* has been criticized for the excessive spectacularization of this injury, yet spectacularization is very much part of the scene. Mbembe speaks of "the spectacle of pain" that is used to instill terror in the slave.[39] Exaggerated cinematic spectacularization, achieved through the iconography of the thriller genre, mimics the production of spectacularized terror.

2. ***Irena's coerced work, as a sex worker and as a mother, is productive in the sense that it is reproductive.*** Irena works as a coerced sex worker; Mold commercializes her sexuality. But Tornatore's script pushes this scenario to its limit by having Irena simultaneously produce babies for the adoption market. She is, at the same time, a coerced sex worker and a coerced biological mother.

Biopolitics is, as has been demonstrated, a form of necro- or thanatopolitics. It distributes death and death-like lives. But it is, most of all, a politics of life and *living*. It is thus necessarily a politics of reproduction, inherently invested not only in "let die" but also in "make live," in Foucault's famous formulation. Foucault insists that biopolitics' investment in death and mortality is itself an offshoot of its investment in fertility and the birth-to-death ratio. Its most important goal is to "optimize the state of life"—bioregulate the reproduction of a population understood in racial terms.[40]

What does Agamben's work, which presents itself as an extension of Foucault's, tell us about the biopolitics of reproduction, about "make live"? Arguably, his erudite work on nudity is a gesture in this direction.[41] One of the images he interprets in *Nudities*, Clemente Susini's wax figures in Tuscany's Museum of Natural History, depicts an anatomical female nude. One can remove various layers, revealing the model's heart, lungs, intestines, etc. "Finally," Agamben writes, "inside the womb, one can make out a small fetus."

Agamben argues that, despite the fact that one can visually unveil its biological layers, the nude remains "obstinately unattainable." From here, he deduces the "impurity, almost the sacredness," of the nude.[42] He goes on to theorize the relation between nudity and knowledge and between nudity and beauty. He never returns to the fetus behind the nude's many veils. Yet the allusion to the nude's sacredness suggests that we are in the proximity of the *homo sacer*. Although he can make out the small fetus behind at least one of the nudes he describes, Agamben does not quite discern its potentiality in the female nude as such. He does not see it, for example, in the performance by Vanessa Beecroft that prompts his essay. Yet that performance could be juxtaposed with the casting scene in *The Unknown Woman* with which I began this chapter. In the various stagings of that performance, Beecroft had a hundred naked women defiantly face the visitors in a museum exhibition space for three hours. In some iterations, the women wore high heels or white masks. In Berlin, the performance Agamben describes, they were oiled from the waist up and wore pantyhose. Lack of facial expressivity was a defining feature of all performances. Nudity was deeroticized so that it could become flesh. When juxtaposed with Tornatore's casting scene, in which an alert eye discerns a potential fetus in a deeroticized female nude, Beecroft's nudities, one realizes, harbor a potential fetus—at least in the eyes of some visitors in the exhibit.

While Agamben's work on nudity can be read as an oblique attempt to address the biopolitics of reproduction and the place of women's nude bodies in it, *The Unknown Woman* leads us to a more straightforward engagement with reproduction. In this, it shares the spirit of studies that have brought ongoing debates on abortion to bear on Agamben's understanding of biopolitics. Penelope Deutscher, for example, entered a dialogue with Agamben in order to draw attention to the conspicuous absence of gender in a theory concerned with life. For Deutscher, the way to reinsert gender into biopolitics is through a study of the language of abortion law.[43] The female body has historically been the site of states' biopolitical attempts to regulate their population by regulating reproduction. As Ruth Miller contends, seen from a biopolitical vantage point, women's work has not been undervalued at all (as was argued in the housework debate we revisited in chapter 2). States have taken reproduction—and therefore women's work—to be the paramount duty of the citizen.[44] For Miller, the paradigmatic space of biopolitical modernity is therefore not the camp but the womb. Agamben neglects this history and its contemporary avatars. Today, many West European women like Tornatore's Valeria do not reproduce, refusing to lend their womb to the state's biopolitical interests. If they do, they reproduce once, late in life, resisting what Dana Luciano calls *chronobiopolitics*—the biopolitical organization of women's sex life.[45] As a result, given the perceived need to replace an aging population, reproduction has been increasingly fragmented and commercialized. Different forms of traffic in women, including sex trafficking, are the illegal answer to a growing *demand* on the market in reproduction.[46]

In a sex-trafficking context, traffickers claim reproductive rights over the bodies they govern. This usually means that they decide whether a pregnancy is aborted. It usually is. *The Unknown Woman* presents us with a woman as reproductive life, a woman who has been transformed into a machine for the production of children for the international adoption market. Counterintuitive as this might be, reproduction is always the horizon of sex trafficking, if often only negatively. In the context of the war in the former Yugoslavia, one of Agamben's examples of a camp, rape was intended as a means of producing "Serbian" children. With Tornatore's film, we move into an entirely new situation, one that tests the limits of Agamben's framework. Nationalist reproductive goals have been commercialized, and children are sold on the international adoption market. What in 1972 Mariarosa Dalla Costa and Selma James called *the capitalist function of the uterus*, referring to women's reproductive tasks, has acquired new dimensions.[47] An East European woman who is not quite white is considered the ideal biological resource for the production of a child who will be white and who will not disrupt the racial continuity of the European family. This is the paradigmatic test of passing.[48] When the phrase *stratified reproduction* is used in feminist literature, it usually refers to social reproduction (housework and child care).[49] *The Unknown Woman* asks its viewer to face the stratification of reproduction *tout court*, a racialized biopolitical mix of biological and social elements.

3. *The fragmentation of reproduction is an effect of new developments in medicine.* In a biopolitical framework, Foucault charges, "bodies are replaced by general biological processes."[50] Tracing this change, Nikolas Rose locates bare life *at the microscopic level*. He writes:

> The fragmentation of the body into transferable tissues which could, often with difficulty, be freed from their marks of origin and re-utilized in other bodies, began with blood and blood products. The elements of reproduction—eggs, sperm, and later embryos—also became separable from any particular body, mobilized around circuits of laboratories, clinics, and other bodies. . . . Molecularization strips tissues, proteins, molecules, and drugs

> of their specific affinities—to a disease, to an organ, to an individual, to a species—and enables them to be regarded, in many respects, as manipulable and transferable elements or units, which can be delocalized—moved from place to place, from organism to organism, from disease to disease, from person to person. . . . [M]olecularization is conferring a new mobility on the elements of life, enabling them to enter new circuits—organic, interpersonal, geographical, and financial. . . . At this molecular level, that is to say, life itself has become open to politics.[51]

One of the effects of the molecularization of life is the need to comparatively grasp the biopolitical dimensions of a range of phenomena, such as blood donation, organ donation, regenerative labor, clinical trial, and international adoption. I am proposing that today *the traffic in women* can serve as an umbrella term through which to understand the new mobility of life, something we might call *the traffic in life*.

Rose's study prompts us to ask a challenging question: At the molecular level, is reproduction still women's work? Is the traffic in life a traffic in women? Melinda Cooper and Catherine Waldby have documented the fact that women (often East European women) are the primary tissue donors in the stem cell industry; they donate embryos, oocytes, fetal tissue, and umbilical cord blood. In other words, if we are tempted to think that molecularization is gender neutral, Waldby returns us to the category *women* via regenerative labor.[52] Ann S. Anagnost's work on the international circulation of blood likewise emphasizes that women sell their blood, given the widespread perception that it is natural for them to lose blood in menstruation anyway. It is one way for some women to become part of an international form of "circulation," one that promises to bring rural populations within the purview of global modernity and its attending consumerisms, but only insofar as they put their blood on the market.[53] In her work on the global traffic in organs, Nancy Scheper-Hughes has shown that women are more likely to be pressured into selling an organ perceived to be disposable; organ donation is considered a womanly thing. Since women are still largely considered responsible for the reproduction of their households, they are more likely to "donate" a kidney to assure the economic survival of their families. They often do so in order to facilitate the marriage of a daughter through a dowry, with organ donation functioning as the linchpin between two forms of traffic ("women flow in one direction and kidneys in the other").[54] In all these instances, the category *women* reemerges as a quasi class, globally. Likewise, *women's work* does not disappear from view;

the concept might require reelaboration and fine-tuning, but it remains a much-needed category of analysis.

4. ***The new reproductive practices are made possible by the fragmentation and dispersal of what used to be called*** **motherhood** ***into a number of discreet units.*** Helena Ragoné identifies three reproductive units at work in a surrogacy situation: the biological mother (who contributes the ovum), the gestational mother (who contributes the uterus and the time of pregnancy), and the social mother (who raises the child).[55] In Irena's case, the first two coincide (she is both a biological and a gestational mother), but she is denied the social dimension of motherhood. She reclaims it first as a nanny, then as a mother. The film prompts us to ask uncomfortable questions about what kinship ties a child might have with various women who have reproduced his or her life: an egg donor, a gestational mother, a biological mother, an adoptive mother, and/or a nanny. Writing about international adoption, David Eng argues for the acknowledgment of multiple, transnational kinship ties (a biological mother and an adoptive mother).[56] By contrast, critics are less willing to acknowledge the fact that a child might have kinship ties to a gestational mother, a woman who carries a fetus in her body for nine months.

It is well-known that transnational adoption is often presented as a narrative about needy children waiting for a Western, middle-class couple, heterosexual or homosexual, to save them from a future of alienation and poverty. While this might often be the case at a microcosmic level, we also need to jump scales and recognize adoption as a global axis of inequality.[57] Comparative methodologies become paramount to such a project. In this context, a comparison between practices of adoption from Asia and East Europe would be instructive. Eng writes about the former: "Dissociating transnational adoption from the historical and economic legacy of war brides, mail-order brides, comfort women, and sex workers thus obscures an understanding of this practice as one of the more recent embodiments of gendered commodification; it is an enduring symptom of an increasingly international gendered division of labor, emerging under the shadows of colonialism and now sustained through the practices of global capitalism."[58] Adoption belongs on the continuum of women's work, a function of the international gendered division of reproductive labor. The legal adoption scene, on which infants (especially white infants likely to come from East Europe) are scarce, is shadowed by the underground world of coerced reproduction.

Alternatively, we could think of Irena as a surrogate mother and compare her predicament to that of surrogate mothers in India, who, assisted by new reproductive technologies, reproduce children commissioned by Western middle-class families. Amrita Pande has called for the recognition of surrogacy as legitimate, income-producing labor.[59] But Irena has not initiated her surrogacy, does not control it, and does not obtain an income from it. She insists, however, on kinship ties to the children she gives birth to and to their adoptive families. She does so not strictly on account of the fact that her biological eggs are used in the transaction but on account of the pregnancy itself. The women Pande interviews speak of the use of their blood and bodily fluids in the transaction in an effort to claim kinship relations.[60] Rather than declare ourselves in a postkinship moment (going back to the argument of chapter 1), we need to carefully unpack the structural relations that overdetermine the new kinship configurations in which the parties involved are situated at ever more stratified poles.[61]

In 1970, Shulamith Firestone gave voice to a feminist fantasy of women freeing themselves from the tyranny of biological reproduction "by any means available." She added: "*Childbearing* could be taken over by technology."[62] The fantasy was another way within second-wave feminism to imagine an end to the familial sexual division of labor. At the same time, Firestone warned that the medicalization of women's bodies could yield unanticipated exploitative results. Over the last two decades, new technologies have indeed come to the aid of biological reproduction, leading to a radical change in its meaning but also to new dilemmas. In 1995, Sarah Franklin wrote: "The meaning of reproductive politics has both expanded and diversified, resulting in a loss of certainty about preexisting feminist strategies, slogans, and frameworks, particularly those grounded on notions of rights and choice."[63] Franklin argued that the new debates on reproductive rights amount to a new debate on kinship. Another decade later, *The Unknown Woman* asks us to reconfirm the urgency to rethink kinship as well as reproductive rights.

If, for the most part, reproductive technologies take us away from biology as the basis of kinship, what happens when biology returns in the context of surrogacy and Irena claims the right to kinship relations to the children she gives birth to? Are we willing to dismiss such claims as *mere biology*? If chapter 1 asked for a reconsideration of feminist second-wave foundational texts like Gayle Rubin's "The Traffic in Women" and Luce Irigaray's "Women on the Market" and chapter 2 for a rereading of the feminist debate on housework, this chapter proposes that it is high time we revisit Firestone's *The Dialectic of Sex*.[64]

5. ***Natality is one possible answer to the highly charged question concerning Irena's agency.*** Can the *homo sacer* act? Can Irena *do* anything in response to the violence perpetrated against her? Judith Butler insists on the possibility of curbing the aggressive impulse in the service of nonviolence, even in the limit case of "the mired and conflicted position of a subject who is injured, rageful, who has access to violent retribution."[65] Ziarek proposes the example of the hunger strike, a form of nonviolent self-hurt, as biopolitical action.[66] Tornatore, on the other hand, does not present us with a peaceful act.[67] Irena's agency (which the film depicts cinematically through her facial stubbornness) eventually expresses itself in the killing of Mold, who, it should be said, has the face of a (highly stylized) evil humanity, but of humanity nonetheless. The bottom line: in order to assert her agency, Irena kills a human being.

This, however, is only the thriller solution to the question of agency. The other answer the film provides is that of agency as the claiming of natality rights. Let us return to Patterson's study of slavery: "In all slaveholding societies slave couples could be and were forcibly separated and the consensual 'wives' of slaves were obliged to submit sexually to their masters; slaves had no custodial claims or power over their children, and children inherited no claims or obligations to their parents."[68] Irena is violently separated from her lover, and she can make no custodial claims to her children. Like her, they are to be circulated as commodities. Only subsequently (once they are in the "right" familial situation) do these children become rights-bearing persons. Irena's act is to claim not only her body but also that which her body has produced, her biological children. Patterson charges that for the female slave, who cannot make claims to her children, social rebirth is synonymous with the restoration of her natality. In this spirit, Irena claims rights of motherhood to one of the children she has produced under conditions of coercion. She does not claim all nine, only the one she thinks is her last, conceived with her lover. The scheming the viewer does not understand throughout the film is aimed at getting access to the adoptive family of four-year-old Thea. Irena wants, in her words, to "take back what's mine."

In the birth scene in the film, Mold assists, visually taking the structural place of the child's father figure (see fig. 3.4). Irena gestures toward the baby but is denied access to it. Can a biological mother who has given birth under conditions of coercion claim a child that has in the meantime been adopted? Regardless of the narrative solution reached by *The Unknown Woman*, the scene brings the question of natality to the fore of the biopolitical debate. It does so in relation to offspring and the fragmented life one might produce but also in relation to one's ancestors (who are not always biologically de-

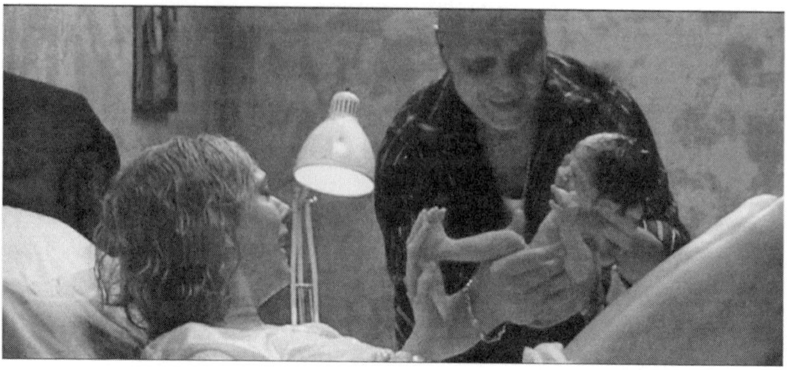

Fig. 3.4. A child is born in conditions of coerced reproduction. Frame from Giuseppe Tornatore's *The Unknown Woman* (2006).

fined). One also becomes a person when one claims rights to one's parents, grandparents, etc. In contemporary Europe, migrant and immigrant youths often find themselves pressured to repudiate their not-so-modern parents from various parts of the world. The situation applies to East European migrants, whose parents are likely to carry an abject communist history in need of European cleansing. Alongside its genre-determined violent solution, Tornatore's film emphasizes the two ends of natality as an agentive framework. On the one hand, Irena claims the rights of motherhood. On the other, beyond the imaginative framework of the film, she could call her (actual or symbolic) mother.

6. ***Killing is not the best model on which to understand contemporary forms of violence.*** *The Unknown Woman* can be said to offer a powerful critique of Agamben because it shows that the definition of the *homo sacer* as someone who "can be killed but not sacrificed," with its emphasis on killing, is inadequate. Tornatore declared in an interview: "In my movie, if you cut all the scenes of violence and you put it all together, it's not more than three minutes in the whole movie. The movie appears so violent because the violence is not shown. The audience is forced to imagine what they don't see. And the imagination of the audience is more violent than anything I can possibly show the audience myself."[69] What kind of violence is the viewer prompted to imagine? The gaps in the film are filled with gender-specific violence; the scene of coerced sex trafficking is, structurally, a rape scene. Tornatore's film reminds Agamben that the female body is subjected to *heterogeneous* kinds of violence.[70] Agamben offers the rape camps during the

war in the former Yugoslavia as an example of a contemporary camp, but he does not discuss rape as a reproductive technology: Bosnian women were raped so that they would produce "Serbian" children. This is not just violence but gender-specific, reproductive violence.

7. ***Sex trafficking imposes the difficult task of thinking the biopolitical through national, global, diasporic, corporate, NGO, and Mafia frameworks.*** These frameworks correspond to a number of overlapping sovereignties at work in any given context. If the interplay between the national and the global has received a lot of critical attention, that between the national, the corporate, and the NGO (nongovernment organization) has not.[71] Technologies of border control that participate in the creation of border vulnerability have been largely corporatized. The refugee camp is in the process of being corporatized.[72] Various forms of reproductive and regenerative labor have been financialized and harnessed by corporate interests. NGOs are exercising their own sovereignty, competing with weak state sovereignties in many parts of the world (the history of the Soros Foundation's work in post-1989 East Europe remains to be written).[73] In many cases, diasporas in the West likewise exercise more sovereignty "back home" than do the weak states that constitute "back home." We also need to account for the sovereignty of a sovereign like Mold. The return of the seemingly private is often glossed by the term *Mafia* (conspiracy is a leitmotif of the thriller genre, which, as we have seen, has penetrated the legal apparatus). The invocation of the Mafia marks a return of bare life to a stateless zone that appears as a perverse *oikos* because its two figures, woman and slave, are standing on the threshold. But the familial, often racialized rhetoric of the Mafia (the "Albanian Mafia," e.g.) is misleading. This is to say not that there are no criminal groups capitalizing on the traffic in women but that a limited focus on Mafia-like structures risks overshadowing the complex assemblage we should refer to as a *camp*, situated at the intersection of a number of overlapping sovereignties.

8. ***A focus on the relationship between Irena and Thea yields a more ambivalent notion of biopolitics, one that supplements Agamben's and is anchored in the possibility of an affirmative reappropriation of life.*** In *The Unknown Woman*, an adoptive mother has been freed from the burdens of reproduction by technology. That technology is the camp. This camp is invisible to us before Irena claims natality rights; all she knows is that she has adopted a child. Adding another twist to the narrative, as required by the genre, Irena turns out not to be Thea's biological mother. As in any adoption

situation, both Irena and Thea nonetheless mourn a loss, unrecoverable in its originary form (a *real* mother, a *real* daughter). A reparative relationship therefore develops between them; this relationship, imperfect as it might be, given that it is tainted by the violence that Irena has endured, makes up for their respective losses. At the end of Tornatore's film, an adolescent Thea waits outside the prison walls for Irena to be released. Thea and Irena will, the viewer is led to assume, develop their relationship into a friendship that challenges us to uncover another meaning of the word *life*—a life that exceeds both the mechanisms of its economic production and the state's biopolitical claims to its protection.[74]

We Are All *Homines Sacri*

One of the most important insights gained from a focus on camp-like situations of traffic in women is a much-needed distinction between coerced and (relatively) noncoerced forms of traffic in women and the conditions that define them. The distinction is most often drawn between migrant women coerced into sex trafficking and migrant women who choose to do sex work (with choice understood to be overdetermined by a number of factors). The latter are located on the margins of their respective societies as well as of the international order. Their work is invisible, undervalued, and stigmatized, but it also has its advocates, who mobilize through unions and other sex workers' organizations. Ann McClintock and Kamala Kempadoo speak of a contemporary global sex workers' movement. They collect their stories and sex workers' and activists' theorizations of sex work.[75] On the other hand, sex trafficking happens not on the margins of the *polis* but outside it or, rather, in a relation of inclusion through exclusion. This means not physical exclusion (sex-trafficking camps are often located at the heart of European cities) but legal exclusion. While sex work is not legal in many countries, it is for the most part *tolerated* by the law and is undertaken by migrant women who have some control of their situation, although they, too, might experience various forms of violence. In contradistinction, coerced sex work is sex and affective labor that one does not control, does not produce an income for the worker, and is performed in dehumanizing, often violent conditions. Despite the rhetoric of occasional heroic rescue, sex trafficking is currently for the most part *abandoned* by the law. Women coerced into sex work can reenter the law in restricted situations, once they formally produce the necessary, thriller-like narrative of victimhood, but these are exceptions to the rule of legal European and global abandonment.

Wendy S. Hesford contends that "victimization narratives presume a process between speaker and audience that moves from identification to persuasion."[76] Although Irena produces a victimization narrative, a function of the legal space in which she finds herself, the film does not allow the viewer to identify with her. Moreover, although the genre of the thriller requires a vulnerable victim and a passive one at that, Irena escapes this role.[77] Hers is a victimization narrative without a victim. *The Unknown Woman* is thus successful in displacing the figure of the victim from the center of the sex-trafficking debate while drawing attention to the necessary narrative of victimization. In doing so, it confirms Agamben's insight that the *homo sacer* cannot be a victim, structurally.

While Agamben's theorization of the contemporary camp as "captured outside" helps us conceptualize the traffic in women, this chapter has pointed to some lacunae in his understanding of the camp. The first is the fact that it is a productive camp. The second concerns the reproductive nature of its productivity. The third describes the fragmented nature of contemporary reproduction as an effect of molecularization. The fourth focuses on the particular fragmentation at stake in motherhood. The fifth revisits the question of agency as it applies to the female *homo sacer* inhabiting a sex-trafficking camp. The sixth concerns violence and its gender-specific heterogeneity. The seventh multiplies Agamben's notion of sovereignty. Finally, the eighth highlights the affirmative potential of life and the possibility of its reappropriation.

To repeat Agamben's controversial wager that "we are all virtually *homines sacri*" in the context of the traffic in women is to acknowledge that we are all a complex, undividable, unrecognizable compound of *zoē* and *bio*.[78] It is to acknowledge that we inhabit this compound unevenly in our stratified relations to protections offered by states and international law as well as in our stratified forms of privilege and precarity. It is also to acknowledge that such relations are further stratified along gender lines. "We are all *homines sacri*" precisely because we are not but could be. "We" too could fall out of capitalist luck and find ourselves situated in a different point on the biopolitical continuum, in situations in which survival means selling an egg or a kidney. Or donating blood. Or gestating somebody else's child.

4

"Give Me Your Passport"

The Traffic in Women in a "Europe without Borders"

In an effort to create what it refers to as an area of "freedom, security and justice," the European Union simultaneously creates a new European wall.[1] Increasingly, this reality has come to be known as *Fortress Europe*. The zigzagging wall around this Europe creates a distinction between Europeans and non-Europeans but also between EU Europeans and non-EU Europeans. Polish women cleaning houses in Berlin are EU citizens, while Ukrainian women doing the same work are noncitizens. Whether East European women can cross European borders easily depends on where in East Europe they come from. But the fact that the movement of some women is curtailed does not mean that they do not work in West Europe. It means only that they work for less money and under more precarious conditions. This chapter is a study of passport-induced precarity as seen through the lens of the traffic in women. If in the midst of the 2011–12 economic crisis it often seems like labor uncertainty and exploitation have been democratized across class, race, and citizenship, I argue that precarity continues to be highly stratified. One instrument of stratification is the passport. The Schengen-based European Union, which advertises itself as a "Europe without borders," makes passports less visible or reduces them to metaphoric uses ("passport to paradise") but transforms

Fig. 4.1. A passport-mediated kiss. Frame from Lukas Moodysson's *Lilja 4-Ever* (2000).

them into much-needed labor documents for those Europeans not "accepted" into the European Union (*admitted* is the verb Rey Chow would use).[2] Passports do not bring labor rights in themselves, but, by filtering mobility rights, some open, and some close, transnational labor trajectories. This is why, in numerous narratives of migration, migrants are asked not whether they have a labor permit but rather whether they have a passport. The Schengen Information System, the digital database that undergirds the regulation of mobility in Europe, is a system of triage that separates legitimate labor from strategically criminalized labor. It does not *exclude* those outside EU borders; it only creates a differential regime for their inclusion.

This chapter was prompted by an image in Lukas Moodysson's *Lilja 4-Ever* (2000), a film that has been consequential for raising awareness about the contemporary traffic in women in Europe. The image shows Lilja, a sixteen-year-old girl from "somewhere in what was once the Soviet Union," in an airport. Andrei, who poses as her boyfriend, is sending her to Sweden, where she will be coerced into sex work. Lilja naively thinks that Andrei will join her in two weeks. They say good-bye and kiss. As Lilja's hands reach for Andrei, the passport she holds is interposed between their faces (see fig. 4.1). An exercise in defamiliarization, this chapter is an invitation to zoom in on this passport. In the history of cinematic kisses, we are faced with a passport-mediated kiss, the metonymy of a passport-mediated love that itself functions as a segue into a passport-mediated traffic in women.

Going back to the argument that the traffic in women spans legal and illegal situations, in addition to Moodysson's *Lilja 4-Ever* I explore in this chapter a second cinematic narrative, Jean-Pierre and Luc Dardenne's *Lorna's*

Silence (2008). In very different ways, the female protagonists of the two films are drawn into two branches of the traffic in women. Although it initially appears that only Lilja is in a situation of coercion, it becomes apparent that the passport mediates the passage of both women into coercion. If in the previous chapter I analyzed a situation of coercion into sex and reproduction, in this chapter I juxtapose a situation of coercion into sex work with one of coercion into marriage. The focus here is on the relation between the traffic in women and passport-mediated European mobility. The interdisciplinary literature on mobility is rich and extensive, but it is surprising how many accounts of European mobility neglect (or actively forget) the passport and its stratifying effects. Recent art cinema, on the other hand, offers a large archive of critically framed passport images. Through a reading of two films, this chapter attempts to bring the interdisciplinary literature on mobility to bear on the materiality of the passport, the object on which transnational mobility, including the traffic in women, pivots. I agree with numerous commentators who contend that a focus on borders results in a restricted analysis of the traffic in women, legal and illegal. The larger stake of this chapter is to propose that we move our analysis of global and European mobility away from a focus on bordering (and EU style debordering) to one on mobile bodies' relation to various passports.

The Passport

Historians of the passport trace identification papers of the passport kind to medieval times. Their appearance coincides with the transition from oral to written modalities of documenting property ownership for the purposes of taxation. In order to travel (without avoiding one's tax or military obligations), one needed an identification paper; one could not "wander" too far, for too long, or on unknown routes.[3] Before the modern passport, documents like passes and letters of introduction served as a way to monopolize what John Torpey calls "the legitimate means of movement."[4] From the fifteenth century to the eighteenth, a variety of more or less enforceable paper records monitored travel. One of the first references to attempts to falsify such papers concerns Gypsies, whose movement was restricted from the early days of Europe.[5]

Having taken their lead from Torpey's pioneering work on the history of the passport, historians generally agree that it is with the French Revolution that we begin to speak of passports in the modern sense. The intense debate on passports during the French Revolution remains symptomatic of the tension passports dramatize in modern times. The right to movement is a testing ground for any claim to freedom. If in its initial stages the Revolution aspired to absolute hospitality, whereby revolutionary France would offer asylum to all who needed it, leading to the prompt abolition of the prerevolutionary passport system, it soon became clear that the movement of people led to instability both politically (revolutionaries moved around) and economically (beggars moved around). Passport obligations were reintroduced by the revolutionary government in 1792. They would be consequential to the birth of citizenship and the governmentality of the Westphalian territorial state. Passports help wall off the territorial state in a process that consecrates its legitimacy. Drawing on both Max Weber and Michel Foucault, historians place the invention of the passport within larger processes of rationalization and bureaucratization, administration and governmentality.

If, for most of the nineteenth century, passports remained a necessity of travel, the end of the century loosened its grip on the control of movement. This period is often celebrated as an open, passportless world. Caren Kaplan quotes the writer and critic C. E. Montague: "Europe lay open to roaming feet. . . . All frontiers were unlocked. You wandered freely about the Continent as if it were your own country."[6] Yet some people's movement remained restricted—that of poor migrants, often generically referred to as *Gypsies*.[7] At the dawn of World War I, borders closed once again as a series of wartime passport measures were taken in response to what was perceived as a state of emergency in mobility matters. Modernist writers and artists found themselves restricted in their travels by what they called the *passport nuisance*, which they imagined as a temporary inconvenience.[8] But the passport measures would never be repealed; we have never overcome what Torpey calls a "state of emergency" in passport matters.[9] Torpey reminds us that it was in the xenophobia-filled atmosphere of World War I that the modern international passport system was standardized and consolidated. It would also be in the wake of World War I that the League of Nations would make the first gestures toward accommodating large numbers of stateless migrants in the new passport order. One of the most heated debates surrounding the passport concerns its role in the genocide of the European Jews.

The vicissitudes of global mobility are captured by the relation the passport maintains with other state-issued identification cards. The passport assigns an identity to the citizen traveling outside the state's borders and a number of trajectories of mobility. But, if the global world is one of transnational movement, the passport is a reminder that movement is a function of statist identification. One must be a citizen of a country, with one's identity established through a national identification card, in order to obtain a passport. Once a passport has been obtained, it can in most contexts be used instead of a national identification card. Conversely, in some circumstances such a card can function as a passport. The global, as seen through the lens of the passport, remains very much striated by statist materialities.

If in the 1990s it looked like the nation-state was in decline and might even disappear, the passport remains a stubborn, powerful reminder that there is no global without the state. Likewise, for now at least, there is no Europe without European states. When the idea of a possible European passport emerged in the wake of the Schengen Agreement, it was quickly put aside. It was argued that citizens of European states should automatically become holders of European passports. The phrase *European Union* was added to the cover of existing national passports. For Schengen Europeans, Europe lies open to roaming feet once again. They are in no need of a passport when traveling within the European Union. Other Europeans, as well as non-Europeans knocking at the door of Fortress Europe, need a passport more than ever. If they find themselves passportless in the European Union, which they often do, they become members of an "invisible state."[10]

What, then, is a passport? An exercise in defamiliarization presents us with an odd booklet. Explicitly or implicitly, the passport retains the archaic framework of a letter through which an authorizing agency in one country introduces one of its citizens to authorities in another country and requests the rights of passage and protection on his or her behalf. The modern passport identifies the citizen through a range of standardized information. There is a legal name, a place of residence, and a date of birth. There is gender: F/M. There is the standard passport photograph, invoking the history of the mug shot. As traces of this history, some passports still contain a physical description (e.g., eye color) or mention identifying marks. There is a signature, carrying the historical baggage of graphology as forensic science and a form of character profiling. More recently, biometric technologies have enabled the attachment of fingerprints and retina or face scans to the passport, allowing it to be plugged into forensic digital databases—the Schengen Information System—and redefining the old booklet as an e-passport. As in the past, when the right to travel needed to be renewed periodically and was often valid for only one trip on a specific route, the modern passport lists its date of issue and expiration. The rest of the passport contains blank pages, which are to be filled with a number of stamps, functioning as an archive of one's mobility and credit history for future travel. Most important among these stamps is the *visa*, which offers a second set of data qualifying the right to movement to specific countries for specific dates and purposes. The international visa system, superimposing itself on the

Fig. 4.2. The passport is foregrounded in a customs scene. Frame from Pawel Pawlikowski's *Last Resort* (2000).

passport system, effectively distinguishes between legitimate and criminalized mobilities. When a given national passport is not sufficient for international travel, additional "passport documents" (Leo Luccasen's phrase), either work or study related, are attached to the passport.[11] On the scene of biometric passport technologies, which often draw on corporate databases, a credit card can be a passport document. The new biometric technologies are meant to prevent forgery and replace outdated security seals, which nonetheless are still nostalgically present on most passports.

In this condensed yet complex media form, the passport answers two interdependent questions: Who are you? and, Where are you from? For many people in the world today the answer to the highly charged question, Where are you from? most likely takes the form of a more or less lengthy narrative. The passport simplifies matters and gives one brief, unequivocal answer—you are from the country that issued your passport. The passport functions as a caption for the body of the global traveler. It clings to the body, making it legible in mobile ways. There is a suggestive frame in Pawel Pawlikowski's film *Last Resort* (2000) in which the film's protagonist, Tanya, places her passport next to her face when hailed by the customs officer (see fig. 4.2). The gesture effectively functions as a response: "Yes, here I am," my face and my passport. It turns out that this passport cannot take Tanya, who is Russian, into the United Kingdom. As she fails to produce additional passport documents (she needs either money or a British fiancé), her mobility becomes restricted, first to the London airport, and then to an "accommodation center" for asylum seekers.

Historians remind us that, in medieval times, the bodies of a range of deviants were marked by tattoos for identification purposes, those tattoos also implying travel restrictions. We like to think that we have become subtler, such that the modern passport testifies to a transition whereby, as Jane Caplan and John Torpey put it, "writing on the body gave way to reading off it."[12] In fact, biometric technologies mark a return to the writing on the body, this time in digital code. Giorgio Agamben theorized his refusal to travel to the United States in 2004 by drawing an analogy between the tattooing of inmates in Auschwitz and the biopolitical identification of travelers to the United States. He argued that what the new passport technologies bring is "the appropriation and registration of the most private and unsheltered element, that is the biological life of bodies."[13] Biometric technologies of passport control archive and stratify life along lines of citizenship. Agamben's protests notwithstanding, the European Union followed its pattern of Americanization in the implementation of what Agamben calls *biopolitical tattoos*. Pawlikowski's image is suggestive but anachronistic: Tanya in fact does not need her passport as her face is already tattooed with the necessary electronic information. The paper passport simply facilitates connection with a digital database.

Despite the recent focus on new passport technologies, the traveling body remains decipherable in traditional ways too. Race continues to determine international movement.[14] So does gender (a wedding band is a useful travel accessory). But the most insidious factor remains class. Tracing the control of movement in nineteenth-century Europe, Lucassen writes: "The main fear among government officials throughout the nineteenth century, as remains the case in present-day welfare states, was that the would-be settler would become a 'public charge' and thus burden the system of poor relief."[15] Passports are instrumental to the administration of the non-European and East European poor. This often means the racialized poor, as is the case with the Roma. Today it often seems like the European Union returns to premodern practices: the Roma picked up on the outskirts of Paris or Rome are identified through dress and the physiognomic, racial reading of the body as well as racialized markers of poverty, like homelessness or presumed criminality.[16] The passport enters the picture only subsequently, to reveal their place of residence, the place to which they are returned once forced on a plane. While the treatment of the Roma has clear racial undertones, it also needs to be understood as an attempt to control the movement of some of the poorest people in Europe. The fear of a passportless world is the fear of an invasion of the poor—the contemporary equivalent to the treatment of beggars following the French Revolution. Most recently, in 2013, the British media warned about an invasion of poor migrant workers from Romania and Bulgaria. Through its digital technologies, the passport system attempts (rather unsuccessfully) to keep the East European poor at a safe, aesthetic distance.

Whether travel is restricted or encouraged, the passport (or its metonymic stand-ins) constitutes an implacable, if often invisible, reality of mobility. One cannot *not* have a passport if one is to be mobile. Ursula Biemann puts the words in flashing caps in her video essay *Remote Sensing* (2001): "TO OWN HER PASSPORT IS TO OWN HER LABOR . . . CIVIL RIGHTS . . . AND SEXUAL GOVERNANCE." Biemann draws attention to the precarity that attaches itself to passportlessness—when one does not own one's labor, one is without civil rights, and one risks losing the governance of one's sexuality. In a study of accommodation centers in Germany, Saskia Witteborn quotes a female asylum seeker: "I have no passport. With a passport, I am a human being."[17]

If one does benefit from protections that come with the ownership of a passport, it is important to remember that passports fall into two categories, casually referred to as *strong* and *weak*. To be the carrier of a strong passport is to be lucky among passport holders—you have elite citizenship status and can go most places. A weak passport is almost useless by itself, as it usually needs special visas or additional accompanying documents to make travel possible. *Strong* and *weak* as descriptive terms draw attention to the fact that, depending on what passport one carries (and in a disjunctive relation to wealth or status), one occupies a strong or a weak position in the global and European economy. Benedict Anderson writes: "Portuguese and Bangladeshi passports, even when genuine, tell us little about loyalties and habitus, but they tell us a great deal about the relative likelihood of their holders being permitted to seek jobs in Milan or Copenhagen. The segregated queues that all of us experience at airport immigration barricades mark economic status far more than any political attachments. In effect, they figure differential tariffs on human labor."[18] This statement rings true for a Ukrainian or an Albanian passport.

The current passport system reinforces birth as a tacit European value and, as such, the underwriting credential for European mobility rights. In rare moments, the tacit becomes explicit, as in a statement made by Umberto Eco speaking in the name of "some European citizens" who addressed "the governments of the continent in which they were born and where they would like to continue living, proud to be part of it."[19] Why would one be proud of a place one happens to have been born in? We obviously do not

Fig. 4.3. Poster in Kiev. Société Réaliste, *EU Green Card Lottery* (2005–).

choose where we are born. To use a Heideggerian word, we are *thrown* into various corners of the world. Birth depends on a throw of a dice; its principle of distribution is luck. Why, then, should the accident of being born Italian come with global and European privileges?

The American Diversity Visa Lottery is one notorious embodiment of arbitrariness, dispensing around fifty thousand work permits ("green cards") a year to applicants around the world. A computer chooses the winners randomly, allotting them to a number of diversity quotas. The program functions as a powerful reminder of the arbitrariness with which identification papers attach to the bodies that carry them. The visa lottery explicitly adds the arbitrariness of luck to that of birth. For the most part, Europeans would like to define their Europeanness in opposition to US practices, the visa lottery included.[20] Yet an analogy between the US visa lottery and the immigration policies of "the United States of Europe" is drawn by Société Réaliste, through an Internet-based art project, *EU Green Card Lottery* (2005–).[21] The site advertises the lottery through posters in various languages and invites visitors to apply (see fig. 4.3). Having been provided statistics about the aging of Europe's population, virtual applicants are told that the European Union needs 1,066,666 migrants per year in order to maintain economic growth. The program's emphasis is on diversity. The visa lottery is presented as a route to EU citizenship, which in turn "allows you to vote and obtain a EU Member State Passport." The program offers comparative information on various EU states in which applicants might settle: GDP, unemployment rate, minimum wage, religion, and language. Applicants are made aware of the fact that married people have two chances to win. The tone of *EU Green Card Lottery* is serious and matter-of-fact. The visitor-applicant becomes acutely aware that the project is an ironic celebration of luck as the route to citizenship and a strong passport. Perhaps Eco should entertain the possibility of taking his chances on the EU lottery.

In addition to the awareness gained from the kind of critical work performed by art projects like *EU Green Card Lottery*, one can glimpse insights into the current passport order in flickering moments of crisis—either when an EU passport is lost or when a desired one is obtained through illicit means. This is when it becomes clear that a strong passport is a most precious possession. Hotels offer safes for the protection of such valuables. Travel agencies include passport advice in their travel packages. The bottom line is, Whatever you do, wherever you go, do not lose your passport! More practical advice follows, encouraging travelers to sew their passports to their jackets or hide them in their undergarments. The signature accessory of the tourist, the fanny pack, is a very visible (and comic) attempt to keep one's passport safe. Ingenious reactions to passport-loss anxiety have led to more discreet devices for safely storing passports (neck pouches, belts, bra stashes, socks).[22] The passport is often intimately caressing the traveler's skin. Were one to lose one's passport, one would become a *sans papier* and risk going native, losing one's privileges and blending in with the weak, the vulnerable, and the immobile. The anxiety is so deep that it has given birth to numerous narratives belonging to what we might call the *lost-passport* genre.

One memorable lost-passport fictional narrative—in Gianni Amelio's film *Lamerica* (1994)—depicts the situation of an Italian, Gino, traveling to Albania on a sham business trip in the early 1990s. In the course of his adventures in Albania, Gino loses his passport. The deference he accepts as due course when he has his passport in his possession gives way to an incipient awareness of what it means to hold Albanian citizenship. The film tellingly depicts the terror that accompanies such an accident. Throughout the film, the viewer sees Gino running around shouting, "But I am Italian! I am Italian!" As an Italian passport holder, Gino has rights—he has the right to have rights, as Arendt would put it. Without an Italian passport, he is *sans*

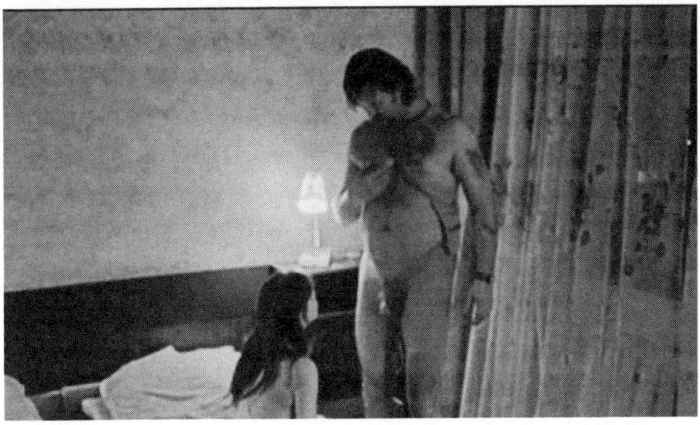

Fig. 4.4. Passport documents compensate for lack of an erection. Frame from Ulrich Seidl's *Import/Export* (2007).

papier. "We are all without papers here," an Albanian official declares. Gino thus has to travel to Italy like all Albanian migrants—illegally, on an overcrowded boat across the Adriatic Sea.

As if to suggest that one had better not find oneself in such a situation, a number of cinematic fictional narratives dramatize situations in which their protagonists do everything they can to protect their passports. Striking in this category is an image in Ulrich Seidl's *Import/Export* (discussed in chapter 2). During a trip to Ukraine, Paul's stepfather, Michael, keeps his papers literally on him, in a belt that he wears across his chest and never takes off. This belt sticks to him like a second skin. Michael even washes in it. In a central scene in the film, having hired a Ukrainian sex worker, Michael orders her to sniff his shoes and bark, all the while explaining to his stepson that this is what money can buy in Ukraine. Michael, however, is a working-class Austrian man with very little money. It is the other kind of valuable stored in his belt that can buy things in Ukraine. Michael performs linguistic and gestural machismo successfully, and, if the viewer is tempted to dismiss his performance because he cannot have an erection, it is clear that the power of his self-identification as "I, Austria" rests not in his sexual prowess but in the belt attached to his body (see fig. 4.4). This belt produces his inflated sense of masculinity. The viewer does not get a chance to peek into the belt; its contents remain invisible, a comment on the invisibility of the passport in a "Europe without borders." Yet the loss of this much-cherished prosthesis would be the symbolic equivalent of castration.

Passport Love: Lilja

The first text this chapter analyzes at length is Moodysson's *Lilja 4-Ever*. In it, a young woman from "somewhere in what was once the Soviet Union" remains without her passport once she steps into Sweden. As in many other cinematic texts, the sentence "Give me your passport" announces narratives of coerced traffic in women—sexual or otherwise. The distinction explored in chapter 3 between coerced and noncoerced traffic in women is also determined by the passport: women who are passportless or are holders of weak passports are vulnerable to coercion. Throughout the Swedish part of Moodysson's film, the viewer sees Lilja in the back seat of a car, being moved around, bought and sold. These images of forced mobility are interposed with scenes in which Lilja is systematically raped by countless Swedish men. In these scenes, the camera is positioned somewhere close to Lilja's head, such that the viewer is forced to endure the ensuing visual discomfort, grunting sounds, sweat, and affective violence with Lilja—not in her place, but *near* her. Moodysson explains in interviews that he wanted his viewer to know from the beginning what would happen to Lilja and then sit back and watch it happen.[23] The story is, in other words, predictable. At the beginning of the film, we know how it will unfold. This is why it is worth rehearsing here—it has become generic, almost a genre in itself.

Faced with Moodysson's film, the outraged critic risks focusing exclusively on the scenes of violence in Sweden. In other words, he or she risks framing Lilja's story through the lens of the traffic in women understood narrowly, as coerced sex trafficking, rather than broadly, on the continuum of *women's work*. In order to grasp the latter interpretation, one must read patiently Lilja's predicament *before* she arrives in Sweden. *Lilja 4-Ever* consists of two distinct yet continuous parts, a before and an after. On the threshold between the two spaces stands a passport. There is spatial continuity between the traffic in women specific to the before side ("somewhere in what was once the Soviet Union") and the traffic in women specific to the after side (Sweden). Thus, Lilja lives in a decrepit, dysfunctional socialist housing project "somewhere in what was once the Soviet Union." In Sweden, she is locked in an apartment in another socialist housing project. The former is the abject side of European socialism, the latter its success story. Give or take a few shades of gray—a parallel to the snow-induced spatial continuity in Seidl's *Import/Export*—the view from Lilja's window is the same.

"Haven't you ever thought of leaving here?" asks Andrei, Lilja's pretend boyfriend and a local recruiter in a pan-European trafficking business. The conversation occurs in his car as he drives past block after block of depressing Soviet apartment buildings. These are the urban landscapes that have famously lent their grayness to Cold War rhetoric (including cinematic rhetoric) and to abundant fantasies of a colorful, exciting West.[24] "This country is shit," he continues. "There's nothing to do here. . . . Sweden is a paradise compared to here. You can really relax there."[25] Lilja is silent, a look of concentration on her face. "And the people, even the people are different. They're kind, not like here." For Lilja, whose life is a series of encounters with people who have lost all capacity for compassion, the fantasy of Swedish warmth is highly appealing. The motif comes back even more ironically when Lilja needs to make believe that she would be picking vegetables in Sweden. "Perhaps it's warmer in Sweden," she whispers timidly, having admitted that she does not really know where Sweden is, other than "somewhere in the EU . . . or whatever it's called." Andrei's final argument is economically implacable: "Besides, you can earn really good money. You know, in a month you can earn what a doctor makes here in a year." Andrei proceeds to warn against the risks of being left behind. "You'll be left in this shithole," Lilja later taunts a friend, echoing this speech. Aside from the fact that "there's nothing to do here" and that therefore one is doomed to a life of boredom and stagnation (as opposed to relaxation), there are risks: "You know what my cousin did? He sold one of his kidneys because he didn't have money. Would you sell a kidney?" The conclusion: "You don't deserve a life like that." In the next scene, the viewer studies the minute movements of Lilja's face as she watches a few elderly homeless people crawling in the winter slush outside Andrei's car. Yes, Lilja will go to Sweden. Moodysson's script is explicitly didactic in amassing all possible arguments that might persuade Lilja that the dream of Sweden is worth pursuing. One or two would have sufficed—for Lilja and the viewer. As seen through Moodysson's didacticism, Andrei's argumentation skills are poor, and Lilja is excessively naive, but the point the film seems to be making is that Lilja does not need much persuasion. She can see the red herring in the story Andrei sells her, but she is ready to go. The scene is filmed in a car because she is already on her way. The film troubles the legal assumption that "perfect victims" of sex trafficking (and Lilja is fairly close to perfect) are distinguishable from economic migrants (Seidl's Olga, e.g.). The traffic in women, as conceptualized in this book, offers a framework to discuss the two on a continuum.[26]

Andrei is not a believable character because he is a fantasy; he has stepped out of Lilja's projections about life in West Europe. He is the fantasy of the local boyfriend who works in the West. A boyfriend is a luxury for Lilja, who has sex for subsistence money with older European men traveling to "somewhere in what was once the Soviet Union" to enjoy the relatively inexpensive sex industry. Andrei is young, handsome, cool, and seemingly compassionate. He offers Lilja a ride in his car and insists that he does not want anything in return. "You think I am ugly?" Lilja wonders. Andrei takes Lilja to McDonald's. He plays electronic games. He drives a Western car. When he eventually has sex with Lilja, he is playful; the scene recalls children at play. These are rudiments of the modernity that Lilja imagines—all perceived in a dizzying succession that does not allow for a pensive pause. It is crucial to understand Lilja's passage into coerced sex work in Sweden in relation to her incipient love for Andrei. He is equipped with the accoutrements that signify the promise of transnational upward mobility. Once one works abroad, one drives a car. One has a cell phone. One eats at McDonald's. One earns more than a local doctor. One can relax—existentially. Lilja falls in love with Andrei, who mediates her desire for an upward mobility ending in a Western, working-class, normative life.

In order to locate Lilja's predicament within the traffic in women broadly understood, one needs to start at the beginning, with her mother. Lilja's initial familial situation is barely sketched in *Lilja 4-Ever*, but as the film progresses the viewer can assemble it retrospectively. Lilja's mother lives in a city that was built to serve a Soviet submarine base known locally as "the Pentagon." She worked in the kitchen. She got to know a soldier who was temporarily stationed at the submarine base. She became pregnant, he was transferred, and she never heard from him again. She raised Lilja alone. She is in her forties and is bitter and resentful. With the collapse of the Soviet Union, she lost her job. To make ends meet, she prostitutes herself occasionally. Her city is in ruins. The nouveau riche of the new economy (local and European) can be seen only in the local sex club. And they are not in the business of creating jobs. Lilja's teacher taunts her with a Soviet-inspired, cynical aphorism ("A golden future awaits you") that applies to the city as a whole. As in Mungiu's *Occident*, it seems that everyone wants to leave. Lilja's mother has recourse to "one of those dating agencies" that have mushroomed across East Europe. She eventually meets a man, presumably an immigrant returned home in search of a wife, who promises to take her to America. In the would-be East European immigrant's anachronistic imagination, the future is either in the European Union or in America (or a blurred combination of the two). This future necessarily passes through a transnational marriage—and the never-mentioned accompanying papers. At the request of her new husband, the mother leaves Lilja behind. Once in America, she does not send Lilja the promised checks. The viewer is left speculating as to why (in the absence of access to digital media, Lilja is waiting for a letter). Mothers usually do send checks. Indeed, mothers usually take their children along, eventually. Moodysson's film unfolds in the temporal gap between the mother's departure and the promise of family reunification.

Lilja 4-Ever dramatizes the question of what happens to the children left behind by women who commute for work or marriage across the globe. Most of the time, they are cared for by other women in the extended family (grandmothers, aunts). What happens when these families (in this case, Lilja's aunt) fail them?[27] Lilja belongs to a second generation of East European women who live on the horizon of a transnational upward-mobility narrative. They can be coerced into sex trafficking, among other things, as a result of *conditions* created by their mothers' participation in the traffic in women, broadly understood.

Profoundly disappointed and hurt by her mother's departure, Lilja comes to understand it. She slowly learns to reintegrate the memory of her mother into her daily life. "Now I understand why my mother left," she whispers as she contemplates a windowless abandoned building. But her "now I understand" involves more than spatial understanding. She comes to slowly grasp the fact that the only way out for her mother and for herself is the traffic in women. The cynical Soviet slogan "A golden future awaits you" finally arrives at its destination. Having learned from her mother, Lilja wants to put herself in circulation on the traditional model, as Andrei's girlfriend.[28] Andrei, on the other hand, has moved from the old, traditional traffic in women (which already in Lilja's mother's generation could be local and/or transnational) to its newer and more violent version. Once Lilja puts herself in his hands, he trades her on the European sex market. He is the linchpin that connects the before and the after in Moodysson's film—and the local and European traffic in women.

Lilja already forms a couple with her friend Volodya, a boy of about eleven. Throughout the film, Lilja and Volodya offer each other glimmers of a form of reciprocity that seems to have become scarce in their world. We see them whispering in bed, eating, drinking, wrestling—literally keeping each other warm in what seems to be a very cold post–Cold War world. One wonders where the East Europe known for its humanity (the East Europe that Ulrich Seidl celebrates) has disappeared in Moodysson's film. Lilja's mother has raised her daughter for sixteen years but abandons her quite easily. Her aunt effectively steals the roof over Lilja's head and encourages her to "go to town and spread [her] legs." Her neighbor scolds her daily. Her teacher humiliates her. Her best friend betrays her. The social worker is at best indifferent. It is against this radically alienating, unnecessarily heartless East European background that Moodysson places Lilja's friend-

Fig. 4.5. Volodya studies Lilja's passport. Frame from Lukas Moodysson's *Lilja 4-Ever* (2000).

ship with Volodya. In this social and emotional wasteland, Volodya can be humanized because he is young, traumatized, and imaginative. He and Lilja become one another's siblings, parents, friends, and would-be lovers. But Volodya is too young; he cannot protect Lilja. He certainly is not "man enough" to act on his fantasy that he and Lilja could form a family ("I come home from work, you bake the bread"). He is not even a survivor; he sniffs glue and talks about death. Lilja's fantasy of Sweden is haunted by the prospect of leaving Volodya behind. Perhaps she can take him to Sweden, too, find a job for him, too. Volodya is not persuaded. The tension builds as he stares at Lilja's fake passport, the ticket to Sweden. He holds the precious document in his hands (see fig. 4.5) before ostentatiously throwing it away. In the air there is a mixture of passport suspicion (passports do not come gratis) and passport jealousy (can I have one?).

Moodysson's film yields renewed eloquence once we focus on the passport that takes Lilja to Sweden. "Is it for me?" Lilja asks Andrei, as if in response to a gift. "Now your name is Katya." Why? "There could be problems at the border. So they won't ask unnecessary questions." The exchange draws attention to the fact that traffickers *exploit* the functioning of the current passport system, which creates the demand for the commodification of illegal migration and produces Lilja's vulnerability. We know that today the border is no longer materialized as a territorial dividing line between states. To a large extent, it has become airport based and as such is found in multiple locations within the European Union. Borders are slowly becoming camp-like border zones. Films like *Lilja 4-Ever* show us that the new wall around Europe is not a line to be crossed but a dwelling place. Lilja is vulnerable because she inhabits her camp passportless, theoretically in Sweden as a citizen of a former Soviet state, but effectively stateless in a precarious borderland. She cannot partake of the protections offered by the Swedish state because the same state is part of the deportation regime that produces her vulnerability.[29] Moodysson filmed *Lilja 4-Ever* in Tallinn, Estonia, and cast the Russian actress Oksana Akinshina to play the role of Lilja, but decided to refer to the setting of the film as "somewhere in what was once the Soviet Union." This is, arguably, a place, but, significantly, it is not a state (like Sweden). This means that Lilja is effectively stateless before and after. She is raped on both sides of the equation, but no state makes it its business to punish the violence and protect her.

The close-ups of Lilja's face as she is repeatedly raped are risky. In the context of the traffic in women and coerced sex trafficking in particular, it would be too easy for the viewer to identify them with the very face of suffering.[30] Lilja is young, innocent, and religious—an ideal object of empathy. Yet Moodysson signals all his maneuvers; he consistently shows the viewer what comes next. Unlike journalistic images of pain and suffering, Moodysson's frames are hyperfictional; they do not claim to realistically capture the face of the other—here, the trafficked woman. What remains is the viewer's affective response to a necessarily failed depiction of suffering. Prompted by the film, the viewer is moved to begin a search for its unrepresentable face. Moodysson's film wants to function as the beginning of the journey, not its end.

The last scene of *Lilja 4-Ever* presents us with a highway. In an ironic take on Hollywood's open road endings mapped onto celebratory accounts of European travel, we are reminded that there are no available routes for someone like Lilja in Europe. When all hope is gone, Moodysson gives Lilja wings as a "passport to heaven."[31] Secular viewers see only blood on a highway. The angry soundtrack—*Mein Herz Brennt* by the heavy metal band Rammstein—accompanying the jerky movements of a handheld camera in the last cuts of the film tracks the secular reaction to the film rather than Moodysson's winged redemptive scenario. Since Lilja shares her mother's fantasy of America, once the viewer brings her back to earth, she finds herself wishing Lilja could get a real passport to America, wherever that might be.

Passport Love: Lorna

If Moodysson's *Lilja 4-Ever* is explicitly didactic when it comes to the imbrication of the traffic in women and the European passport system, the other text I discuss here, Jean-Pierre and Luc Dardenne's *Lorna's Silence* (2008), is subtler. Viewers might not see the passport in it or, initially, the traffic in women. The passport is present in the film through its relation to the national ID, in this case Belgian. The film stages a narrative at the intersection of labor, gender, and citizenship—and the passport question. Lorna is a stronger agent than Lilja, but the film slowly introduces the viewer to more surreptitious forms of coercion, this time into marriage.

In 2007 Lauren Berlant published a remarkable essay on two of Jean-Pierre and Luc Dardenne's films, *Rosetta* (1999) and *The Promise* (1996). The essay, titled "Nearly Utopian, Nearly Normal," prompts reflection on the passport at the same time as it asks for a range of marginalia occasioned by the Dardennes' more recent *Lorna's Silence* (2008). Arguing that the brothers' films focus on the Belgian working class in the context of global migration, Berlant writes:

> It matters that these films are organized around not migrants whose migration is animated by hope of a better good life, but citizens who thought that the traditional forms of social reciprocity would provide scenes for life-building, not the attrition of being. For legal citizens (here, of Europe), the difference between having papers or not determines which economies you can participate in, yet the ease of attaining the paper identity that performs a simulacrum of social ballast puts into question the legal/illegal distinction. In the economic lifeworld of these films, citizens without capital and migrants are *almost* in the same boat, and all might be called survivalists, scavengers bargaining against defeat by the capitalist destruction of life.[32]

Berlant revised this formulation when she included the essay in *Cruel Optimism* (2011) to say: "Citizens without capital and migrants with fake papers are in proximate, interdependent boats structurally and affectively."[33] Between the two versions of the essay, Berlant moves from arguing that migrants and citizens without capital are "*almost* in the same boat" to suggesting that they are in "proximate, interdependent boats." I am interested in probing what is at stake in this transition, in an effort to explore the temptation behind Berlant's initial formulation. The impetus for this exercise comes from the fact that this temptation has been exacerbated in the current economic crisis, such that today many commentators insist that precarity has been democratized across the migrant/citizen distinction.[34] My argument is that precarity continues to be highly stratified by, among other things, differential access to mobility and various passport options.

It is as if the Dardennes released *Lorna's Silence* in 2008 to respond to Berlant's italicized *almost*—the idea that Belgian citizens without capital and migrants/immigrants are "*almost* in the same boat." A sense of continuity between the Dardennes' films is assured by the fact that the actor who plays the troubled boy in *The Promise* (Jérémie Renier) has matured into the petty criminal young man in *The Child* (2005) and is "the junkie" in *Lorna's Silence*. This last film, however, does not have Renier's character at its center. Lorna occupies this place, a migrant in search of the good life, in an odd, complex relationship with a Belgian citizen without capital. I believe, however, that, while the Dardennes' *Lorna* acknowledges the structural affinities between the Belgian citizen (Renier's character, Claudy) and the new immigrant class (Lorna), it accents Berlant's *almost* somewhat more forcefully and more ironically than her own italics. Indeed, the accent on *almost* is a function of various papers (IDs and passports) and the ease or difficulty of obtaining them.

Lorna is an Albanian immigrant living in Belgium, more exactly, in a gray, industrial-looking Liège. She is played by the Kosovar actress Arta Dobroshi, who speaks an accented French that she learned for the role. Jean-Pierre Dardenne declared in an interview: "In order for the story to work, she [Lorna] had to come from a country outside the European Union. She is Albanian, but she could just as well have been Brazilian or Russian."[35] Lorna is an immigrant, and, as such, she could be East European or non-European. In the film, she has a menial day job at a dry cleaner, washing and ironing—a job we need to add to the list of occupations belonging to the category *women's work*. Lorna also has a second job, a night job: marriage. She has entered a specific marital contract: she married Claudy, a Belgian drug addict, for whom she initially procures drugs. In exchange, she gets a Belgian ID. The contract is mediated by a Mafia-like structure run by an Italian, Fabio (played by the Belgian-Italian actor Fabrizio Rongione), who has plans to subsequently marry Lorna off to a man referred to as "the Russian." Lorna also has an Albanian boyfriend, Sokol (played by the Kosovar actor Alban Ukaj); they save money so that they can marry and open a snack bar. Lorna is thus trafficked by a European structure with three levels: Fabio, representing a pan-European criminal trafficking ring; Claudy, the Belgian man, representing the neocolonial traffic in care and emotion; and Sokol, the boyfriend and future husband, representing the traditional traffic in women through marriage. This might not be the reason why *Lorna's Silence* won the prize for best screenplay at Cannes in 2008, but the screenplay, based on a real story of a false marriage, is a complex theoretical statement on the imbrication of three forms of European traffic in women.

In a central scene in the film, Lorna briefly meets her boyfriend, Sokol. He is a migrant worker and is traveling between jobs. In a parking lot, at a

Fig. 4.6. "I love you" is mediated by a Belgian ID.
Frame from Jean-Pierre and Luc Dardenne's *Lorna's Silence* (2008).

crossroads, squeezed between cars, and listening to the honking of a van urging them to hurry, Lorna shows Sokol her new Belgian ID (see fig. 4.6). They kiss passionately over it. "I am so happy to be with you," he declares. It is a special "I love you." The scene pressures us to consider whether in the contemporary world of migration the sight of an ID can genuinely make one fall in love or rekindle an old love.[36] What the sight of an ID does is promise the normative life in which Lorna and Sokol own a snack bar and build a family in the rooms above it. It is a fantasy of working-class labor and conservative family dynamics. "Tell me you love me," Lorna murmurs. Before they part, Sokol asks Lorna to show him her Belgian card again. They kiss good-bye over it. What David Eng, drawing on Berlant, calls the *intimate sphere* becomes a site where the tensions of the private and the public, the national, the European Union, and the global, come together in this ID-mediated kiss.[37]

We do not see Claudy's papers precisely because he has them. When Lorna takes him to a hospital, she is surprised that she does not have to pay: "Just bring his card tomorrow." Claudy is sutured to the Belgian welfare state and receives care and survival assistance. While Lorna wakes up every morning to go to work, he struggles with his addiction. When Claudy calls Lorna in the middle of the night ("Lorna . . . Lorna . . . Help me . . . Help me . . ."), she is resistant because, unlike him, she has to wake up in the morning to go to her crappy job. "Perhaps I'll look for a job," Claudy proposes in passing. In the meantime, he tries to find things to do to keep his mind off drugs—like ride a bike. "It'll give me something to do." Claudy is at the bottom of class society, *almost* like Lorna, but in the world of identification papers this is an important *almost*.

Lorna acknowledges her proximity to Claudy. She is not willing to participate in his murder. Once he dies, she is not willing to forget him. She revolts against the fact that his death is utterly uneventful. *Lorna's Silence* marks this death through an eloquent silence. We see Lorna lovingly shopping for a man's shirt, and the viewer subsequently realizes that the shirt is to be used for Claudy's burial. Lorna's gesture of love is to insist that *she* mark Claudy's death. She literalizes her mourning by manufacturing an imaginary pregnancy. If she is pregnant, if only in her imagination, Claudy is mourned. If his life is worth mourning, it means that his life was worth living. Retrospectively, after he dies, Lorna transforms Claudy into a person.

Yet Lorna also acknowledges the distance between Claudy and herself. They are not in the same boat because they are situated differentially across the international and European division of labor. Because Claudy is a beneficiary of the European core/periphery divide, which translates into access to the Belgian welfare state, his class position is ambiguous. He is a Belgian nobody. Except for Lorna, everyone in the film calls him "the junkie." He is used by the marriage Mafia because, as a junkie, he is thought to be disposable. As far as the Belgian state is concerned, his murder is not worth investigating. In a European frame, however, his abjection appears in a slightly different light. He is a Belgian citizen; he can always sell his citizenship privileges. He can sell marriage. The commodification of his marital options comes as an effect of immigration policies that congeal around family reunification. As Caroline H. Bledsoe and Papa Sow argue: "Individuals may try to select themselves—and, of course, others—into family relationships that offer immigration advantage. . . . [S]ocial formations assemble around the inner perimeters of the allowable family reunification categories, producing both distortion and opportunity."[38]

Lorna's pride in her ID reveals her attachment to the promise of citizenship in an EU state. "I will be Belgian soon," she declares in the first scene of the film, her face beaming with pride. To be proud in this context is not to feel superior. On the contrary, this is pride in being like everyone else—like the black bank clerk, for example. This, too, is a narrative of international upward mobility—from a criminalized, subproletarian underground to a normative, working-class surface. In order to get there, Lorna needs to engage in a particular form of labor: she marries. Her brief love for Claudy and her attachment to the papers her marriage to him procures (which make possible her love for Sokol) are impossible to disentangle. Claudy is as abject as one gets in Belgian society. Even members of his family reject him in absolute terms. Even so, he can patronize Lorna's upward mobility. "It's the slot itself, the function of the patron or benefactor, that is eroticized," Bruce Robbins charges.[39] This is why abject figures like Claudy (or Seidl's Erich) can be loved once they occupy what Robbins calls the *fairy godmother* structural position. Although (perhaps *because*) they are *not* in the same boat, Lorna and Claudy love each other, briefly and frugally. They marry for the papers, but once they find themselves under the same roof, performing rituals of couplehood meant to prove the warmth of the marital sheets to authorities, the performance yields real emotions—love.

Discussing the upward-mobility narrative, Robbins argues that, for the most part, relations of erotic patronage (through which a patron helps out the upwardly mobile character) take nonmarital forms. He writes: "This erotic uncertainty again seems characteristic of upward mobility in our time. It reflects a narrative in which the goal of advancement has broken free from customary heterosexual bondings that refer explicitly or implicitly to marriage and the reproduction of the patriarchal family and for better or worse has come to reside increasingly in looser, half-formed relationships, neither biologically reproductive nor necessarily heterosexual, that seem to fit social units other than the family."[40] It is important to emphasize that in a transnational, migration context these relationships often *do* take the marital form. Patronage here consists in the procurement of papers that give access to the welfare state and its protections. Moreover, in a marital context, reproduction involves much more than biological reproduction; affective work is reproductive, too, and it is this work that upwardly mobile disciples often perform. Yet I agree that there is something that Robbins would consider queer about the kind of relation that develops between Lorna and Claudy, even if it is marital (theirs is a fake marriage but a marriage nonetheless) and reproductive in a broad sense. This queerness is best dramatized in the sex scene between Claudy and Lorna.

Sex between Lorna and Claudy is literally a gesture.[41] Lorna methodically takes her clothes off to reveal a healthy, beautiful body and offers to hold an emaciated Claudy. This is not to say that she does not desire him. In this sex scene, one that is truly unique in the history of cinema, it is clear that her sexual initiative is driven by desire but that it also exceeds desire, doing work, affective work on the continuum of care. Lorna extends a hand to Claudy in the form of a sex act. It is her idiosyncratic, ethical response to his middle-of-the-night exhortations that she help him. At the same time, the sex scene marks a displacement in her position in the tripartite traffic in women in which she participates. She is not supposed to have sex with "the junkie." Both Fabio and Sokol forbid it. But she is an agent, a strong agent. The sex scene she initiates is a function of her desire, will, and newly found ethics. It is the central scene in the most furtive of love stories. Adapting Laura Marks's notion of haptic cinema, Joseph Mai describes the Dardennes' aesthetic as "sensuous realism."[42] The scene *touches* the viewer in a haptic sense, inviting participation in its affective mix, without making it necessary or even possible to touch in an erotic sense.

Importantly, the story does not end here, with an acknowledgment of Lorna's agency and ethics. The Dardenne brothers made a film that can be included in an art gallery dedicated to the vicissitudes of women's search for passports in contemporary Europe. In this gallery, *Lorna's Silence* could be placed next to Tanja Ostojić's photograph and performance "Looking for a Husband with EU Passport" (2000–2005; see fig. 4.7). Ostojić's project dramatizes the aggression that papers inflict on bodies like Lorna's.[43] It stages the violence inherent in the agentive situation of looking for a husband with an EU passport. Like the bodies in the first scene of Tornatore's *The Unknown Woman* (see chapter 3), Ostojić's shaved naked body is not eroticized. Ostojić is provoking the viewer/beholder to visualize the life of a body offered up for sale in exchange for a passport. The mug shot aesthetics suggest that the photograph already contains, *in nuce*, the future passport photograph that the performance makes possible. The twist, however, is that this is not a standard passport photograph but a midshot. A standard passport photograph would elide the gendered body of the future passport holder.[44] This body is put to work, in Ostojić's case as well as in Lorna's, in the service of obtaining papers.

Lorna is not in Claudy's boat because her search for papers is *not* easy, passing as it does through three forms of traffic in women before it can offer minimal access to a welfare state that decriminalizes her labor or, why not, allows for the possibility that, like Claudy, she might want to sleep in each morning and decide to *not* work. We know that not all precarity is equal when we realize that Lorna wants access to the European precariat.[45]

Lorna is an upstart in the economy of citizenship, which means that in the world of her everyday Belgian existence others regard her with suspicious eyes (her name, her language, her dress, her mannerisms, her ways of handling money, all are markers of her racialization). She is the new, East European Rastignac in the *comédie humane* of contemporary Europe. Being an upstart citizen means that Lorna can easily lose her fortune, which is always threatened and precarious. She is a Belgian citizen through most of *Lorna's Silence*, yet she does not benefit from the state's protections. Her belonging is fragile. The viewer soon realizes that she does not in fact *own* her

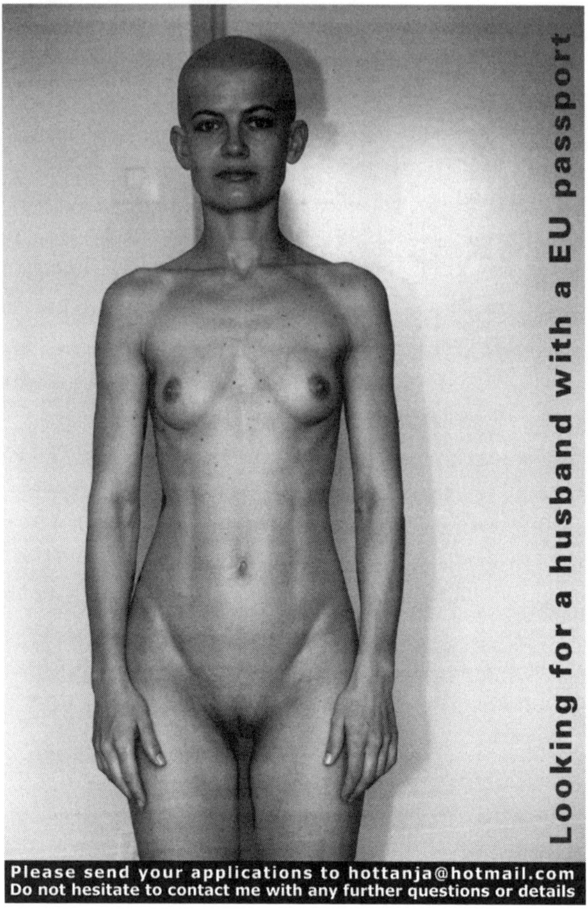

Fig. 4.7. Tanja Ostojić, the "ad" from "Looking for a Husband with EU Passport" (2000–2005). Participatory web project/combined media installation. Photograph by Borut Krajnc. Copyright/courtesy of Tanja Ostojić.

ID.[46] If at the beginning of the film her relationship with Fabio is ambiguous—they could be business partners, even friends—Lorna slowly but purposely acknowledges that she is under his control. The viewer realizes retrospectively that all their interactions occur in his car, with him driving Lorna around. Lorna's agentive participation in the traffic in women gives way to an understanding of its coerced dimensions. The viewer's gradual acknowledgment of this coercion culminates in the realization that Lorna is not in control of her reproductive rights. Fabio, with Sokol's consent, decides that her (imaginary) pregnancy is to be aborted. As we have seen in chapter 3, access to reproductive and natality rights is one crucial site of female agency in the context of the traffic in women viewed through a biopolitical lens. Lorna claims reproductive rights through her insistence that it is her choice to continue her (imaginary) pregnancy.

At the end of the film, once she realizes that she can be killed, Lorna runs into a forest but does not take her purse (and, presumably, her ID) with her. Even when materially there, some papers come with baggage that nullifies their weight, rendering their carrier effectively stateless. Ever stubborn and resistant, at the end of the film Lorna talks to her imaginary unborn baby, with whom she now forms a "we." Her relationship with this baby is the equivalent of Lilja's friendship with Volodya. As in *Lilja 4-Ever*, this, too, is a scene by the side of a highway, and here, too, there is nowhere to go. This is the limit of "Europe without borders." If until this point the Dardennes' film uses only ambient sound, after a transition in which Lorna listens to birdsong in the forest, Beethoven's Piano Sonata no. 32 becomes the background to the last few cuts of the film, taking Lorna and the viewer into an alternative space, an elsewhere that functions structurally not unlike Lilja's heaven. Two responses seem possible. First, the images of the forest and the accompanying music open up a space that displaces the viewer's emotional response to Lorna onto a larger, free-floating affective field in which a meditation on the experience produced by the film begins. Second, the viewer resists the transfer into the elsewhere and holds on to the narrative that has just come to an end, in the hope that Lorna could have her own America in the world of everyday sound, her snack bar and her conservative family, EU ID in her pocket.

Passport Plans

By the end of both *Lilja* and *Lorna* viewers are often left crying and, through their tears, ideally working both with and against the melodrama, asking that most famous "carnal question": What is to be done?[47] Berlant mentions that the Dardennes' *Rosetta* led to the Belgian government implementing the "Rosetta Plan," meant to facilitate the employment of Belgian youths who are, like Rosetta, likely to "fall through the cracks."[48] We should make it our task to ask what a "Lorna Plan" might look like and who (what national or global institution) would implement it. Even more challenging would be the prospect of a "Lilja Plan." Passports are reminders that both Lorna and Lilja need a state (preferably a strong state) in order to make claims to the rights of mobility, labor, and protection and to participate, if they so "choose," in the less coercive and less precarious forms of the contemporary traffic in women.

As for mobility, Berlant's take on it is refreshing: "Mobility is a nightmare, not a dream, and property and propriety signify *having something* and keeping it, and being able to return to it. The end of mobility as a fantasy of upwardness, and the shift to the fantasy of stop-loss is itself a subtle redirection of the fantasy bribes transacted to effect the reproduction of life under the present economic conditions."[49] This is an important correction to the myriad accounts celebrating transnational mobility as a route to upward mobility *tout court*. Lilja and Lorna are in search of a place where they can settle and rest. They do not want to be on the move. Papers, passports included, guarantee the right to stay rather than move. At the same time, any displaced person knows that, once on the move, one is always on the move. Rest might be an attractive horizon, but migration has its own *durée*. We see Lorna in a call center and are reminded that this has become a ubiquitous institution of urban life precisely because, when one finds oneself on moving sands, one travels even when one stays (Zygmunt Bauman's metaphor).[50] More than the border, the call center (or the Internet café) at the heart of the global city is the site where one meditates on mobility today. We see Lorna in a booth, every day the same booth, speaking Albanian. She greets the cashier with familiarity. Lorna, whose cell phone meets some of her communication needs, comes to the call center regularly. There is a home (not always "back home") one travels to, whether in actuality or virtually, even if all one wants is rest.

The situation would seem to require the simultaneous right to mobility and to rest. It is in this spirit, although in a different language, that Michael Hardt and Antonio Negri urge: "The multitude must be able to decide if, when, and where it moves. It must also have the right to stay still and enjoy one place rather than being forced constantly to be on the move."[51] In light of the narratives retraced here, we should find it legitimate to ask for global passports for global citizens, which would allow them both to travel and to return to places where they need or desire to stay. The debate on European mobility will remain a symptom of globalization from above as long as we do not filter it through the materiality of the passport. As such, it risks reinforcing ideas about a "Europe without borders" and, indeed, a "feminism without borders."[52]

In *Another Cosmopolitanism*, Seyla Benhabib celebrates nonnational forms of belonging like long-term residency, denizenship, binationality, and transnationality that she sees currently evolving in Europe. Benhabib cannot, however, avoid the question of passports: "Wouldn't perhaps a true cosmopolitan politics require that every human child receive a passport as a world citizen in addition to his/her local identification papers?"[53] In a truly cosmopolitan Europe, such a passport would undo the connection between birth, family, and citizenship that underlies our otherwise "imagined communities." In the meantime, no analysis of the political economy that underwrites the traffic in women is complete without an account of the current passport system.

5 Ways Out

Hospitality and Free Love

When Andrea Štaka's *Das Fräulein* (2007) first presents its viewer with the image of Ana, the young Bosnian protagonist, placing her bag in a locker in the Zürich railway station, the scene is unremarkable. She must be taking a stroll through the city while waiting for her train; the locker offers a temporary solution to the burden of her luggage. When the scene is repeated on a subsequent day, the viewer is confused: Ana takes her bag into a public restroom, changes her shirt, brushes her teeth, and places the bag back in the locker. It soon becomes clear that she lives out of the locker at the railway station. The locker is her metonym of home. Ana is permanently in transit. The scene has become remarkable.

In the economy of Štaka's film, Ana is a foil to two other women, Ruža and Mila, both ex-Yugoslav immigrants settled in Switzerland. At the same time, she challenges an absent but familiar East European figure (Seidl's Olga). While acknowledging the circulation of women as part of the fabric of the new Europe's historical moment, *Das Fräulein* offers alternative scenarios of women's transcontinental movement. Its viewer is called on to anticipate by now familiar trajectories of the traffic in East European women (domestic work or sex work) and is subsequently forced to inquire into the racializing rationale of his or her anticipation. Coming at the end of this book, Štaka's film is a reminder that cinema is both a symptom of a historical moment and an art form; it dramatizes the contemporary traffic in women but offers at the same time an archive of experimentation in creative realignments. This chapter will focus on one such experiment.

Going back to the argument of chapter 1, this chapter explores imaginative ways out of the traffic in women. Sociologists, legal studies scholars, and political theorists evaluate valuable legal, political, and economic solutions (immigration policy, labor protections) that improve women's everyday lives in the contemporary care industry, which, as we have seen, is mediated by the traffic in women. What happens when we jump scales and imagine how we can get out of a culture of traffic in women altogether? If, as we have seen in chapter 1, exchange as such is gendered, can we change our modes of exchange? Glossing Claude Lévi-Strauss, Elizabeth Cowie writes: "What is important here is that exchange is not itself constitutive of the subordination of women; women are not subordinate because of the fact of exchange but because of the *modes* of exchange instituted."[1] Can we imagine exchange differently?

Throughout the past century, the answer to this question has revolved around the notion of the gift as the alternative to exchange understood on a traffic-in-women model. In this chapter, I return to the work of Mauss and Lévi-Strauss, in order to assess the promise of two types of gift: hospitality and free love. I show that hospitality, often considered the utopian response to questions of migration, retains a traffic-in-women structure. At the end of the chapter and of the book, I turn briefly to an alternative form of exchange: free love. Through a focus on Štaka's protagonist, Ana, the chapter also identifies a generational shift in the narrative of East/West European mobility and, possibly, in the traffic in women.

Three Ex-Yugoslav Women

There are three immigrant women in *Das Fräulein*: Ana, Ruža, and Mila. Štaka's camera takes its time introducing the viewer to Ana's most important foil, Ruža. The scene begins with a close-up of Ruža's face as she wakes up (see fig. 5.1*a*). The succession of images is suggestive of the immigrant's morning disorientation: the night's dream work was dense and tense; it takes a while to recover from it and gather oneself in the light of the new day. We know that modernism has been obsessed with the threshold between wakefulness and sleep (Kafka, Proust). Štaka's film injects this tradition with a dose of immigration politics. We are all confused waking up; the moment is highly undecidable. Yet some of us are more confused than

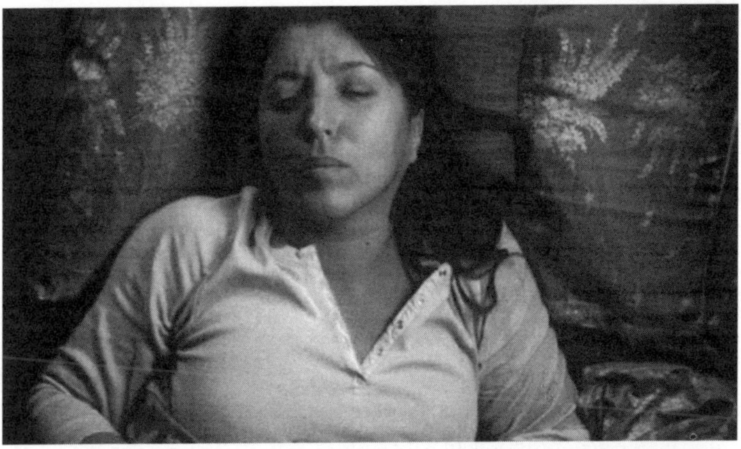

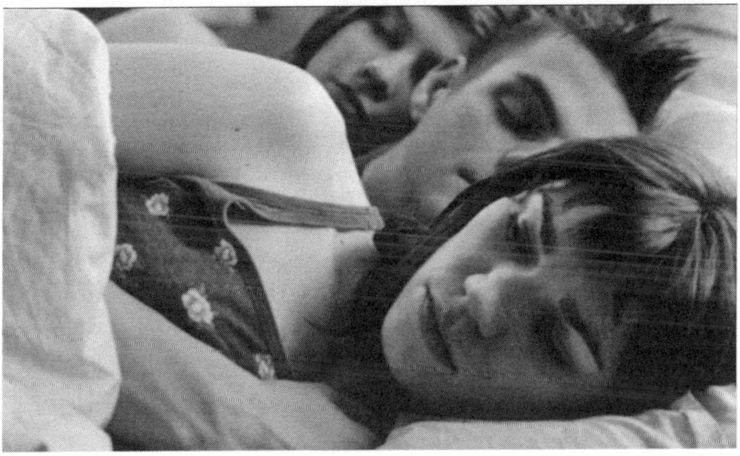

Fig. 5.1. Ruža (*a*) and Ana (*b*) wake up. Two frames from Andrea Štaka's *Das Fräulein* (2007).

others or are confused in different ways. Ruža struggles to gain her footing in the new day. The temporality of migration (then and now, here and there, coexist in this moment) is captured by the close-up of Ruža's face.[2]

Thus begins another day for Ruža, one in a line of identical days. Although "we lived well," as she puts it, Ruža emigrated from Yugoslavia in the 1980s. She now owns a restaurant in Zürich. She worked hard to get where she is, and this daily labor—physical and emotional—has left scars. She has become the perfect West European worker, more hardworking and conscientious than the proverbial Swiss. Her success story is that of the well-adjusted immigrant. The highly controlled camera movements of

Das Fräulein present Ruža as joyless and a killjoy. She is on track, but she goes through her routine mechanically, without any trace of enthusiasm. She does not talk to her employees. The men who gather to watch a football game are sent home in the midst of the excitement with a succinct "Time to go, gentlemen." There is a Swiss admirer lingering around, but she does not allow him to come close. The only thing that seems to excite Ruža and give her some satisfaction is counting her money, carefully saved in an old cookie box, at the end of the day. In the first part of the film, this is the only task that Ruža undertakes in her native language (numbers stubbornly resist translation); the rest of her activities are conducted in Swiss-German. Her life revolves around an emotionally charged saving project that has taken on a life of its own, as she does not seem to be saving for anything in particular. Her life is a perfect economy in which nothing is wasted—time, words, emotion, sexual energy. As a well-adjusted immigrant, she does not indulge in either a life or a past.

It is in relation to Ruža that the film first introduces the idea of the gift, albeit in passing. Once Ruža goes to work, the viewer witnesses a brief scene in which she rejects an item delivered in error. "A gift," the delivery man jokes. "I don't need any gifts," comes the blunt reply. It is Štaka's way of announcing that this will be a film about gifts and the possibility of gift giving as framed by the question of East/West European migration. This is where Ana, the new migrant figure, comes in.

Ana hitchhikes to Switzerland. She is twenty-two, but she looks preoccupied and mature as her gaze lingers on the snowy Alps. If *Das Fräulein* places Ruža in a recognizable socioeconomic framework, it makes a point of confusing the viewer's sense of Ana's status. Thus, Ana gives a woman asking for change a handful of coins, although it later becomes clear that this is the only money she has. Stopped by a couple in the street and asked for cigarettes, she ends up at a party smoking a joint and telling stories about growing up in Sarajevo during the war. She, too, is disoriented waking up; she does not seem to know where she is and whose arm is holding her (see fig. 5.1*b*). While the viewer is teased to make guesses about Ana's situation, Ana herself seems comfortable not being anchored in any recognizable categories.

Once Ana enters Ruža's restaurant, the two women's stories are explicitly intertwined. This is the point when Mila, the third ex-Yugoslav immigrant, enters the film. Ana offers to help Mila, an employee in Ruža's restaurant, who has cut her finger. As Ruža mercilessly pressures Mila to return to her counter, Ana bandages Mila's finger and steps in and does her work. When Ana leaves the restaurant, Ruža follows her and offers to pay her. "I just wanted to help," Ana responds. The film pauses for what seems to be a long time. Confused, Ruža offers to hire Ana. "No thanks, I'm not from here," comes the equally baffling reply. This, the viewer is aware, is a desirable job for "someone like Ana" (the traveling East European woman)—Mila had just asked for it for a niece—yet Ana does not seem invested in having a job and, by extension, in the promise of settling in Switzerland. The free gift leaves Ruža not only puzzled, not knowing what to do with the money she is holding, but also quite angry. The viewer is equally disconcerted. Ana troubles the cinematic economy within which we have become familiar with the "type" of the East European migrant woman. The feeling is reinforced formally as the segments that depict Ana are, when compared to the tightly controlled camera movements that follow Ruža, rather chaotic framings and pans. As David Fleming puts it, Ana is striving to "escape" not only our socioeconomic recognition but also the camera's attempts to frame her.[3]

Further confusion ensues as the film unfolds and the viewer witnesses additional gestures of Ana's gift giving. Ana offers to go home with a man she has just met in a bar who finds the offer dubious and refuses her. In a street scene, she instinctively offers to pick up the bag an elderly man has dropped. He responds aggressively with, "What do you want? Get lost, leave me alone." Back in Ruža's restaurant, she carves vegetables into miniature works of art, she chats with customers, she asks for music, and she prepares Ruža's to-go meal—all gestures that Ruža finds gratuitous in the context of her bland but efficient restaurant. When Ana hosts a birthday party for Ruža, the latter, always resistant and annoyed, starts dancing and eventually has sex with her Swiss admirer. Before the encounter with Ana, both gestures would have been unimaginable waste for Ruža. Ana's party registers as a miniature feast, the gift of a symbolic banquet.

Štaka's narrative is disconcerting when considered according to the logic of the interlocking economies of money and migration. Ruža has lived her life trying to accommodate herself to her new habitus and become a respectable Swiss citizen. Mila pursues the familiar alternative path of saving money so that she can build a house "back home" and retire to Croatia. In the old context of migration, only these two trajectories seem to have been possible. Mila is a docile wife, a mother, and a worker engaged in "women's work." She struggles to build the house "back home." In contradistinction, Ruža is a single, childless woman and a business owner. She, too, works hard but has no desire to return. Is a third way possible? Ana is an unattached free spirit who resists the pressures of both work and family. She repeatedly states that she is in Switzerland temporarily. "We all thought that," retorts Mila. But Ana is not interested in Ruža's papers, the guarantee of at least provisional settlement and a path of access to the Swiss good life. Mila seems to offer the viewer something of an explanation when she proposes, "You young people travel for fun these days. . . . We left home to earn money. . . . You're spoiled." The diagnosis is, however, profoundly unsatisfactory because Ana is neither spoiled nor into fun.

Ana's sleeping around would almost seem to fit the familiar scenario whereby she would move from bed to bed in exchange for *something*. The old man's question, "What do you want?" very much haunts the viewer, too. Ana needs to *want* something—whether money, objects, or a roof over her head. But she does not ask for or accept money or other forms of compensation. Furthermore, she has sex only in the form of gift giving: free love. This is not, it should be said, uncomfortable or awkward sex. After Ruža's party, Ana spends the night with a man who works in the restaurant; the scene is very much a lovemaking scene, with Ana's face in ecstatic, joyful pleasure as she whispers, in Bosnian, "Stay with me."

A further encounter with a man in a club clarifies Ana's free love philosophy. Ana accompanies him to his apartment, where she simply falls asleep. The viewer subsequently witnesses a different morning routine. The man is tender and thoughtful to Ana and tells her to use whatever she needs in his apartment. It is an incipient domestic scene. Ana thanks him for having "looked after me." "I would like to look after you again," he responds. To the viewer sympathetic to Ana's homelessness, this offer sounds like celestial manna. He or she is called on to fill in the domestic sketch with the fantasy of a future. Having considered the offer for a few seconds, Ana disappears. She does not want to trade in care.

Ana offers free gifts in a traffic economy. She is very much overdoing the cliché of "Eastern Europe."[4] If other films we have looked at in this book repeatedly present us with scenarios in which "women like her" seem to be destined to certain labor and sexual trajectories (the prospect from which Ruža flees, furiously), Ana overdoes the cliché. She offers what is expected of her gratuitously, free labor and free love. And she does it in a meticulous, profoundly self-aware, philosophical way. Free love is to the economy of love and sex what gambling is to the economy of money. In a central scene in the film, Ana takes a terrified Ruža to a casino, where Ana happily gambles her meager earnings. Ruža's stern reproach, "You just threw your money away," is countered by Ana's, "I don't give a damn about money." Ana squanders both money and love, lightly and joyfully.

How can the viewer, steeped in a political economy of profitable exchange, make sense of Ana? It helps to know that she is haunted by the war in the former Yugoslavia. "Everybody asks me about it," she tells Ruža, as if waiting for an invitation to narrativize the trauma, an invitation Ruža never issues. The film allows the viewer to think that Ana is different on account of having grown up in war-torn Sarajevo. In one scene, the man who eventually refuses her gift of the night tells her the story of his studies in New York. "My brother and I always wanted to go there," she replies. "So? Why didn't you?" asks the man. The answer is that her brother killed himself after the war. Throughout the film, the viewer cannot forget that Ana carries a small box containing her dead brother's baby teeth with her in her European travels. This is her baggage.

In the present of the film, Ana is sick and dying of leukemia. She spits blood and has a number of fainting spells. The image on the screen often becomes blurry as it attempts to represent her illness visually. It is the thought of death that guides her travels through Europe as well as her refusal of a job and papers. Without papers, she cannot go to a hospital, and she cannot buy much-needed medicine. It seems, however, that Ana chooses to live on the horizon of death, joyfully. She lives differently because she lives in the non-economical temporality of death. "Hey," Ana calls in a flashback scene, facing Sarajevo, "I am alive!" She is alive precisely because she is acutely aware that she is dying. Of course, we all live in the extended duration of dying, but for the most part we manage to forget our existential condition. Ana, on the other hand, cannot forget.

Ruža eventually takes Ana to a hospital, ready to use her savings to pay for her care. In a moving scene, on her way to the hospital Ana meditates on the similarity between the sensation of thirst and that of longing, a reference to the Bosnian folk belief that the dead become thirsty on their journey to the other world, a journey for which Ana seems to long. The film ends with Ana refusing Ruža's offer of care and thumbing a ride by the side of the road next to a man whose hitchhiking sign reads *Genève*. Ana, whose dying is figured as a form of prolonged thirst, is taking the road to Geneva as a way of reminding us of promises of European hospitality. The intertext here is the idea that one can imagine a way out of the imbrication of exchange and migration via hospitality—a practice of gifting.

Unlikely Diasporas

Das Fräulein dramatizes Ana's death in order to demonstrate how her presence transforms those around her. Once she meets Ana, waste enters Ruža's life. She laughs and dances, uselessly. She has useless sex. She claims her useless past—old pictures, old loves. Visually, color enters the grayness of her life (life in Switzerland can be gray, too).[5] Ana teaches her that in order

Fig. 5.2. Mila treasures a photograph of the house she is building in Croatia. Frame from Andrea Štaka's *Das Fräulein* (2007).

to be a respectable Swiss citizen one need not be a tabula rasa without an East European past. One does not have to forgo speaking one's language for the sake of speaking better German (it will never be good enough anyway). One does not have to be alone.

Ruža is not dying, at least not immediately, but Ana's inquiries about the possibility of returning "home" bring up the immigrant's dilemma vis-à-vis death: "I don't know where I want to be buried." "Who cares when one is dead?" Ana responds. But Ruža does care. Does one die abroad, among foreigners, like Oedipus, without mourners? Or does one heed the fantasy of home as a place of mourning and memory? In the world of migration, home is not where you want to live but where you want to die. One belongs wherever one is ready to welcome death. At the same time, the question of death and burial leads to a potentially wasteful, joyful, and ultimately politicized immigrant life.

Ana's presence affects Mila even more. Mila decides that the house on the Croatian coast for which she and her husband have been saving is not her dream anymore. Ana helps Mila detach from her narrative of return. Mila has lived her life in Switzerland, and she wants to live her old age in Switzerland. She wants to be close to her children, who have grown up in Switzerland and for whom Croatia is not even the illusion of home. Mila has been carrying and showing everyone a photograph of her Croatian house under construction (see fig. 5.2). At this point, the photograph loses its indexical value and is recognized as a fantasy. In a subsequent scene, the viewer watches Mila as she takes in the image of a spider she momentarily glimpses on her television set. The black spider builds its house around it, wherever that happens to be. The house in Croatia, attractive as it might be in its promise of middle-class retirement after a life of labor in a foreign land, will remain, like many such houses built around the world today, half built. The Croatian coast has in fact become excessively expensive, one of Mila's friends warns her, too expensive, and not only for locals but also for Croatian immigrants who have presumably moved up in the world, having worked abroad for a lifetime. It is the end of the Balzacian saving venture for Mila. She wants to use the money patiently collected in a tin box in her freezer to buy a new coat (saving has its own iconography in *Das Fräulein*). She thus moves from a narrative of exile to one of diaspora. If in exile she desires to return "home" and constructs a life oscillating between there and here, in diaspora she settles emotionally in Switzerland and forms lateral relationships with Swiss citizens, other ex-Yugoslav migrants and immigrants, and other immigrant communities.[6]

Ana's presence in Zürich reveals that, while there might not be a Yugoslavia anymore, there is certainly a Yugoslav diaspora. Like "Eastern Europe," itself a Cold War restaging of an Enlightenment creation, Yugoslavia, an early twentieth-century invention acknowledged as such by the people who lived in it, often serves as a diasporic congealer. Serbs, Croats, and Bosnians meet in Zürich and discover affinities from what they ironically remember as the good old times, even if those times were not exceedingly good. Štaka, herself the child of ex-Yugoslav parents, assembled an ex-Yugoslav cast—with the Bosnian Ana played by the Croat actress Marija Škaričić, the Croat Mila played by the Bosnia-Herzegovina-born Ljubica Jović, and the Serbian Ruža played by the Serbian actress Mirjana Karanović—in order to reflect, cinematically, this reality. At the beginning of *Das Fräulein*, the community congregates around the football game and is primarily male, with the women observing from the margins. The women speak German among themselves and are suspicious of each other. Ana's presence challenges them to bond over the few things they share, problematic as those might be: Serbian language and music but also a sense of sociality.[7] Ruža's party concludes with a dance, which begins as a slow *sevdalinka* and moves into a lively *kolo*, with the ex-Yugoslav dancers momentarily forming a circle.

"Why do you speak German to me? You are from Belgrade, aren't you?" the Bosnian Ana asks the Serbian Ruža, with false naïveté. Ana warns the ex-Yugoslav community about the risks of losing one's language, even when this language is decidedly not one's own. This is the very predicament of the refugee, as Hannah Arendt knew: "We lost our language, which means the naturalness of reactions, the simplicity of gestures, the unaffected expression of feelings."[8] The three ex-Yugoslav women speak versions of a language that goes by the name of Serbo-Croatian, the official language of the former Yugoslavia. A few words and grammatical inflections betray their Serb, Croat, or Bosnian background. By the end of the film, however, the three women have reclaimed their language. They each speak their idiom, which is nonetheless intelligible to all three. It is Štaka's way of taking issue with what is perceived as the absolute *need* to live in the language of the "host" country.

Ana challenges Ruža to entertain the possibility that "I've made it" does not have to mean "I am now like them." She comes from Sarajevo to tell the Yugoslav diaspora that it is not necessary to try so hard to adjust. Perhaps Europe, if it indeed aspires to be the "former West," should adjust to their presence, too?[9] Most importantly, Ana challenges the ex-Yugoslav community to be hospitable. Once she offers her labor gratuitously, Ruža welcomes her in the restaurant. Later in the film, once she realizes that Ana does not have a place to spend the night, she offers her the key to her restaurant. All the members of the ex-Yugoslav community slowly take "the little Bosnian" stranger in, unconditionally, without asking questions, although, as Mila puts it, "nobody knows what you are doing here." The question of religion (is the little Bosnian Muslim?) remains productively unasked as the film does not allow Ana to live her difference as racialized religiosity. At the end of the film, Ruža reaches out to Ana in a reparative friendship. In one of the most eloquent images of touch explored in this book, she caresses Ana's head.

Welcome!

Throughout *Das Fräulein*, it is clear that Ana is resistant to certain forms of hospitality while being deeply invested in others. She defiantly and tragically refuses the hospitality of the hospital. ("The view is different, but they all smell the same.") She is not interested in any hotel-like hospitalities. When asked where she lives, she responds, "With friends." But her friends are strangers, men she meets on a nightly basis in bars or clubs. This, however, seems to be the point: What kind of hospitality can there be between strangers who momentarily find themselves under the same roof? In more general terms, what kind of gift is hospitality?

Hospitality, we know from Mauss, is a structure of exchange: my welcoming you into my house obliges you to reciprocate with an equal gesture. The reciprocity is captured by the French word *hôte*, which translates as either *host* or *guest*, depending on which side of the reciprocal relation one finds oneself on. At the heart of hospitality, Émile Benveniste argues, is a certain "compensatory relationship."[10] As a structure of exchange, hospitality builds friendships, social bonds, alliances, and solidarity. The Greek word for hospitality, *xenia*, is often translated as *guest-friendship*. The term refers to a relation between individuals *and* larger social groups.

Although it has a religious core, which has never been completely secularized, the practice of hospitality has been frequently invoked in contemporary conversations on migration, globalization, and border control.[11] Mapping itself onto the transnational upward-mobility narrative, hospitality becomes an ironic axis of inequality that operates a stable, nonreciprocal distinction between hosts and guests. Transnational narratives of upward mobility become hospitality narratives the moment they present us with the figure of the patron as host.[12] There are host countries, whose native inhabitants play the role of individual hosts, speaking the host language, and there are a range of more or less welcome guests, often figured as parasites.[13] Questions regarding what makes a host, who can be considered a guest, and what can be shared in the name of hospitality have acquired renewed urgency in the last decades. In the wake of Jacques Derrida's 1996 seminar on hospitality, the relation of hospitality has often come to be seen as *the* ethical relation, raising the question of welcome vis à-vis an unknown and unanticipated, uninvited stranger—today, the migrant foreigner. "Hospitality is culture itself. . . . [H]ospitality is coextensive with the ethical problem," writes Derrida.[14] The ethics of hospitality are opposed to the contemporary hospitality industry, an institutionalized form of hospitality through which touristic forms of hospitality (accommodation and commensality) are sold to those who can afford to buy them. The question is, How does one in a secular world—offer hospitality to strangers who cannot or refuse to pay, often not even in gratitude?

In Kant's modern articulation of the concept, hospitality is underwritten by a universal trade or commerce (*Verkehr*). In the name of this commerce, and in order to avoid war, Kant divorces hospitality from philanthropy and posits it as a right. For him, hospitality implies "the right of an alien not to be treated as an enemy upon his arrival in another country." Kant elaborates: "He may request the *right* to be a *permanent visitor* [*Gastrecht*] (which would require a special, charitable agreement to make him a fellow inhabitant for a certain period), but the *right* to visit [*Besuchsrecht*], to associate [*sich zur Gesellschaft anzubieten*], belongs to all men by virtue of their common ownership of the earth's surface; for since the earth is a globe, they cannot scatter themselves infinitely, but must, finally, tolerate living in close proximity, because originally no one had a greater right to any region of the earth than anyone else."[15] The global resonances of Kant's 1795 formulations ("the earth is a globe") are eloquent. The world was becoming (more) global in the wake of European colonialism, a fact that triggered the need for universal tolerance and hospitality. "Originally," that is, in natural terms, no one could claim ownership of the surface of the earth, which anyone could traverse freely. No one could ask anyone else for a passport. Politically, however, once we enter the purview of states, globalization arguably also triggers the need to set limits on hospitality through law. Kant emphasizes the temporality of hospitality. Paradoxically, even the *permanent* visitor, if granted permission, is a fellow inhabitant only for a limited time. For we always need to remember that the guest, as J. Hillis Miller puts it, remains both "a friendly presence and alien invader . . . perhaps the first emissary of a host of enemies."[16] Today, in the discourse on immigration, the unquestionable *need* for limited hospitality is figured in the language of invasion; were there to be no limits, the parasite guest would invade and eventually devour the host. Kant helps us understand that this is a profoundly Eurocentric worry, stemming from the history of colonialism, European guests having acted greedily and violently when welcomed generously by native peoples.[17] Kant's proposal is, therefore, of a limited cosmopolitanism based on a temporally conditioned hospitality that neutralizes the figure of the invading enemy and opens up the possibility of global alliance.[18] Note, however, the ensuing paradox. We have on the one hand the cosmopolitan right to receive hospitality and on the other the *limited* duty to offer it. Our crisis in hospitality occurs in the gap.

Taking up the question of hospitality in the today of the 1990s (in the wake of 1989), Derrida maintained that hospitality is necessarily limited by clear conditions and restrictions (materialized in various papers) while at the same time unfolding the horizon of radical openness, the free gift of an unconditional yes to the uninvited guest. He concluded that hospitality is productively caught in this aporia. On the one hand, it presupposes the existence of a propertied master who in one way or another *owns* the space of hospitality and whose mastery hospitality reinforces (one of the meanings of *host* is "master of guests," as J. Hillis Miller points out).[19] The master has a chance to exercise his power over his guests, set limits, and draw borders delimiting their mobility and inclusion/exclusion. He orchestrates and oversees the rituals of hospitality. On the other hand, hospitality raises the possibility of unconditional welcome to a visiting radical other and maintains its dramatis personae in the horizon of this possibility.[20] For Derrida, the resulting aporia is "our" European inheritance when it comes to welcoming others across the threshold of the household, the nation, or the European Union. His challenge is that any inheritance must be received, inhabited, and passed on creatively and responsibly.

Hospitality thus has an ambivalent structure, its ambivalence sheltering the germs of violent inhospitality. Philippe Lioret's film *Welcome* (2009) bears witness to this inhospitality. There is a minor character in the film, a neighbor whose neighborly job is to report acts of hospitality to the police. Ironically, on the threshold into this neighbor's apartment there is a doormat that reads "Welcome" (see fig. 5.3). The fact that this Frenchman's welcome is in English would suggest a certain cosmopolitanism. Yet he has limited his sense of hospitality to exclude migrant foreigners. The neighbor makes calculations and decides that cosmopolitan rights of welcome do not attach to "illegals": "It's illegal. . . . We don't want trouble. . . . Look at the state he's in! They have lice. They steal."[21] In recognition of the violence inherent in the hospitality that Lioret's film dramatizes, Mona Hatoum created an art object titled *Doormat* (1996) (see fig. 5.4). In Hatoum's hands, the doormat remains recognizable as a welcome sign, but it is made entirely of pins, inflicting pain on those who misinterpret its selective interpellation. The violence inherent in the injunction *welcome* becomes painfully visible.

The neighbor in Lioret's film is the master of his house. He makes decisions regarding the trespassing of his threshold. His doormat reads "Welcome," but the door is unequivocally closed. Hospitality is also a question of space. How does one, in architectural terms, navigate the paradox that hospitality is a form of openness dependent on privacy?[22] Put differently, if hospitality is dramatized on the threshold of the household, can we have a threshold without a door? Even an open door is still a door, announcing its potential closure and exclusion of those not interpellated by the welcome sign. Lioret's film uses the neighbor figure to foreground the question of what it would mean to be hospitable to people who need hospitality most. What would it mean to envision welcoming architectural spaces in no need of a welcome doormat?

Welcome reminds us that hospitality often finds itself at odds with the laws of the land as the French host is faced with the Kantian question, Can one lie when, as the master of the house, one is asked whether those looked for (by the police, for the purposes of deportation) are guests in the house? No, Kant responded, truth is the first imperative. *Perhaps*, according to Derrida's absolute law of hospitality, which trumps one's duty to truth. What is clear is that *the* law of hospitality is often, though not always, in contradiction with absolute *laws*, placing the host in the urgency of an aporetic decision between (Derridean) ethics and (Kantian) duty. Does one uphold

Fig. 5.3. The threshold of the racist neighbor's apartment features a welcome mat. Frame from Philippe Lioret's *Welcome* (2009).

Fig. 5.4. Mona Hatoum, *Doormat* (1996), stainless steel and nickel-plated pins, glue, and canvas, 1¼ × 28 × 16 inches (3 × 71 × 40.5 cm). Photograph by Stephen White. Courtesy White Cube.

the law of absolute hospitality when this means becoming guilty of a crime, what French jurisprudence calls a *délit d'hospitalité* (crime of hospitality)?[23]

One other question imposes itself: Is this tradition the only European tradition of hospitality? One could always invoke the fact that one of the first things travelers to East Europe noticed in the early 1990s was hospitality. People opened their houses, and they opened themselves to manifold encounters with foreign guests (mostly West European and American). One should not, however, be too quick to idealize such signs of East European hospitality. Judith Still writes: "Travellers' tales of any place perceived as 'simpler' than our own may tell of relatively abundant hospitality."[24] This is the risk faced by Ben Jelloun's *French Hospitality*, a book that celebrates the Maghrebian tradition of welcome by way of critiquing its French counterpart.[25] "We" are better hosts than "you" is a self-Orientalizing gesture. For Still, the praise of alternative, multicultural forms of hospitality also risks tacitly reinforcing the assumption that hospitality is practiced more faithfully by those who are thought to have a stricter division between the sexes.

We fall into the trap of eliding gender if we are tempted to offer, for example, the hospitality of the Roma as a counterpoint to European hospitality. One could recall the hospitality offered to the guest in Tony Gatlif's *The Crazy Stranger/Gadjo dilo* (1997). In stark contrast to recent French inhospitality to the Roma, the Frenchman in Gatlif's film is taken in by the Roma community in Romania, offered shelter, food, and entertainment. The celebration of this tradition, however, is a path with many pitfalls, not only because we end up idealizing nomadic forms of hospitality (a tendency also found in celebrations of youth culture or queer communities), but also because we forget that the ultimate gesture of Roma hospitality in Gatlif's film is the right to marry a Roma woman.

The Traffic in Hospitality

We have arrived at the point where we need to ask, What is the relation between the exchange in hospitality (both a service and a sign) and the exchange in women? Let us remember that Lévi-Strauss thought that women are the most precious gifts. Let us also remember that "when one gives," as Émile Benveniste puts it, "he must give the most precious things he has." One gives "with largesse."[26] Pushed to its ultimate consequences, this means that the supreme form of hospitality—what Derrida calls *hyperbolic hospitality*—would be to offer one's women—figured as dependents of the master of the house—as gifts. It is a way for the guest-stranger to become, structurally, a brother-in-law and a friend.[27] Seen from this angle, hospitality is a practice of kinship.

Having advocated the promises of hospitality, at the end of his seminar Derrida had to confront this problem. He ended the seminar by recounting two biblical stories. One story is that of Lot in Sodom, who invites two disguised angels into his house. When the people of Sodom ask him to hand the angels over so that they can abuse them, Lot feels that he must protect his divine guests at any cost and offers his own virgin daughters up for abuse instead (Genesis 19). The other story is that of the man in Judges 19–21 who is asked to hand over his Levite guest. This host, too, offers his virgin daughter instead, but, as his invitation is not heeded, the Levite makes another offer, giving them his "concubine." The men rape the woman all night. When she returns in the morning, the Levite cuts her into twelve pieces and sends the pieces through the land of Israel. Derrida concludes: "Are we the heirs to this tradition of hospitality? Up to what point? Where should we place the invariant [*l'invariant*], if it is one, across this logic and these narratives? They testify without end in our memory."[28]

Hospitality has a traffic-in-women structure. The master of the house has the power to dispose of the women in his household and offer them to his guests. Hospitality creates homosocial alliances and solidarity through the traffic in women. Through hospitality, the stranger, an other unlike the (male) host, becomes a *semblable*, "like" him, and thus, on the basis of the newly transacted symmetry, possibly a friend. The sexual offering of the women of the house hyperbolizes the fact that hospitality is in fact often premised on women's work. The cooking for, the cleaning for, and the serving of the guests are the jobs of the women of the house, with the (male) host performing some symbolic gestures.[29] Women are in charge of the elaborate etiquette, the choreography of polite gestures and rituals, that hospitality involves. They are likewise responsible for something we might call *the affect of hospitality*, that something in the air that makes certain houses hospitable and others not.[30]

Derrida's rhetorical question at the end of his seminar suggests that Europeans necessarily inherit this tradition of hospitality, both at its violent (rape) and at its softer (labor) ends. They are also responsible for the decision as to where to draw the line. The placing of the "invariant," that which does not change, that which comes to be perceived as destiny, involves a decision. While for the most part his seminar is affectively invested in the promise of unconditional, absolute, lawless hospitality, the traffic in women returns Derrida to the question of law as the buffer against the hyperbolization of ethics.[31] It might be undesirable to advocate for some forms of hospitality.

The task, then, would be to creatively rewrite the laws of hospitality and reposition its invariant when it comes to the traffic in women. This is what Pierre Klossowski's trilogy *The Laws of Hospitality* set out to do in the 1950s, unequivocally reframing the traffic in hospitality as a traffic in women. Erotic literature in the tradition of Sade and Bataille, the trilogy intervenes in the hospitality debate from within the tradition Derrida uncovered in the 1990s. Klossowski puts hospitality in front of his reader in all its structurality and pushes its implications to its ultimate, scandalous consequences. Sade's challenge, as Maurice Blanchot proposes, is to "say everything": Klossowski's novels "say everything" about hospitality.[32] Importantly, he frames the problem of hospitality as at the same time religious and modern. Equally important, hospitality is thoroughly sexualized.

In Klossowski's trilogy, the traffic in women is where one begins; it is a fact. There is a house, and there is marriage. There is a master of the house (*maître de céans*), who is an enlightened patriarch but king of his domain nonetheless.[33] His prerogative is to set down the laws of the house, including the laws of hospitality. As the master of the house, the husband in Klossowski's novels, Octave, revives/invents a hospitality ritual. The letter of this law is spelled out on the wall above the bed in his guest room. We should note in passing that the (bourgeois) house is equipped with a guest room, the spatial, architectural prerequisite for the hospitality that Octave envisions. What the law requires is that he offer his wife, Roberte, "a rare and precious object," to guests in his house, strangers, "whomever comes to dine at his table and to rest under his roof from a day's wearying travel." As if answering many of Lévi-Strauss's critics who objected to his concept of the traffic in women in the name of women's emancipation, Klossowski positions Roberte as, at the same time, an object of exchange and a modern woman (she has the Kafkaesque job of censor). As an object of exchange, she circulates between her husband and the men to whom he generously offers her. Roberte's agency, on the other hand, manifests itself in choosing to be an accomplice in Octave's practice of hospitality, although she disapproves of it because, as the narrator puts it, it is practiced "at her expense." Her fidelity to her husband (her "labor of love") manifests itself in her active participation in his practice of hospitality as infidelity.[34] Or so the author would have us believe.

In Klossowski's framework, the scene of repeated sexual encounters between Roberte and her husband's guests necessitates the husband's presence. Always opening the door at the right time, Octave sees Roberte being "taken by surprise" by the guest.[35] What he sees is her surprise, that which is unanticipated in the encounter and that which Octave himself does not know in his own "property" and therefore in himself. Through this blink-of-the-eye snapshot, Roberte surprises Octave, the master.[36] In his surprise, the host is vulnerable and therefore less in control, less of a master, less of a host. Klossowski plays with the fact that adultery is traditionally often understood as a violation of the laws of hospitality (think of Paris's abduction of Helen).[37] In the economy of his novels, the outcome of a practice of hospitality as invited cuckoldry is the interruption of the host's mastery. The master becomes a guest in his own house ("whereupon the host shall be master in his house no more"). As such, he is in no position to offer hospitality at all. He is on the same footing as the guest, with whom he now shares an "essential relationship."[38]

In the two stories Derrida recounts, masters give their daughters or their mistresses away but not their wives. In this logic, a wife is so thoroughly the master's property that she is an essential part of his identity. To give one's wife away—graciously—is to give oneself away, one's identity as a master and one's self-mastery. The master becomes a guest, but the two positions are not exchangeable because Octave's guests do not reciprocate the gesture, which remains without response, a free gift. The host has experienced the pure "risk of losing." As for the always-present risk of gratitude as a form of reciprocity, if anybody is "grateful in advance," it is Octave.[39] The result: there are only guests in the house. And a hostess.

Of course, this is all Octave's scheming, his design. It is as if God orchestrated the death of God: Does this make him less of a god? Roberte always returns to Octave; the end result of each sexual encounter is the reinforcement of the marital bond. Octave takes her in his arms. The strangers are *invited* into the house by Octave, who waits for them on the threshold of his house and calls on them to come inside and liberate him. In other words, they come by invitation, not visitation; it is arguable whether they can take the host by surprise. If this is a form of theft, as Tracy McNulty contends, it is invited theft, the theft of an object the master has offered up for thieving.

McNulty proposes that Klossowski's *Laws of Hospitality* offers "a highly developed critique of the logic of exchange."[40] What notion of critique is at work here? It would seem that Klossowski himself repeats a traffic-in-women structure, with a twist. The hostess is the twist. She is already present in the tradition of hospitality (McNulty discusses Sarah as hostess in Genesis), but Klossowski gives her center stage. She has nonetheless been actualized in her essence as hostess through the traffic in women. The method coincides with the problem. One gets out of the traffic in women through the traffic in women. Roberte accepts the premise of the traffic in women and uses it as a tactic against itself. Again, this is all Klossowski's scheming, his design, and the reader is ultimately his guest, even if Klossowski, too, is a guest in his own novel.

While Klossowski and his commentators are interested in bringing the figure of the hostess to bear on the theater of hospitality, the question that haunts *Das Fräulein*, this chapter, and the end of this book is that of hospitality as the question of the woman guest. Prompted by Octave, Roberte receives male guests. Can she receive women guests? Would this scene be different if it were staged between women?

Lesbians, Queers, Free Love

It is well-known that for the feminist second wave one of the most persuasive forms of resistance to the traffic in women has been the lesbian alternative. If we go back to "The Traffic in Women," we are reminded that, having unpacked the overlap in Freud's and Lévi-Strauss's understanding of the position and circulation of women within a system whose limit is for both the incest taboo, Rubin suggests that the incest taboo presupposes a "prior, less articulate taboo on homosexuality." "What would happen," Rubin goes on to ask, "if our hypothetical woman not only refused the man to whom she was promised, but asked for a woman instead? If a single refusal were disruptive, a double refusal would be insurrectionary." The lesbian is the figural agent of this insurrectional double move. She withdraws herself from the market and demands a woman for herself. If heterosexuality works to render natural what is social and cultural, such that women do not question the inevitability of the marriage market, the lesbian troubles this naturalism. Marriage, Rubin reminds us, "presupposes individuals disposed to marry."[41] As a corollary to the traffic in women, heterosexuality produces this disposition. Seen from this perspective, the lesbian is a structuring taboo; her very existence opens the horizon of an enduring doubt regarding the much-needed disposition to marry.

Monique Wittig gave this idea some of its most lucidly radical formulations. Lesbians are not women, Wittig famously argued, because they are escapees from the traffic in women. "The only thing to do," she wrote, "is to stand on one's own feet as an escapee, a fugitive slave, a lesbian."[42] To be a lesbian is to be a not-woman, insofar as, according to the logic of traffic, a woman is defined in relation to a man. What Wittig called *lesbian society* is premised on the ontology of the lesbian as a not-woman. Her sexual practice is not a choice or a preference but is inherently political. Lesbian political struggle is for Wittig a form of class struggle. Its goal is the destruction of the political and economic categories *men* and *women* and of the naturalized division of labor that sustains them. This idea met with a lot of resistance in the 1980s but might be worth revisiting today, when the international division of labor brings back the economic category *women* (ever more broadly understood) as one pole of the international class struggle.

Wittig cautioned against an easy dismissal of Lévi-Strauss's theorization of the traffic in women in the context of modern societies, in which arguably traffic is eluded by many emancipated women. She insisted that to be single is still to be defined—albeit negatively—in relation to the institution of marriage and that the traffic in care remains a pervasive dimension of the traffic in women. She wrote: "If you are unmarried, you will have to be available to take care of the sick, the aged, the weak (as nuns and volunteer workers do), whether they belong to your family or not." The archaic and the modern often cohabit comfortably. Stressing that the traffic in women is a social and historical reality, Wittig nonetheless insisted: "Thanks to our action and our language, shifts are happening . . . and since, as Lévi-Strauss said, we talk, let us say that we break off the heterosexual contract."[43] It is a manifesto-like provocation that many took on. Under the banner of lesbian, one refused to go to market and worked to create parallel markets for the circulation of commodities, signs, and bodies.

The radicalism of the lesbian has often been misunderstood. A major point of dispute has been its assumed separatism. As a consequence, Wittig's materialist radicalism has often translated into utopian visions of all-women communities that are most often far from what Wittig meant by *lesbian society*. Here is Teresa de Lauretis's gloss: "Well, the phrase 'lesbian society' had everyone in an uproar. . . . They said Wittig was a utopist, an essentialist, a dogmatic separatist, even a 'classic idealist.' . . . Wittig's 'lesbian society' did not refer to some collectivity of gay women but was the term for a conceptual and experiential space carved out of the social field, a space of contradictions in the here and now that need be affirmed and not resolved."[44] Going back to chapter 1, one way in which to imagine such a conceptual and experiential space carved out of the social field is on the model of the feminist bookstore.

Perhaps an even more insidious and therefore more damaging development over the last twenty years is the fact that the lesbian alternative has come to be seen as the default solution to the traffic in women. It has—ironically if one thinks of the scandalous dimension of Wittig's *The Lesbian Body*—been made to look easy, almost a cliché.[45] When Fatih Akin made his film *The Edge of Heaven* (2007), for example, he felt that he needed a lesbian East-West couple.[46] The only way for Akin to make sure that a trafficking pattern (local and international) is not reproduced in the new generation is to have the new relationship be between lesbian women. What is troubling about *The Edge of Heaven* is the ease with which an antitraffic position registers as lesbian, which in the context of the debate surrounding Turkey's application to join the European Union is also a stand-in for modern.

It is because of such opportunistic representations of the lesbian, coupled with charges of separatism, identity politics, and, paradoxically, asexuality, that the lesbian alternative has faced increasing resistance, including from new generations of feminists. The word *queer* gained a lot of its attractiveness in the transatlantic world of gender and sexuality studies as part of this resistance.[47] What *queer* promises is to multiply desires and desirous bodies, leading to social networks that exceed the model of the traffic in women (which is why *queer* should be structurally incompatible with marriage). While most queer theorists claim allegiance to second-wave feminism, their rhetoric often forecloses a sustained critique of the traffic in women and women's work. As I suggested in the introduction, Lee Edelman's work is emblematic here. *No Future* is a radical critique of reproduction, but it does not engage the extensive feminist literature on the subject.[48] Edelman does not revisit feminist critiques of the figure of the child (Firestone's passionate call that childhood should be abolished, e.g.)[49] or the myriad feminist critiques of reproduction. Although one could well describe Štaka's Ana as queer, my turn to free love at the end of this book comes as an effort to return to the tradition of radical feminism. The impetus behind this book has been not simply to *state* that our conversations regarding sexuality should not be split from the feminist project and its histories but to actually work from within the tradition of radical feminism and perhaps even revisit some of its East European figures. I hope to have demonstrated the kind of work that can still be done with a concept like the traffic in women. Perhaps a similar project can be undertaken with free love.

Das Fräulein is instructive because it brings to the fore a female vagabond, a modern-day *pícaro*. Although she works, Ana would be happy with the label *parasite*. She wanders through Europe and squanders her resources and energies. Rather than being an instance of libertinage, her travels belong to the tradition of free love. Let us remember that free love is indeed a form of love. It is *free* love, unconditional, uneconomic, gratis; but it is also *free* in the tradition of the freedom of consciousness that Klossowski's Roberte invokes. The strangers whom Ana encounters are not serialized, even if they do not always have names. They are loved—for a night or lon-

Fig. 5.5. Ana continues her travels. Frame from Andrea Štaka's *Das Fräulein* (2007).

ger. Ana can give her love because she does not have a father, a husband, or a boss. Like Antigone, she has only a dead brother. Her homelessness needs to be understood in this context: she is not dependent on a master of the house because she does not have a house. She is not homeless; she is houseless. This is why she cannot accept the hospitality offered to "people like her" through houses like the hotel or the hospital, which comes with strings attached. At the end of the film, Ana thumbs another ride, continuing her European travels (see fig. 5.5).

To speak of free love today risks various anachronisms, yet some of its tenets feel very contemporary, especially in the context of the traffic in women. Free love, as it was theorized by early twentieth-century materialist feminists like Alexandra Kollontai, is decidedly and resolutely antimarriage. It is also antireproductive; it emerged, as a concept, in response to the acknowledgment of the state's biopolitical investment in reproduction. It works with a materialist awareness of an economy not only of marriage but also of sex and love. Its critique of marriage emerged in tandem with a critique of what in the discourse of the time was called *prostitution*, a term that in retrospective can be read as *sex work*, to refer to women's sex and affective labor more generally. (Kollontai wrote: "The sale of women's labour . . . is closely and inseparably connected with the sale of the female body.")[50] In the context of the traffic in women, free love is an attempt to subtract women and their reproductive labor from various networks of exchange and reimagine relation starting from a reconfigured notion of love.

In 2004, Hans Weingartner's film *The Edukators/Die fetten Yahre sind vorbei* offered one of the harshest critiques of the 1968 generation and, with that, of the European political landscape of the early years of the twenty-first century. Having reached maturity and accessed power, 68'ers turned out to be more conservative than their parents. In a grand inquisitor–inspired scenario, the film asks what the 68'er-turned-banker does when faced with a new generation of youthful idealists. It mercilessly suggests that he turns them in to the police. The only hope in a sobering European historical moment is that the three young protagonists discover that, as revolution after revolution fails and revolutionaries become respectable conservative citizens, good revolutionary ideas survive. In Weingartner's film, as in Štaka's, free love is such an idea.

We see Ana in Zürich, which is not in the European Union but is in Schengen. *Das Fräulein* does not seem particularly invested in the distinction as long as Switzerland *feels*, for all intents and purposes, like Europe.[51] The brilliance of Štaka's film is to have presented us with a Europe where the host is an immigrant community. This situation could be understood on a pattern whereby settled immigrants extend hospitality to new migrants (guests make good hosts), but this does not seem to be the point the film is making. In the logic of *Das Fräulein*, this *is* Switzerland. Or at least there is no other Switzerland. The host country is already a Babel. And there is no going back to a purer European precedent. Visually, as with the locations in the other films we have explored in this book, Zürich is not recognizable as a tourist destination. Ruža's restaurant is situated in a postindustrial, gray area. The only other space in the film is a romantic mountainous landscape, the backdrop to meditations about death.

In a strict, formal sense, the host is always male, hence, as we have seen, the innumerable East-West sexualized encounters involving an East European woman traveler and a Western male host. "What would a foreigner woman be?" is the question that haunts Derrida's seminar.[52] An answer was not ventured. Scattered remarks on the figure of the sister nonetheless gesture toward such an answer. As we have seen in chapter 1, the sister is a potential woman-friend. Kollontai speaks of a "love-comradeship" that opens the possibility that "men and women will strive to express their love not only in kisses and embraces, but in joint creativity and activity."[53] Possibly a lover, the sister disassociates the imbrication of friendship with brotherhood. She is not necessarily a *brother*'s sister. Let us remember that, in her past, Roberte has traded in charity as a sister in the Red Cross. She has traded, in other words, in the hospitality of the hospital, before becoming an accomplice in Octave's hospitality.[54] But the kind of hostess she becomes in light of the new hospitality hardly makes her a sister. While the guests in her house, including Octave, partake of a new relation, she is not a partner in it, although the relation itself might carry residual traces of her enabling difference. The question is, In her nonrelational singularity, can Roberte mediate a relation to the female foreigner? In more immediate terms, can the French hostess welcome the East European woman—as a guest, a sister, or a friend and not as a domestic servant, nanny, or nurse?[55]

In *Das Fräulein*, Ana's dying presence mediates these questions. In the strict sense that Georges Bataille gives to the term, the viewer *sacrifices* Ana.[56] Death, Bataille believed in a Nietzschean fashion, is a joyful festival, a gift. Ana squanders herself in this spirit. Cinema, in its very medium, is instrumental to this dramatization. *Das Fräulein* begins with an intriguing scene in which a man cuts young, green branches of a tree in an orchard in spring. In a sense, the film cuts such a young branch so that we can witness what happens in the wake of the cut. The gesture resonates in the alternative public sphere that art cinema has created over the last decades. It is a reminder that cinema can cyclically return to its mandate as "the most important art."[57] This time around, across a tumultuous twentieth century, the phrase marks cinema's hospitality to parasitic readings framed by the debate on the traffic in women.

Notes

Introduction

1. Gianni Riotta, "Umberto Eco: 'It's Culture, Not War, That Cements European Identity': The Writer and Semiologist Advocates a Sexual Revolution to Make Us All 'European,'" *The Guardian*, January 26, 2012.

2. On the global resonances of this argument, see Barbara Ehrenreich and Arlie Russell Hochschild, eds., *Global Woman: Nannies, Maids, and Sex Workers in the New Economy* (New York: Metropolitan, 2002).

3. The literature on the history of Europe is extensive. For an overview, see Anthony Pagden, ed., *The Idea of Europe: From Antiquity to the European Union* (Cambridge: Cambridge University Press, 2002).

4. Daniel Defoe, *Robinson Crusoe*, ed. Michael Shinagel (New York: Norton, 1993), 294.

5. See Dipesh Chakrabarty, *Provincializing Europe: Postcolonial Thought and Historical Difference* (Princeton, NJ: Princeton University Press, 2000).

6. Scholars speak of *Eastern Europe*, *eastern Europe*, and *East Europe*. Today, there is a growing resistance to the label *Eastern Europe*. This is because the adjectives *eastern* and *western* imply a comparison. One *OED* definition of *eastern* explains the term as "designating the more easterly part of a country or region." "Eastern Europe" is "more Eastern" than other parts of Europe. This implication not only solidifies the Western/Eastern dichotomy but also encourages a hierarchy within *eastern*—some East European countries are "more Eastern" than others. The other problematic meaning of *Eastern Europe* comes from the fact that *Eastern* continues to carry the Cold War baggage of "the Eastern bloc." Another *OED* definition of the adjective *eastern* thus lists the following: "Of, relating to, or designating the Soviet Union and its allies, esp.

the Communist states of eastern and central Europe. Now *hist.*" In an effort to avoid such anachronistic invocations of *Eastern Europe*, I choose to use *East Europe*. I write *Eastern Europe* (placed within [admittedly jarring] scare quotes) when I am quoting or referencing the historical, essentializing use of the phrase in other scholars' and writers' work.

7. On the history of "Eastern Europe," see Larry Wolff, *Inventing Eastern Europe: The Map of Civilization on the Mind of the Enlightenment* (Stanford, CA: Stanford University Press, 1994). On Europe's relation to the Balkan, see Maria Todorova, *Imagining the Balkans* (Oxford: Oxford University Press, 1997).

8. Czesław Miłosz speaks of specifically Central European "ways of feeling and thinking" that can be grasped from the literature of the region but also of "a perception of [Central Europe's] common destinies and of peculiar traits that make it different from its big neighbours, West and East." Czesław Miłosz, "Central European Attitudes," in *In Search of Central Europe*, ed. George Schöpflin and Nancy Wood (Cambridge: Polity, 1989), 116–24, 116–17, 118. For a response to Miłosz, see Iver B. Neumann, "Russia as Central Europe's Constituting Other," *East European Politics and Society* 7, no. 2 (1993): 349–69.

9. Edward Said, *Orientalism* (New York: Vintage, 1979). The recent emergence of *Eurasia* as a regional designation has constituted one attempt to critically rethink the Orientalizing resonances of the adjective *Eastern*. See Mark Von Hagen, "Empires, Borderlands, and Diasporas: Eurasia as Anti-Paradigm for the Post-Soviet Era," *American Historical Review* 109, no. 2 (2004): 445–68.

10. A rhetoric of paternalism permeates the language of scholars and intellectuals who have made it their task to "promote" East Europe. Pointing out that West Europeans are uninformed and uninterested in East European cultural realities, Karl Schlögel, a historian of East Europe, writes: "Even though it is partly true that the East is more 'backward' and not as modern, that is no reason for the absurdly fanciful ideas we have about Eastern Europe. When we read the reports, we sometimes gain the impression that the East consists of nothing but chaos, crime and collapse, and we are surprised, when we actually go there, to see that children go to school, do their work and lead, admittedly strenuous, but otherwise normal lives. In short, east of Berlin is also Europe, a different Europe that still has to be discovered and assimilated." Karl Schlögel, "Europe Tests Its Boundaries: A Searching Movement," *Eurozine*, November 24, 2004, http://www.eurozine.com/articles/2004-11-24-schloegel-en.html (accessed May 26, 2013).

11. In 1993, the Polish sociologist Piotr Sztompka proposed that, in order to fully integrate, East Europeans needed to acquire "civilizational competence": "a complex set of rules, norms and values, habits and reflexes, codes and matrixes, blueprints and formats—the skillful and semi-automatic mastery of which is a prerequisite for participation in modern civilization." Piotr Sztompka, "Civilizational Incompetence: The Trap of Post-Communist Transition," *Zeitschrift für Soziologie* 22, no. 2 (1993): 85–95, 88.

12. *Transitland* is a collaborative East European video art project initiated on the twentieth anniversary of 1989. See *Transitland: Video Art from Central and Eastern Europe, 1989–2009* (Budapest: Ludwig Museum, 2009); and http://transitland.eu (accessed May 26, 2013). *Transitland* could offer a point of comparison to a more recent art project, initiated in the Netherlands, and suggestively titled *Former West*, a variation on *post-West*, that attempts to rethink, from within the West, the hegemony of Western Europe. See http://formerwest.org (accessed May 26, 2013).

13. Jacques Derrida, *The Other Heading: Reflections on Today's Europe*, trans. Pascale-Anne Brault and Michael B. Naas (Bloomington: Indiana University Press, 1992), 48.

14. Chakrabarty's nod to East Europe is brief and parenthetical. He writes about "internalist histories of Europe in which Europe was described as the site of the first occurrence of capitalism, modernity, or Enlightenment": "These 'events' in turn are all explained mainly with respect to 'events' within the geographical confines of Europe (however fuzzy its exact boundaries may have been)." In the logic of "first in Europe, then elsewhere," the parentheses on Europe's boundaries deserve further consideration. A country like Albania does not belong to "first in Europe"; it has historically been "elsewhere." Within the contemporary European Union, the "two velocities theory" reiterates the long-standing perception that some East European countries need to wait patiently for their European destiny, which will surely come, but at a different speed. "Eastern Europe" is a postcolonial case study in what Chakrabarty calls "the art of waiting." Chakrabarty, *Provincializing Europe*, 7–8.

15. In a different context, Terry Smith offers useful insights into provincialism *tout court*, applicable to East-West European cultural realities. Terry Smith, "The Provincialism Problem," *Art Forum* 13, no. 1 (1974): 54–59.

16. On the East Europeanness of the "Eastern European Jew," see Tony Kushner, "Racialization and 'White European' Immigration to Britain," in *Racialization: Studies in Theory and Practice*, ed. Karim Murji and John Solomos (Oxford: Oxford University Press, 2005), 207–25.

17. For an analysis of the European Capitals of Culture initiative, see Ginette Verstraete, *Tracking Europe: Mobility, Diaspora, and the Politics of Location* (Durham, NC: Duke University Press, 2011).

18. James Clifford, "Traveling Cultures," in *Cultural Studies*, ed. Lawrence Grossberg, Cary Nelson, and Paula Treichler (New York: Routledge, 1991), 96–116.

19. See Evelyn Nakano Glenn, *Unequal Freedom: How Race and Gender Shaped American Citizenship and Labor* (Cambridge, MA: Harvard University Press, 2002).

20. Étienne Balibar, *We, the People of Europe? Reflections on Transnational Citizenship*, trans. James Swenson (Princeton, NJ: Princeton University Press, 2004).

21. Pierre Bourdieu and Loïc Wacquant accused American scholars of exporting American conceptual particularisms, like *race*, to contexts to which they are alien (Brazil, Europe), thus facilitating the globalization of "American problems." Pierre Bourdieu and Loïc Wacquant, "On the Cunning of Imperialist Reason," *Theory, Culture and Society* 16, no. 1 (1999): 41–58.

22. See, e.g., Sadik Jalal al-'Azm, "Orientalism and Orientalism in Reverse," in *Orientalism: A Reader*, ed. A. L. Macfie (Edinburgh: Edinburgh University Press, 2000), 217–38.

23. J. G. A. Pocock, "Some Europes in Their History," in Pagden, ed., *The Idea of Europe*, 55.

24. This use of the phrase *traffic in women* is often associated with the work of Kathleen Barry. See Kathleen Barry, *Female Sexual Slavery* (New York: New York University Press, 1984), and *The Prostitution of Sexuality* (New York: New York University Press, 1996).

25. Gayle Rubin, "The Traffic in Women: Notes on the 'Political Economy' of Sex," in *Toward an Anthropology of Women*, ed. Rayna R. Reiter (New York: Monthly Review Press, 1975), 157–210.

26. Reading Claude Lévi-Strauss, Elizabeth Cowie speaks of "the bodily movement

of women from one place to another via a matrimonial ceremony." She quotes Jacques Lacan's invocation of "the *voyage* on which wives and goods are embarked." Elizabeth Cowie, "Woman as Sign" (1978), in *The Woman in Question*, ed. Parveen Adams and Elizabeth Cowie (Cambridge, MA: MIT Press, 1990), 117–33, 128–29.

27. The adjective *coerced* has emerged in the debate surrounding the UN Trafficking Protocol (2000). The protocol distinguishes between coerced and noncoerced sex work, with the former being defined as "trafficking." I use the adjective *coerced* in this sense throughout this book to refer to illegal, violent forms of sex trafficking, although the impetus behind the book is to problematize, in a Marxist framework, both coercion and choice in relation to labor (more on this in chapter 3).

28. I draw on Kamala Kempadoo's definition of *coerced sex trafficking*: "trafficking not as the enslavement of women, but as *the trade and exploitation of labor under conditions of coercion and force*." Kamala Kempadoo, "Introduction: From Moral Panic to Global Justice: Changing Perspectives on Trafficking," in *Trafficking and Prostitution Reconsidered: New Perspectives on Migration, Sex Work, and Human Rights*, ed. Kamala Kempadoo, Jyoti Sanghera, and Bandana Pattanaik (Boulder, CO: Paradigm, 2005), vii–xxxiv, viii.

29. Melissa Ditmore, "In Calcutta, Sex Workers Organize," in *The Affective Turn: Theorizing the Social*, ed. Patricia Ticineto Clough (Durham, NC: Duke University Press, 2007), 170–86.

30. Michel Foucault, *The Order of Things: An Archaeology of the Human Sciences* (New York: Pantheon, 1970), 232.

31. Michel Foucault, *The History of Sexuality*, vol. 1, *An Introduction*, trans. Robert Hurley (New York: Vintage, 1990), 140.

32. See Lee Edelman, *No Future: Queer Theory and the Death Drive* (Durham, NC: Duke University Press, 2004). For responses to Edelman within queer theory, see José Esteban Muñoz, *Cruising Utopia: The Then and There of Queer Futurity* (New York: New York University Press, 2009); Elizabeth Freeman, *Time Binds: Queer Temporalities, Queer Histories* (Durham, NC: Duke University Press, 2010); Michael D. Snediker, *Queer Optimism: Lyric Personhood and Other Felicitous Persuasions* (Minneapolis: University of Minnesota Press, 2008); and Robert L. Caserio, Lee Edelman, Judith Halberstam, José Esteban Muñoz, and Tim Dean, "The Antisocial Thesis in Queer Theory," *PMLA* 121, no. 3 (2006): 819–28.

33. The growing literature on this phenomenon addresses the fragmentation and commercialization of "care products" offered both by the welfare state and by an extended family. On the welfare side, see Trudie Knijn, "Marketization and the Struggling Logics of (Home) Care in the Netherlands," in *Care Work*, ed. Madonna Harrington Meyer (New York: Routledge, 2000), 232–48. On the family side, see Bettina Haidinger, "Transnational Contingency: The Domestic Work of Migrant Women in Austria," in *Women and Immigration Law: New Variations on Classical Feminist Themes*, ed. Sarah van Walsum and Thomas Spijkerboer (New York: Routledge-Cavendish, 2007), 163–82. See also Alice Anderson, "Europe's Care Regimes and the Role of Migrant Care Workers within Them," *Journal of Population Aging* 5 (2012): 135–46.

34. See Louis Althusser, "Ideology and Ideological State Apparatuses," in *Lenin and Philosophy and Other Essays* (New York: Monthly Review Press, 2001), 85–126.

35. Kirsten Drotner, "Toppling Hierarchies? Ethnicity, Digital Literacy and Holistic Media Research" (keynote address delivered at the conference "Digital Crossroads," Utrecht, July 2012).

36. On Ostojić's authorial intentions for *Untitled/After Courbet (L'origine du monde)*, see Marina Gržinić and Tanja Ostojić, eds., *Integration Impossible? The Politics of Migration in the Artwork of Tanja Ostojić* (Berlin: Argobooks, 2009).

37. Lauren Berlant argues that affect theory is a new phase in the history of ideology theory. See Lauren Berlant, *Cruel Optimism* (Durham, NC: Duke University Press, 2011). The twist I am alluding to is very much an affective twist. The nanny *loves* her charge, but the affective mix that we call *love* needs to be understood as reproductive work. In the old framework, the housewife's class interest could not be separated from that of the husband/breadwinner. The housewife was, for the most part, conservative; she lent her conservatism to the reproduction of the attitudes needed to sustain the division of labor in the new generation (her children). The transnational nanny engaged in the same work is less supportive of the status quo as her allegiances are split between her charge and her family "back home."

38. See, e.g., Ali Behdad, "On Globalization, Again!" in *Postcolonial Studies and Beyond*, ed. Ania Loomba, Suvir Kaul, Matti Bunzl, Antoinette Burton, and Jed Esty (Durham, NC: Duke University Press, 2005), 62–79; and Stephen Greenblatt et al., *Cultural Mobility: A Manifesto* (Cambridge: Cambridge University Press, 2010).

39. Defoe, *Robinson Crusoe*, 220.

40. Defoe's nationalism is not necessarily tied to a culturally or ethnically bounded sense of nationhood. For Defoe, the "true-born Englishman" is a "heterogeneous thing." See Daniel Defoe, *The True Born Englishman* (1700). Defoe was an enthusiastic advocate of naturalized immigration to England (Crusoe's father is a German immigrant). See Daniel Statt, "Daniel Defoe and Immigration," *Eighteenth-Century Studies* 24, no. 3 (1991): 293–313. That being said, Defoe does not entertain the possibility of Friday becoming a "true-born Englishman."

41. On classification, see Liisa Malkki, "Citizens of Humanity: Internationalism and the Imagined Community of Nations," *Diaspora* 3, no. 1 (1994): 41–68.

42. Imre Szeman, "Remote Sensing: An Interview with Ursula Biemann," *Review of Education, Pedagogy, and Cultural Studies* 24 (2002): 91–109, 108.

43. The care industry capitalizes on the essentialist view that women are naturally inclined to care—care about and care for. Today, the premise of this difference gives women access to transnational caring jobs. Their participation in the industry at the same time reinforces the essentialist assumption (that women, as a group, internationally, are better suited for such jobs)

44. Bridget Anderson, *Doing the Dirty Work? The Global Politics of Domestic Labor* (London: Zed, 2000), 152–54.

45. Siddharth Kara, *Sex Trafficking: Inside the Business of Modern Slavery* (New York: Columbia University Press, 2009), 88.

46. On the denial and erasure of race in Europe, see David Theo Goldberg, "Racial Europeanization," *Ethnic and Racial Studies* 29, no. 2 (2006): 331–64.

47. Rosi Braidotti, "On Becoming European," in *Women Migrants from East to West: Gender, Mobility and Belonging in Contemporary Europe*, ed. Luisa Passerini, Enrica Capussotti, Dawn Lyon, and Ioanna Laliotou (New York: Berghahn, 2007), 23–44, 34.

48. Stuart Hall, "Pluralism, Race and Class in Caribbean Society," in *Race and Class in Post-Colonial Society: A Study of Ethnic Group Relations in the English-Speaking Caribbean, Bolivia, Chile and Mexico* (Paris: Unesco, 1978), 150–82.

49. Shu-mei Shih describes the moment when "passing as white becomes an economic activity, and whiteness, for those who can pass, can be sold and acquired at determined values and prices." Shu-mei Shih, "Comparative Racialization: An Introduction," *PMLA* 123, no. 5 (2008): 1347–62, 1356.

50. Karim Murji and John Solomos, "Introduction: Racialization in Theory and Practice," in Murji and Solomos, eds., *Racialization*, 1–28, 16.

51. Fatima El-Tayeb, *European Others: Queering Ethnicity in Postnational Europe* (Minneapolis: University of Minnesota Press, 2011).

52. Goldberg writes: "Those sex-workers parading today in Amsterdam's famous red light district, as elsewhere, on display each evening as tourists flock by, drawn by the smell of sex or transfixed on the spectacle, are overwhelmingly from Asia, the Caribbean, Latin America and Eastern Europe. The former three regions represent exoticized sites of sexual attraction, male and female, the preferred destinations of Europe's thriving tourist sex trade today, a point driven home in the wake of the devastating Indian Ocean tsunami, Christmas 2004." Goldberg, "Racial Europeanization," 353. Goldberg does not return to the fourth region on his list, East Europe, itself an exoticized site of sexual attraction and a destination for sex tourism. Two questions emerge: Why do we find it difficult to speak of race in relation to East Europe once we acknowledge the constructedness of the concept? What are the consequences of this elision?

53. Because East European women are often too easily perceived by scholars to be white, the study of their coerced sex trafficking is considered a form of white hysteria (the media is outraged about their situation because they are white). For the most vehement critique of white hysteria explicitly connecting it to the whiteness of East European women, see Jo Doezema, *Sex Slaves and Discourse Masters: The Construction of Trafficking* (London: Zed, 2010).

54. Robert Miles, *Racism and Migrant Labour* (London: Routledge & Kegan Paul, 1982).

55. For a repositioning of Jewishness within the racial field in the United States, see Jennifer Glaser, "The Jew in the Canon: Reading Race and Literary History in Philip Roth's *The Human Stain*," *PMLA* 123, no. 5 (2008): 1448–64.

56. *Moving People, Moving Images: Cinema and Trafficking in the New Europe*, ed. William Brown, Dina Iordanova, and Leshu Torchin (St. Andrews: St. Andrews Film Studies, 2010), is limited to an assessment of coerced sex trafficking, but it documents the range of films and film festivals that have become invested in this phenomenon.

57. Thomas Elsaesser, *European Cinema: Face to Face with Hollywood* (Amsterdam: Amsterdam University Press, 2005), 101.

58. On the global dimension of European art cinema, see Rosalind Galt and Karl Schoonover, eds., *Global Art Cinema: New Theories and Histories* (Oxford: Oxford University Press, 2010).

59. Janet Harbord, *Film Cultures* (London: Sage, 2002), 60.

60. On precedents for thinking about the usefulness of cinema in various social contexts, see Charles R. Acland and Haidee Wasson, eds., *Useful Cinema* (Durham, NC: Duke University Press, 2011).

61. Miriam Hansen, *Babel and Babylon: Spectatorship in American Silent Film* (Cambridge, MA: Harvard University Press, 1991), 2. See also Miriam Hansen, "Early Cinema, Late Cinema: Permutations on the Public Sphere," *Screen* 34, no. 3 (1993): 197–210.

62. Rita Felski writes: "Anyone surveying the scholarship on the present and future of Europe cannot help being struck by the sovereignty of the social sciences. . . . Where, in the debates about the present and the future of Europe, are the art historians, the literary scholars, the philosophers, the cultural critics? Not entirely absent to be sure, but their role remains modest, often marginal." Rita Felski, introduction to "A New Europe?" ed. Rita Felski, special issue, *New Literary History* 43 (2012): v–xv, v.

Chapter 1

1. *Occident* is the word Romanians used during the Cold War to refer to the West. The term is synonymous with a certain Europe, Europe as the West.

2. Gayle Rubin, "The Traffic in Women: Notes on the 'Political Economy' of Sex," in *Toward an Anthropology of Women*, ed. Rayna R. Reiter (New York: Monthly Review Press, 1975), 157–210.

3. Luce Irigaray, *This Sex Which Is Not One*, trans. Catherine Porter and Carolyn Burke (Ithaca, NY: Cornell University Press, 1985).

4. Emma Goldman, "The Traffic in Women," in *Red Emma Speaks: An Emma Goldman Reader*, ed. Alix Kates Shulman (Amherst, NY: Humanity, 1998), 175–89, 145.

5. Emma Goldman, "What I Believe," in ibid., 48–60, 57.

6. Laura Kipnis, *Against Love: A Polemic* (New York: Vintage, 2004).

7. Mariarosa Dalla Costa and Selma James, "Women and the Subversion of the Community," in *Materialist Feminism: A Reader in Class, Difference and Women's Lives*, ed. Rosemary Hennessy and Chrys Ingraham (New York: Routledge, 1997), 40–53, 47.

8. For an overview of where capitalist notions of economy intersect this history, see Linda Nicholson, "Feminism and Marx: Integrating Kinship with the Economic," in *The Second Wave: A Reader in Feminist Theory*, ed. Linda Nicholson (New York: Routledge, 1997), 131–46.

9. Marcel Mauss, *The Gift: The Form and Reason for Exchange in Archaic Societies*, trans. W. D. Halls (New York: Norton, 2000), 5.

10. Claude Lévi-Strauss, *Structural Anthropology*, trans. Claire Jacobson and Brooke Grundfest Schoepf (New York: Basic, 1963), 83.

11. Claude Lévi-Strauss, *Elementary Structures of Kinship*, trans. James Bell, John von Sturmer, and Rodney Needham (Boston: Beacon, 1969), 51. For a critique of the universalism of the incest taboo, see Robin Fox, *The Red Lamp of Incest: An Enquiry into the Origins of Mind and Society* (Notre Dame, IN: University of Notre Dame Press, 1984). For a critique of the assumed heterosexuality of this narrative of origins, see Monique Wittig, *The Straight Mind and Other Essays* (Boston: Beacon, 1992), 10.

12. Lévi-Strauss, *Elementary Structures of Kinship*, 481, 483.

13. Elsewhere, Lévi-Strauss puts it in even more unambiguous terms: "A certain kinship tie, the brother-in-law relationship, . . . is both sexual and political-social; and, owing to its complexity, the brother-in-law relationship may perhaps be regarded as an actual institution." Claude Lévi-Strauss, "The Social Use of Kinship Terms among Brazilian Indians," *American Anthropologist*, n.s., 45, no. 3 (July –September 1943): 398–409, 398, quoted in Marcela Coelho de Souza, "The Future of the Structural Theory of Kinship," in *The Cambridge Companion to Lévi-Strauss*, ed. Boris Wiseman (Cambridge: Cambridge University Press, 2009), 80–100, 86.

14. Rubin, "The Traffic in Women," 198.

15. Mauss, *The Gift*, 78.

16. Lévi-Strauss, *Structural Anthropology*, 35.

17. Rubin, "The Traffic in Women," 543.

18. Louis Althusser and Étienne Balibar, *Reading Capital*, trans. Ben Brewster (London: Verso, 2006), 25.

19. Lévi-Strauss, *Structural Anthropology*, 61. Another version of this statement reads: "What is communicated in marriage is *almost* of the same nature as those who communicate (women, on the one hand, men, on the other)" (ibid., 297 [emphasis added]).

20. Ibid., 51, 47.

21. Claude Lévi-Strauss, *The View from Afar*, trans. Joachim Neugroschel and Phoebe Hoss (Chicago: University of Chicago Press, 1992), 60.

22. Claude Lévi-Strauss, "Postface," *L'homme: Revue française d'anthropologie*, nos. 154–55 (2000): 713–20, 717, quoted in Coelho de Souza, "The Future of the Structural Theory of Kinship," 93.

23. Judith Butler, *Antigone's Claim: Kinship between Life and Death* (New York: Columbia University Press, 2000), 66.

24. Ibid., 10. On incest, see Gillian Harkins, *Everybody's Family Romance: Reading Incest in Neoliberal America* (Minneapolis: University of Minnesota Press, 2009).

25. Butler, *Antigone's Claim*, 29.

26. Judith Butler, "Is Kinship Always Already Heterosexual?" *differences: A Journal of Feminist Culture Studies* 13, no. 1 (2002): 14–44. Butler references recent work in anthropology in support of her narrative, which she interprets in a "post-kinship" sense. See, e.g., Janet Carsten, *After Kinship* (Cambridge: Cambridge University Press, 2004); and Sarah Franklin and Susan McKinnon, eds., *Relative Values: Reconfiguring Kinship Studies* (Durham, NC: Duke University Press, 2001). It is worth quoting Carsten's gloss on her title: "The title, *After Kinship*, is of course, playful; the message of this book appears to be that 'after kinship' is—well, just more kinship (even if it might be of a slightly different kind)." Carsten, *After Kinship*, xi. Recent anthropological literature on kinship signals a renewed interest in the now-classic anthropological concept. This literature attempts to move away from biologism toward "families we choose," with Lévi-Strauss's structuralism understood (hastily, I think) as a form of biologism.

27. Butler, "Is Kinship Always Already Heterosexual?" 14–15.

28. For a critique of this narrative of progress, see Elizabeth A. Povinelli, *Empire of Love: Toward a Theory of Intimacy, Genealogy, and Carnality* (Durham, NC: Duke University Press, 2006).

29. Butler, *Antigone's Claim*, 22–23.

30. David L. Eng, *The Feeling of Kinship: Queer Liberalism and the Racialization of Intimacy* (Durham, NC: Duke University Press, 2010), 137. The intellectual history of this debate unfolds along structuralist and poststructuralist lines. The critique of structuralism has often too easily conflated the term with immutability in an attempt to propose poststructuralist alternatives for change. Eng's project is invested in the following question: "Why do we have numerous poststructuralist accounts of language but few poststructuralist accounts of kinship?" (ibid., 15). Eng proceeds to offer a critique of the Oedipus complex as structuralist; the alternative, "queer diasporas," is poststructuralist. Ferdinand de Saussure and Lévi-Strauss would be quick to remind us that immutability and mutability are both key dimensions of structuralist analysis and that structuralism is, in this sense, itself poststructuralist. See esp. Claude Lévi-Strauss, "Do Dual Structures Exist?" in *Structural Anthropology*, 132–66.

31. In a different context, Chow writes: "Much 'subject work' has, in other words, too hastily put its emphasis on the 'post' of 'poststructuralism,' (mis)leading us to think that the force of structure itself is a thing of the past." Rey Chow, "The Politics of Admittance: Female Sexual Agency, Miscegenation, and the Formation of Community in Franz Fanon," in *Franz Fanon: Critical Perspectives*, ed. Anthony C. Alessandrini (London: Routledge, 1999), 35–36.

32. Michael Warner, *The Problem with Normal: Sex, Politics and the Ethics of Queer Life* (Cambridge, MA: Harvard University Press, 2000), 123.

33. On this important point, and for an account of the role of kinship theories in

the analysis of sexuality, see Elizabeth Freeman, "Queer Belonging: Kinship Theory and Queer Theory," *A Companion to Lesbian, Gay, Bisexual, Transgender and Queer Studies*, ed. George E. Haggerty and Molly McGarry (Oxford: Blackwell, 2007), 295–314.

34. Michel Foucault, *The History of Sexuality*, vol. 1, *An Introduction*, trans. Robert Hurley (New York: Vintage, 1990), 108/*Histoire de la sexualité*, vol. 1, *La volonté de savoir* (Paris: Gallimard, 1976), 143, 108.

35. Foucault, *The History of Sexuality*, 104, 113.

36. Gayle Rubin, "Thinking Sex: Notes for a Radical Theory of the Politics of Sexuality," in *Pleasure and Danger: Exploring Female Sexuality*, ed. Carole S. Vance (London: Pandora, 1992), 267–319. It is often held that, in "Thinking Sex," Rubin replicated what is taken to be Foucault's move from alliance to sexuality. For a rebuttal of this evolutionist reading (which is thought to replicate a parallel move from feminist theory to queer theory), see Rubin's interview with Judith Butler: Gayle Rubin, "Sexual Traffic," *differences: A Journal of Feminist Cultural Studies* 6, nos. 2–3 (1994): 62–99.

37. The first issue of *m/f*, published in Britain in 1978, included Elizabeth Cowie's reading of Lévi-Strauss, which triangulated (and thus multiplied) the "two faces of second-wave feminism." See Elizabeth Cowie, "Woman as Sign," in *The Woman in Question*, ed. Parveen Adams and Elizabeth Cowie (Cambridge, MA: MIT Press, 1990), 117–33.

38. Irigaray, *This Sex Which Is Not One*, 170.

39. Cowie interrogates this premise: "If, however, women are exchanged in kinship structures because they have value for the group, then the group must have already entered culture to the extent of recognizing women as socially valuable. . . . [S]exual division as social must already exist in order for women to be available for men to exchange in an organized way, and for women to be 'valued' as an object of exchange." Cowie, "Woman as Sign," 126. See also Sherry B. Ortner, "Is Female to Male as Nature Is to Culture?" in *Woman, Culture, and Society*, ed. Michelle Zimbalist Rosaldo and Louise Lamphere (Stanford, CA: Stanford University Press, 1974), 67–87.

40. Irigaray, *This Sex Which Is Not One*, 172, 173, 174.

41. Ibid., 170.

42. This is Irigaray's take on what Jean-François Lyotard condenses in the question, "What is the desire named Marx?" See Jean-François Lyotard, *Libidinal Economy*, trans. Iain Hamilton Grant (Bloomington: Indiana University Press, 1993), 114–15.

43. Irigaray, *This Sex Which Is Not One*, 181.

44. Ibid., 191, 196, 197.

45. Ibid., 208, 209, 216, 214, 215.

46. The notion of literature toward which Irigaray gestures was developed in response to Habermasian theories of communication as a form of trading in signs. See esp. Jean-Luc Nancy, *The Inoperative Community*, ed. Peter Connor, trans. Peter Connor, Lisa Garbus, Michael Holland, and Simona Sawhney (Minneapolis: University of Minnesota Press, 1991). The privileging of literature as an experimental space for the thinking of relation has often been justifiably critiqued, most recently by Catherine Malabou. See Catherine Malabou, "The New Phantoms of Subjectivity: From the Book without Author to Neural Transparency" (lecture, University of California, Los Angeles, May 5, 2009). It is important to note that the notion of literature at work here comes from a tradition suspicious of literature itself (see Georges Bataille, *The Hatred of Poetry* [1947], available today as *The Impossible*, trans. Robert Hurley [San Francisco: City Lights, 2001]). It is therefore often divorced from the literary and is generous enough to include, among other forms of writing, Malabou's work in neuroscience or, indeed, a film like *Occident*.

47. Milan Women's Bookstore Collective, *Sexual Difference: A Theory of Social-Symbolic Practice*, trans. Patricia Cicogna and Teresa de Lauretis (Bloomington, IN: Indiana University Press, 1990), 50. (*Sexual Difference* was originally published in 1987 under the title *Non credere di avere dei diretti* [Don't think you have any rights].) The bookstore is not, of course, the only imaginative space where women take themselves to market. At the other end of the imaginative spectrum, Linda Williams charges that women's cinematic pornography can be read as such a space. Linda Williams, *Hard Core: Power, Pleasure and the Frenzy of the Visible* (Berkeley and Los Angeles: University of California Press, 1989), 249.

48. The female sociality that the Milanese women envision is premised on the debt a daughter has to repay to her symbolic mother. Gratitude is a necessary ingredient of this payment, arguably bringing reciprocity back at the level of affect.

49. Jacques Derrida, *Politics of Friendship*, trans. George Collins (London: Verso, 2006), viii, 149.

50. Jacques Derrida, *On Touching: Jean-Luc Nancy*, trans. Christine Irizarry (Stanford, CA: Stanford University Press, 2005), 22.

51. Derrida, *Politics of Friendship*, 177.

52. Lévi-Strauss, *Structural Anthropology*, 38, 309.

53. Peter Wade, "Race, Ethnicity and Nation: Perspectives from Kinship and Genetics," in *Race, Ethnicity and Nation: Perspectives from Kinship and Genetics*, ed. Peter Wade (New York: Berghahn, 2007), 1–31, 10.

54. Benedict Anderson, *Imagined Communities: Reflections on the Origin and Spread of Nationalism* (London: Verso, 1991), 7.

55. Camille Robcis, *The Law of Kinship: Anthropology, Psychoanalysis and the Family in France* (Ithaca, NY: Cornell University Press, 2013).

56. Carsten, *After Kinship*, 155, 162.

57. Orban quoted in "Romania and Bulgaria Join the European Family," *The Parliament*, January 15, 2007, 28–29, 28.

58. Victor Hugo, "Congrès de la Paix, Paris: Discours d'ouverture (21 août 1849)," in *L'Europe? L'Europe*, ed. Pascal Ory (London: Omnibus, 1998), 165.

59. François Guizot, The *History of Civilization in Europe*, trans. William Hazlitt (London: Penguin, 1997), 30.

60. Anthony Smith, "National Identity and the Idea of European Unity," *International Affairs* 68, no. 1 (1992): 55–76, 70.

61. Eco quoted in Gianni Riotta, "Umberto Eco: 'It's Culture, Not War, That Cements European Identity': The Writer and Semiologist Advocates a Sexual Revolution to Make Us All 'European,'" *The Guardian*, January 26, 2012.

62. Beyza Ç. Tekin, *Representations and Othering in Discourse: The Construction of Turkey in the EU Context* (Amsterdam: John Benjamins, 2010), 202.

63. Jürgen Habermas, *Europe: The Faltering Project* (Cambridge: Polity, 2009).

64. http://www.euprizeliterature.eu/what-eupl (accessed May 26, 2013).

65. This is a striking line in Andrei Codrescu's film *Romania: My Old Haunt* (PBS, 2002).

66. On the neoliberal zeal of Cold War exiled scholars and writers, see Mark Von Hagen, "Empires, Borderlands, and Diasporas: Eurasia as Anti-Paradigm for the Post-Soviet Era," *American Historical Review* 109, no. 2 (2004): 445–68.

67. See also Svitlana Taraban, "Birthday Girls, Russian Dolls, and Others: Internet Bride as the Emerging Global Identity of Post-Soviet Women," in *Living Gender After*

Communism, ed. Janet Elise Johnson and Jean C. Robinson (Bloomington: Indiana University Press, 2007), 105–27.

68. Arlie Russell Hochschild, "Love and Gold," in *Global Woman: Nannies, Maids, and Sex Workers in the New Economy*, ed. Barbara Ehrenreich and Arlie Russell Hochschild (New York: Metropolitan, 2002), 15–30.

69. It will be asked, What of cases when women marrying transnationally marry men they love? Laura Kipnis (*Against Love*) notes the consistency in our love choices, which visibly bear the signs of racial, class, and other affinal appurtenances. We are very predictable in our love. The counterpoint to Kipnis's argument is a book like Stephanie Coontz's *Marriage, a History: How Love Conquered Marriage* (New York: Penguin, 2005). Coontz writes: "Today most people expect to live their lives in a loving relationship, not in a rigid institution. Although most people want socially sanctioned relationships, backed by institutional protections, few would sacrifice their goal of a loving, fair, and flexible relationship for those protections" (10). The point Kipnis is making is precisely that love has conquered marriage—leading to what Coontz calls the *love revolution*. Today it is through love that the institution of marriage does its economic and political work—for heterosexual and homosexual couples alike. What Coontz does not consider is Goldman's or Irigaray's distinction between different kinds of love.

70. Melissa Ditmore, "In Calcutta, Sex Workers Organize," in *The Affective Turn: Theorizing the Social*, ed. Patricia Ticineto Clough (Durham, NC: Duke University Press, 2007), 170–86.

71. See Kipnis, *Against Love*.

72. Michael Hardt, "Affective Economies," *boundary 2* 26, no. 2 (1999): 89–100, 98.

73. See Hochschild, "Love and Gold."

74. West European women have their own emancipation anxieties. Enrica Capusotti writes about "Italian women's renegotiation of their position within contemporary transnational processes: women migrants are exploited for the self-representation of Italian women to finally become modern, emancipated and fully Western." Enrica Capusotti, "Modernity versus Backwardness: Italian Women's Perceptions of Self and Other," in *Women Migrants from East to West: Gender, Mobility and Belonging in Contemporary Europe*, ed. Luisa Passerini, Dawn Lyon, Enrica Capussotti, and Ioanna Laliotou (New York: Berghahn, 2007), 195–211, 13.

75. Habermas, *Europe: The Faltering Project*, 159.

76. Irigaray wrote in 1977: "Exogamy doubtless requires that one leave one's family, tribe or clan, in order to make alliances. All the same, it does not tolerate marriage with populations that are too far away, too far removed from the prevailing cultural codes." Irigaray, *This Sex Which Is Not One*, 172. At stake is a distinction between global kinship markets and European markets. As an effect of the new wave of space-time compression today exogamy often tolerates marriages into faraway populations. At the same time, Europe remains a cultural entity with pervasive effects for kinship. In terms of marriage markets, this means that for the Romanian mother in *Occident* the (white) European husband has become in a certain sense one of ours in ways in which a Saudi man has not.

77. The impetus here is not to renationalize women, as if to say, "These are our women; they should stay home, where they belong, circulate within the nation or not at all." This was the spirit of the debate in Slovenia spurred by Damjan Kozole's *Slovenka* (2009). The female character in that film supports her studies at the University of Ljubljana through sex work. *Slovenka* was released during the Slovenian presidency of the European Union, prompting questions of whether Slovenka (a stand-in for Slovenia) is

prostituting herself to the European Union. The underlying assumption was that she should circulate within proper Slovenian national boundaries.

78. On metropolitan racialization as a practice of relational comparison, see Shu-mei Shih, "Comparative Racialization: An Introduction," *PMLA* 123, no. 5 (2008): 1347–62.

79. Cleaning toilets is often seen as the bottommost rung of the feminized migrant labor market. See Katarzyna Marciniak, "Foreign Women and Toilets," *Feminist Media Studies* 8, no. 4 (2008): 337–56.

80. "Export material" is a line in another Romanian film on the traffic in women, *Asphalt Tango* (1996), directed by Nae Caranfil. A number of Romanian films participate in this critical debate: e.g., Didi Danquart's *Offset* (2006); Cristian Nemescu's *California Dreamin'* (2007); and Bobby Păunescu's *Francesca* (2009).

81. This argument parallels accounts of men's predicament in postcolonial cultures. Frantz Fanon famously describes the position of the black man fearing emasculation by competition with black women, precisely because the latter have access to white society through sexual transactions. The male figures in these cultures are never simply male but also castrated in relation to the privileged world into which "their" women are circulated. For a reading of Fanon's description of the woman of color's desire for the white man and his elision of her ensuing emotional ambivalence, see Chow, "The Politics of Admittance."

82. The question is reminiscent of Wolfgang Becker's dramatization of this generation's predicament in *Good Bye Lenin!* (2003). Thomas Elsaesser writes about this film: "The physical territory of the GDR has been occupied in a most arrogant and heartless manner by the West Germans, taking over houses, villas, offices and institutions, but as a moral territory it is also still occupied by the feelings, memories, faded dreams and dashed hopes of its socialist inhabitants. To counter this double occupancy, the son's nightly broadcasts become ever bolder and yet totally convincing recordings of the West's televisual news images of the fall of the wall, allowing that other utopian reality of a socialist paradise to coexist peacefully with the new post-unification capitalist state and consumerism, as if the ultimate addressee of his manipulation was not his mother but he himself and his generation." Thomas Elsaesser, "Double Occupancy: Space, Place and Identity in European Cinema of the 1990s," *Third Text* 20, no. 6 (2006): 647–58, 658.

83. It should be possible to speak of promise in relation to Europe while engaging the actual politics of the European Union, however vulgar they might seem from the standpoint of a strictly philosophical perspective. For the risks of the latter choice, see Rodolphe Gasché, *Europe, or the Infinite Task: A Study of a Philosophical Concept* (Stanford, CA: Stanford University Press, 2008).

Chapter 2

1. Christoph Huber, "Ulrich Seidl's Song for Europe," *Cinema Scope* 33 (2008): 24–28, 26.

2. Seidl's film claims membership in a cinematic tradition in which film critically frames gestures—a touch, a look, the movement of a hand. "Making gestures citable" is one of the greatest achievements of the actor, Samuel Weber writes, reading Walter Benjamin. Seidl made a point of using nonprofessional actors, in an effort to "cite" spontaneous, unscripted gestures. See Samuel Weber, *Benjamin's -abilities* (Cambridge, MA: Harvard University Press, 2010), 97.

3. *Core Europe* is a phrase made famous by Jürgen Habermas in a letter he cosigned

with Jacques Derrida, "February 15, or, What Binds Europeans Together: A Plea for a Common Foreign Policy, Beginning in the Core of Europe," reprinted in Daniel Levy, Max Pensky, and John Torpey, eds., *Old Europe, New Europe, Core Europe: Transatlantic Relations After the Iraq War* (London: Verso, 2005), 3–13.

4. Seidl's 1990 documentary *Good News* began a long-term project of documenting the everyday lives of migrant workers—first in Austria, then in Europe generally. Stefan Grissemann refers to Seidl's project as "docu-fictional anthropology." Stefan Grissemann, *Sündenfall: Die Grenzüberschreitungen des Filmemachers Ulrich Seidl* (Vienna: Sonderzahl, 2007), 19.

5. In another scene in *Import/Export*, an immigrant woman attends a course on Austrian job application procedures. She is praised when she learns the appropriate way of introducing herself: "Hi, this is Andrea Milica. I was born in Yugoslavia. I am looking for a job as a cleaning lady." The scene suggests that the woman's expertise is based in her gender and place of birth/citizenship. Half of all migrant and immigrant women in Austria are employed as domestic workers. See Bettina Haidinger, "Transnational Contingency: The Domestic Work of Migrant Women in Austria," in *Women and Immigration Law: New Variations on Classical Feminist Themes*, ed. Sarah van Walsum and Thomas Spijkerboer (New York: Routledge-Cavendish, 2007), 163–82, 172.

6. In Rabelais's *Gargantua and Pantagruel*, Panurge debates the pros and cons of marriage. Among other things, he claims, one is at a disadvantage in one's old age if one is not married. Were he to fall ill, who would care for him? François Rabelais, *Gargantua and Pantagruel*, trans. M. A. Screech (London: Penguin, 2006), 444. Seidl pushed this argument to its logical consequences in an earlier film, *Loss Is to Be Expected* (1992), which features an elderly Austrian man looking for a wife to cook for him.

7. Barbara Ehrenreich, "Maid to Order," in *Global Woman: Nannies, Maids, and Sex Workers in the New Economy*, ed. Barbara Ehrenreich and Arlie Russell Hochschild (New York: Metropolitan, 2003), 85–103, 87.

8. Karl Marx, *Capital*, trans. Ben Fowkes (London: Penguin, 1990), 716.

9. Friedrich Engels, *The Origin of the Family, Private Property and the State* (London: Penguin, 1985), 35. On this work's historical oscillation between "productive" and "reproductive," see Jeanne Boydston, *Home and Work: Housework, Wages, and the Ideology of Labor in the Early Republic* (New York: Oxford University Press, 1990).

10. Selma James listed the tasks involved in reproductive labor: "First it [a human being] must be nine months in the womb and must be fed, clothed and trained; then when it works its bed must be made, its floors swept, its lunch box prepared, its sexuality not gratified but quieted, its dinner ready when it gets home, even if this is eight in the morning after night shift. . . . This is how labor power is produced and reproduced when it is daily consumed in the factory or the office. *To describe its basic production and reproduction is to describe women's work.*" Selma James, "Introduction to *The Power of Women and the Subversion of the Community*," in *Materialist Feminism: A Reader in Class, Difference and Women's Lives*, ed. Rosemary Hennessy and Chrys Ingraham (New York: Routledge, 1997), 33–39, 37.

11. On the general strike, see Mariarosa Dalla Costa, "A General Strike," in *All Work and No Pay: Women, Housework, and the Wages Due*, ed. Wendy Edmond and Suzie Fleming (Bristol: Falling Wall, 1975), 125–27.

12. Silvia Federici, "Wages against Housework," in *The Politics of Housework*, ed. Ellen Malos (Cheltenham: New Clarion, 1995), 187–94, 191. Although often the feminist call was to get women out of the home, work was not idealized as a solution.

Mariarosa Dalla Costa and Selma James wrote: "Women refuse the myth of liberation through work. For we have worked enough. We have chopped billions of tons of cotton, washed billions of dishes, scrubbed billions of floors, typed billions of letters, wired billions of radio sets, washed billions of nappies by hand and in machines. . . . We must refuse the development they are offering us." Mariarosa Dalla Costa and Selma James, "Women and the Subversion of the Community," in Hennessy and Ingraham, eds., *Materialist Feminism*, 40–53, 51. The Los Angeles Wages for Housework Committee argued: "When we fight for jobs, we fight for the right to be exploited, we fight for the right to do more work." Los Angeles Wages for Housework Committee, "Sisters Why March?" in Edmond and Fleming, eds., *All Work and No Pay*, 123–24, 124. Retracing the history of this debate, Kathi Weeks emphasizes that "wages for housework" was at the same time a demand, a provocation, and a perspective; its spirit was antiwork and sometimes postwork. Kathi Weeks, *The Problem with Work: Feminism, Marxism, Antiwork Politics, and Postwork Imaginaries* (Durham, NC: Duke University Press, 2011), 128.

13. Pat Mainardi, "The Politics of Housework," in Malos, ed., *The Politics of Housework*, 83–87, 83 (emphasis added).

14. Federici, "Wages against Housework," 187.

15. Ellen Malos, introduction to Malos, ed., *The Politics of Housework*, 1–33, 28.

16. For a history of this debate, see Deborah Dinner, "The Universal Childcare Debate: Rights Mobilization, Social Policy, and the Dynamics of Feminist Activism, 1966–1974," *Law and History Review* 28 (2010): 577–628.

17. Vivien Leone, "Domestics," in *Radical Feminism: A Documentary Reader*, ed. Barbara A. Crow (New York: New York University Press, 2000), 516–20, 516.

18. Wendy Edmond, "The Single Housewife," in Edmond and Fleming, eds., *All Work and No Pay*, 42–44, 43.

19. Power of Women Collective, "The Home in the Hospital," in ibid., 69–89, 69.

20. Juliet Mitchell, *From Feminism to Liberation* (Cambridge, MA: Schenkman, 1971), 121.

21. Ukeles enumerates the tasks of maintenance work in her "Manifesto for Maintenance Art 1969!": "Clean your desk, wash the dishes, clean the floor, wash your clothes, wash your toes, change the baby's diaper, finish the report, correct the typos, mend the fence, keep the customer happy, throw out the stinking garbage, watch out don't put things in your nose, what shall I wear, I have no sox, pay your bills, don't litter, save string, wash your hair, change the sheets, go to the store, I'm out of perfume, say it again—he doesn't understand, say it again—it leaks, go to work, this art is dusty, clear the table, call him again, flush the toilet, stay young." Mierle Laderman Ukeles, "Manifesto for Maintenance Art 1969!" reprinted as "Artist Project: Mierle Laderman Ukeles Maintenance Art Activity (1973) with Responses from Miwon Kwon and Helen Molesworth," *Documents* 10 (1997): 5–22, 6.

22. Anne McClintock made a similar argument on the margins of popular sadomasochistic theatrical enactments: "Prostitutes testify that men frequently enact scripts framed by the 'degradation' of domesticity: paying large sums of money to sweep, clean, launder, and tidy, under a female regime of verbal taunts and abuse. . . . [T]he spectacle of the male 'slave' on his hands and knees, naked as a newt and scrubbing the kitchen floor, throws radically into question 'Nature's' edict that differences in gender entail natural divisions of labor." Anne McClintock, "Maid to Order: Commercial Fetishism and Gender Power," *Social Text* 37 (1993): 87–116, 93, 97.

23. Marcel Proust, *Swann's Way*, trans. Lydia Davis (New York: Penguin, 2003), 8.

24. Central here is what Saskia Sassen has referred to as "the feminization of survival." Saskia Sassen, "Global Cities and Survival Circuits," in Ehrenreich and Hochschild, eds., *Global Woman*, 254–74, 265. East European countries like Ukraine, Moldova, Romania, and Bulgaria (EU *and* non-EU countries) are following in the footsteps of the Philippines and Sri Lanka, facilitating "survival circuits" through the export of women's labor. The need for domestic labor in West Europe was met in the postwar period by women from former European colonies (Algerians in France, West Indians in Britain) as well as women from poorer parts of Europe (Spain, Italy, Portugal). A wave of Filipina domestic workers then met the increasing demand for domestic work. They are now being followed by women from Central and East Europe. Women from the former Soviet Union come next, their situation as non-EU citizens leading to increased labor precariousness. The last ring in the global care chain in this region consists of Polish women who do domestic work in Germany and who hire Ukrainian women to clean their houses and care for their children in Poland. For this history, see Bridget Anderson, *Doing the Dirty Work? The Global Politics of Domestic Labor* (London: Zed, 2000).

25. For the numbers, see Judith Treas, "Why Study Housework?" in *Dividing the Domestic: Men, Women and Household Work in a Cross-National Perspective*, ed. Judith Treas and Sonja Drobnič (Stanford, CA: Stanford University Press, 2010), 3–18.

26. The old patterns take us back to histories of colonialism and slavery and a phenomenon I am referring to as *Americanization*. See Evelyn Nakano Glenn, "From Servitude to Service Work: Historical Continuities in the Racial Division of Paid Reproductive Labor," *Signs: Journal of Women in Culture and Society* 18, no. 1 (1992): 1–43; and Amy Kaplan, "Manifest Domesticity," *American Literature* 70, no. 3 (1998): 581–606.

27. In an exchange with Gayatri Spivak, Judith Butler describes the private sphere as "a *dark* domain . . . , necessarily *dark*, [where] slaves and children and the disenfranchised foreigners took care of the reproduction of material life": "These spectral humans, deprived of ontological weight and failing the tests of social intelligibility required for minimal recognition include those whose age, gender, race, nationality, and labor status not only disqualify them for citizenship but actively 'qualify' them for statelessness." Judith Butler and Gayatri Chakravorty Spivak, *Who Sings the Nation State? Language, Politics, Belonging* (London: Seagull, 2007), 14–15.

28. We can assume that Olga makes about 500 euros a month at a rate of about 2.2 euros per hour. Haidinger, "Transnational Contingency," 169.

29. Think, alternatively, of the irony of reading Vivien Leone's words today: "The rallying call of Women, Unite! never had a more urgent objective than to solve the Servant Problem, because the Servants are Us. All of us." It would seem that the "us" of "Women, Unite!" has never been more stratified. Leone, "Domestics," 520.

30. Historically, this work has often been done by slaves, indentured servants, and racially and ethnically marginalized groups. See Judith Rollins, *Between Women: Domestics and Their Employers* (Philadelphia: Temple University Press, 1987).

31. A strong rebuttal of the assumption that feminism is to blame for this development is offered in Linda Bosniak, "Citizenship, Noncitizenship, and the Transnationalization of Domestic Labor," in *Migration and Mobilities: Citizenship, Borders and Gender*, ed. Seyla Benhabib and Judith Resnik (New York: New York University Press, 2009), 127–56.

32. Lisa Adkins argues that the last two decades have witnessed the dispersal of reproductive labor across the social body, such that this labor is no longer subject to the logic of patriarchal exchange in the private sphere. While I agree that some aspects of reproductive labor have been dispersed, I believe that Olga's presence in the Austrian

household pressures us to consider the production of an international private sphere, with its own attendant patriarchalism. Lisa Adkins, "Feminism After Measure," *Feminist Theory* 10, no. 3 (2009): 323–39.

33. André Bazin developed his thoughts on "total neo-realism" on the margins of a scene in Vittorio De Sica's and Cesare Zavattini's *Umberto D.* (1952) in which a maid is making coffee: "The girl gets up, potters about in the kitchen, chases away the ants, grinds the coffee . . . and all these 'unimportant' actions are recorded for us in strict temporal continuity." André Bazin, "Umberto D.," trans. Jim Hillier, in *Cahiers du Cinéma: Neo-Realism, Hollywood, New Wave*, ed. Jim Hillier (Cambridge, MA: Harvard University Press, 1985), 180–81, 181. On Akerman's revision of neorealism, see Ivone Margulies, *Nothing Happens: Chantal Akerman's Hyperrealist Everyday* (Durham, NC: Duke University Press, 1996). On Viennese actionism, see Malcolm Green, ed., *Brus, Muehl, Nitsch, Schwarzkogler: Writings of the Vienna Actionists* (London: Atlas, 1999).

34. Kathleen McHugh, "One Cleans, the Other Doesn't," *Cultural Studies* 11, no. 1 (1997): 17–39, 35.

35. Freud's words on the mother seducer acquire new resonances once we acknowledge the possibility that the child's intimate hygiene is the purview of the mother's surrogate. The result is a new family romance: "The seducer is regularly the mother. But here, however, fantasy touches the ground of reality, for it was really the mother who, by her activities over the child's bodily hygiene inevitably stimulated, and perhaps even roused for the first time, pleasurable sensations in her genitals." Sigmund Freud, "Femininity," in *The Standard Edition of the Complete Psychological Works of Sigmund Freud*, ed. James Strachey, 24 vols. (London: Hogarth, 1956–74), 22:112–35, 120.

36. Bridget Anderson quotes a Filipina maid working in Paris: "The only thing I cannot do is go to bed with her husband. If only I can go to bed with her husband maybe she will ask me to because I am doing everything." There is a small niche of the domestic labor market for maids who are required to clean in the nude. Ads for domestic work mention work the domestic would do, like cleaning, cooking, etc., and sometimes add "no sex." Anderson, *Doing the Dirty Work?* 16. Juxtaposed with McClintock's description in "Maid to Order" of sadomasochistic reenactments of the domestic scene, this suggests the existence of a libidinal economy, a structure of desire caught up with housework.

37. As if coming to offer a comment on European cleanliness, the British short film in *Visions of Europe*, Peter Greenaway's *European Showerbath* (2004), imagines Europe as a shower. Europeans of various stripes elbow each other for a place under it. Some of them are bigger than others. As the space gets tighter, water resources scarcer, and would-be showerers more numerous, it becomes clear that some Europeans might remain dirty. Their job, it seems, will be to clean the shower.

38. Catherine Hall, "The History of the Housewife," in Malos, ed., *The Politics of Housework*, 34–58, 34.

39. Transnational marriage was the focus of Seidl's documentary *The Last Real Men* (1994).

40. Nancy Folbre, "The Invisible Heart," in *Global Dimensions of Gender and Carework*, ed. Mark Zimmerman, Jacquelyn S. Litt, and Christine E. Bose (Stanford, CA: Stanford University Press, 2006), 211–15.

41. On outsourced elder care, see Brett Neilson, "Globalization and the Politics of Aging," *CR: New Centennial Review* 3, no. 2 (2003): 161–86.

42. Rollins, *Between Women*, 183.

43. Sigmund Freud, *Civilization and Its Discontents*, trans. James Strachey (New York: Norton, 1961), 30.

44. Seidl is skeptical about digital media. Once in front of a computer in the context of the cybersex business, Olga could have used the Internet to look for a job in Austria. Instead, Seidl has her receive a letter from a friend, inviting her to come to Austria. Once there, Olga could have used the Internet to Skype with her son and mother. Instead, Seidl's film has her make furtive phone calls. Letters and phones—so-called old media—are preferred to the new so that the Internet can be framed as alienating and exploitative in the cybersex scene. At the level of the medium itself, Seidl's skepticism mirrors concerns over the transition from analog to digital media, which is thought to threaten the cinematic medium and its indexical realism, leading to worries about the death of cinema.

45. Seidl declared in an interview: "I made many journeys to Eastern Europe, and I like the mentality of the people there, their conviviality and hospitality. Also, there is much beauty and ugliness in Eastern Europe, a lot to despair about, but also a lot to love. . . . [T]here is a lot of humanity." Huber, "Ulrich Seidl's Song for Europe," 26, 28.

46. Caroline Freeman, "When Is a Wage Not a Wage?" in Malos, ed., *The Politics of Housework*, 142–48, 147.

47. Mary Romero writes: "Domestics and nannies are relegated to the more physical and taxing part of child work while employers upgrade their own status to mother-managers." I am not sure the term *mother-manager* is plastic enough to capture the labor that family work involves, *after* the middle-class mother-manager is liberated from its most arduous tasks. Today, this includes the production and cultivation of a familial public relations network, the aesthetic staging of the house to meet social and professional expectations, the production and cultivation of social, cultural, and educational relations deemed necessary to good parenting, and training that helps the mother-manager keep up and expand her affective-cognitive capital. It should be acknowledged that, while the domestic worker's labor is exhausting, the mother-manager experiences her own forms of stress, guilt, and fatigue. Mary Romero, "Unraveling Privilege: Workers' Children and the Hidden Costs of Paid Childcare," *Chicago Kent Law Review* 76, no. 3 (2001): 1651–72, 1659.

48. On this distinction, which comes from the history of slavery, see Dorothy E. Roberts, "Spiritual and Menial Housework," *Yale Journal of Law and Feminism* 9 (1997): 50–79.

49. On cinema's investment in touch, see Thomas Elsaesser and Malte Hagener, *Film Theory: An Introduction Through the Senses* (New York: Routledge, 2010), 108. Seidl's documentary *Animal Love* (1996) made the controversial point that pet love should be understood as an effect of the care deficit. His most recent film, *Paradise: Love* (2012), is an exploration of sex tourism as a branch of the global care industry.

50. Laura Steward Heon, ed., *Mona Hatoum: Domestic Disturbance* (North Adams, MA: Mass MoCA, 2001).

51. Maurizio Lazzarato, "Immaterial Labor," trans. Paul Colilli and Ed Emory, in *Radical Thought in Italy: A Potential Politics*, ed. Michael Hardt and Paolo Virno (Minneapolis: University of Minnesota Press, 1996), 133–47, 140, 136.

52. Karl Marx, "Estranged Labor," in *Economic and Philosophical Manuscripts of 1844*, ed. Dirk J. Struik, trans. Martin Milligan (New York: International, 1964), 106–19, 110.

53. Lazzarato, "Immaterial Labor," 137.

54. On the celebration of feminism as an antecedent to the autonomist debate, see Christian Marazzi, "Rules for the Incommensurable," *SubStance* 36, no. 1 (2007): 10–36. For an analysis of the feminist contribution to autonomist Marxism, see also Weeks, *The Problem with Work*; and Sianne Ngai, *Our Aesthetic Categories: Zany, Cute, Interesting* (Cambridge, MA: Harvard University Press, 2012).

55. Wendy Edmond and Suzie Fleming, "If Women Were Paid for All They Do," in Edmond and Fleming, eds., *All Work and No Pay*, 5–12, 12.

56. See Arlie Russell Hochschild, *The Managed Heart: Commercialization of Human Feeling* (Berkeley and Los Angeles: University of California Press, 1983).

57. Rollins, *Between Women*, 186.

58. Citing Gloria Steinem's *Revolution from Within: A Book of Self Esteem* (Boston: Little, Brown, 1992) and Jane Fonda's *My Life So Far* (New York: Random House, 2005), and ignoring the feminist critical literature on the affective dimensions of housework, Eva Illouz argues that feminism (understood as a family-centered form of psychologizing self-help) was an important factor in the formation of what she calls *emotional capitalism*. She writes: "The cultural persuasions of therapy, economic productivity, and feminism intertwined and enmeshed with one another and provided the rationale, the methods, and the moral impetus to extract emotions from the realm of inner life and put them at the center of selfhood and sociability in the form of a cultural model that has become widely pervasive, namely the model of communication." Eva Illouz, *Cold Intimacies: The Making of Emotional Capitalism* (Cambridge: Polity, 2007), 36. It should be clear that, instead of being conducive to emotional capitalism, the feminist housework debate was one of the first sites where its emergence was contested. Arlie Russell Hochschild's recent book, suggestively titled *The Outsourced Self: Intimate Life in Market Times* (New York: Metropolitan, 2012), continues work anchored in this tradition.

59. Franco Berardi acknowledges the geographic distribution of Fordism and post-Fordism. But he mentions it in passing; his site of focus, emphasis, and perspective is immaterial labor: "Today, what does it mean to work? As a general tendency, work is performed according to the same physical patterns: we all sit in front of a screen and move our fingers across a keyboard. We type." Franco Berardi, *The Soul at Work: From Alienation to Autonomy*, trans. Francesca Cadel and Giuseppina Mecchia (Cambridge, MA: MIT Press, 2009), 74 (quote), 85. Olga, too, works in front of a computer screen in one of her jobs, but typing is a marginal task. My interest is in reformulating an Althusserian question: What does post-Fordism look like in an international frame, when considered "from the point of view of reproduction"? See Louis Althusser, "Ideology and Ideological State Apparatuses," in *Lenin and Philosophy and Other Essays* (New York: Monthly Review Press, 2001), 85–126.

60. Dominique Laporte, *History of Shit*, trans. Nadia Benabib and Rodolphe el-Khoury (Cambridge, MA: MIT Press, 2000), 28, 31.

61. Paolo Virno, "Notes on the General Intellect," in *Marxism beyond Marxism*, ed. Saree Makdisi, Cesare Casarino, and Rebecca E. Karl (New York: Routledge, 1995), 265–72, 271.

62. Seidl was unhappy with the fact that Rak, who was chosen for the role of Olga because she did not speak German, learned the language in a very short time: "When she arrived she spoke German rather too well! I wanted her to speak the way a cleaning woman in that situation would: individual words rather than complete sentences." Catherine Wheatley, "Europa Europa," *Sight and Sound* 18, no. 10 (2008): 46–49, http://www.bfi.org.uk/news-opinion/sight-sound-magazine (accessed May 26, 2013).

63. Mattias Frey, "The Possibility of Desire in a Conformist World," in *New Austrian Film*, ed. Robert von Dassanowsky and Oliver C. Speck (New York: Berghahn, 2011), 189–98, 196.

64. The income of citizenship is one of the most influential practical ideas to have emerged from the Western Left in the last two decades. The proposal aims to sever the relation between work and income. The term *basic income*, often used as an alternative

to *income of citizenship*, obscures the fact that citizenship is a prerequisite for the proposed guaranteed income all citizens (and, in some formulations, legal residents) would receive, unconditionally, without work. Some proponents of basic income (see Hardt, "Affective Economies") simultaneously argue for global citizenship, such that the proposed income would not reproduce existing citizenship hierarchies, citizenship remaining for the most part an explicit or tacit condition for basic income. Weeks (*The Problem with Work*) does not extend her insights beyond a national (US) framework when she celebrates the promise of basic income, including its gender-neutral appeal. As we have seen in an international frame, *women* reemerges as an economic category. If, as Weeks suggests, basic income would be a way to acknowledge the reproductive work all of us do for cognitive capitalism, the fact that those who actually do some of its most arduous tasks (Olga) would be excluded from it is unacceptable.

Chapter 3

1. James Ulmer, "The Unknown Man behind 'The Unknown Woman,'" *Cinema without Borders*, January 2008, http://cinemawithoutborders.com/notebook/1447-the-unknown-man-behind-the-unknown-woman.html (accessed May 26, 2013).

2. Recent cultural anthropology has taken up the task of assessing changes in human reproduction in light of new technologies and practices (infertility treatment, surrogacy, organ or ovum donation, etc.). See esp. Faye D. Ginsburg and Rayna Rapp, eds., *Conceiving the New World Order: The Global Politics of Reproduction* (Berkeley and Los Angeles: University of California Press, 1995); Sarah Franklin and Helena Ragoné, eds., *Reproducing Reproduction: Kinship, Power, and Technological Innovation* (Philadelphia: University of Pennsylvania Press, 1998); and Carole H. Browner and Carolyn F. Sargent, eds., *Reproduction, Globalization, and the State: New Theoretical and Ethnographic Perspectives* (Durham, NC: Duke University Press, 2011).

3. Peter Andreas and Timothy Snyder, eds., *The Wall around the West: State Borders and Immigration Controls in North America and Europe* (Lanham, MD: Rowman & Littlefield, 2000).

4. See also Catherine Waldby and Melinda Cooper, "From Reproductive to Regenerative Labour: The Female Body and the Stem Cell Industries," *Feminist Theory* 11, no. 1 (2010): 3–22, 13.

5. See, most importantly, Aihwa Ong, *Neoliberalism as Exception: Mutations in Citizenship and Sovereignty* (Durham, NC: Duke University Press, 2006); and Patricia Ticineto Clough and Craig Willse, eds., *Beyond Biopolitics: Essays on the Governance of Life and Death* (Durham, NC: Duke University Press, 2011).

6. Rappoport became a transnational star after her appearance in *The Unknown Woman*. See Giovanna Faleschini Lerner, "Ksenia Rappoport and Transnational Stardom in Contemporary Cinema," *Journal of Italian Cinema and Media Studies* 1, no. 1 (2013): 7–20.

7. Tornatore quoted in Ulmer, "The Unknown Man."

8. On the politics of whiteness in this film and others, see Sandra Ponzanesi, "Europe in Motion: Migrant Cinema and the Politics of Encounter," *Social Identities* 17, no. 1 (2011): 73–92.

9. Laura Mamo, *Queering Reproduction: Achieving Pregnancy in the Age of Technoscience* (Durham, NC: Duke University Press, 2007).

10. Charles Derry, *The Suspense Thriller: Films in the Shadow of Alfred Hitchcock* (Jefferson, NC: McFarland, 1988).

11. See, e.g., Dina Francesca Haynes, "Used, Abused, Arrested and Deported: Extending Immigration Benefits to Protect the Victims of Trafficking and to Secure the Prosecution of Traffickers," *Human Rights Quarterly* 26 (2004): 221–72; and Jayashri Srikantiah, "Perfect Victims and Real Survivors: The Iconic Victim in Domestic Human Trafficking Law," *Boston University Law Review* 157 (2007): 157–211.

12. For a discussion of the rhetoric of visualization in relation to the traffic in women, see Wendy S. Hesford, "Kairos and the Geopolitical Rhetorics of Global Sex Work and Video Advocacy," in *Just Advocacy? Women's Human Rights, Transnational Feminisms, and the Politics of Representation*, ed. Wendy S. Hesford and Wendy Kozol (New Brunswick, NJ: Rutgers University Press, 2005), 146–72.

13. Giorgio Agamben, *Homo Sacer: Sovereign Power and Bare Life*, trans. Daniel Heller-Roazen (Stanford, CA: Stanford University Press, 1998).

14. The other books in the series are Giorgio Agamben, *Remnants of Auschwitz: The Witness and the Archive*, trans. Daniel Heller-Roazen (Brooklyn, NY: Zone, 2002), *The State of Exception*, trans. Kevin Attell (Chicago: University of Chicago Press, 2005), *The Kingdom and the Glory: For a Theological Genealogy of Economy and Government*, trans. Lorenzo Chiesa (Stanford, CA: Stanford University Press, 2011), and *The Sacrament of Language: An Archaeology of the Oath*, trans. Adam Kotsko (Stanford, CA: Stanford University Press, 2010).

15. Agamben, *Homo Sacer*, 4, 5.

16. Michel Foucault, *The History of Sexuality*, vol. 1, *An Introduction*, trans. Robert Hurley (New York: Vintage, 1990), 143.

17. Agamben, *Homo Sacer*, 13, 65.

18. Ibid., 66.

19. On the sacred, see Mircea Eliade, *The Sacred and the Profane: The Nature of Religion*, trans. Willard Trask (New York: Harcourt Brace Jovanovich, 1987).

20. Agamben, *Homo Sacer*, 82, 85.

21. Ibid., 121.

22. See Carl Schmitt, *The Concept of the Political*, trans. George Schwab (Chicago: University of Chicago Press, 2007).

23. Agamben, *Homo Sacer*, 27.

24. Giorgio Agamben, *Means without End: Notes on Politics*, trans. Vincenzo Binetti and Cesare Casarino (Minneapolis: University of Minnesota Press, 2000), 41, 39.

25. Agamben, *Homo Sacer*, 123.

26. For the critical debate here, exacerbated by the publication of Agamben's *Remnants of Auschwitz*, see Leland de la Durantaye, *Giorgio Agamben: A Critical Introduction* (Stanford, CA: Stanford University Press, 2009).

27. Giorgio Agamben, "We Refugees," trans. Michael Rocke, *Symposium* 49, no. 2 (1995): 114–19.

28. Agamben, *Means without End*, 40–41.

29. Agamben, *Homo Sacer*, 175.

30. Karl Marx, "Estranged Labor," in *Economic and Philosophical Manuscripts of 1844*, ed. Dirk J. Struik, trans. Martin Milligan (New York: International, 1964), 106–19, 110–11.

31. See, e.g., Siddharth Kara, *Sex Trafficking: Inside the Business of Modern Slavery* (New York: Columbia University Press, 2008).

32. Kamala Kempadoo, "Introduction: From Moral Panic to Global Justice: Changing Perspectives on Trafficking," in *Trafficking and Prostitution Reconsidered: New Perspectives*

on Migration, Sex Work, and Human Rights, ed. Kamala Kempadoo, Jyoti Sanghera, and Bandana Pattanaik (Boulder, CO: Paradigm, 2005), vii–xxxiv, xx.

33. Julia O'Connell Davidson, "Will the Real Sex Slave Please Stand Up?" *Feminist Review* 83 (2006): 4–22, 10.

34. Orlando Patterson, *Slavery and Social Death: A Comparative Study* (Cambridge, MA: Harvard University Press, 1982), xi, 13 .

35. Achille Mbembe, "Necropolitics," trans. Libby Meintjes, *Public Culture* 15, no. 1 (2003): 11–40; Ewa Płonowska Ziarek, "Bare Life on Strike: Notes on the Biopolitics of Race and Gender," *South Atlantic Quarterly* 107, no. 1 (Winter 2008): 89–105.

36. Mbembe, "Necropolitics," 21.

37. Hannah Arendt, *The Origins of Totalitarianism* (New York: Harcourt, Brace & World, 1966), 444–45.

38. Mbembe, "Necropolitics," 21.

39. Ibid., 21.

40. Michel Foucault, *"Society Must Be Defended": Lectures at the Collège de France, 1975–1976*, trans. David Macey (London: Picador, 2003), 241 (first two quotes), 243, 246 (last quote).

41. The other essay of interest here is a short fragment on pornography: Giorgio Agamben, "The Idea of Communism," in *The Idea of Prose*, trans. Michael Sullivan and Sam Whitsitt (Albany: State University of New York Press, 1995), 73–75.

42. Giorgio Agamben, *Nudities*, trans. David Kishik and Stefan Pedatella (Stanford, CA: Stanford University Press, 2010), 79.

43. Penelope Deutscher, "The Inversion of Exceptionality: Foucault, Agamben, and 'Reproductive Rights,'" *South Atlantic Quarterly*, 107, no. 1 (2008): 55–70.

44. Ruth A. Miller, *The Limits of Bodily Integrity: Abortion, Adultery, and Rape Legislation in Comparative Perspective* (Aldershot: Ashgate, 2007), 12.

45. Dana Luciano, *Arranging Grief: Sacred Time and the Body in Nineteenth-Century America* (New York: New York University Press, 2007), 9.

46. The legal traffic in women is a gendered biopolitical regime, too. Aihwa Ong writes about Indonesian maids working in neoslavery conditions in Malaysia: "During the two-year contract, the foreign maid is not permitted to have sex, or to marry a local citizen. To ensure that she will not have biological recourse to citizenship, the foreign domestic helper is tested every six months to check for HIV and pregnancy. Pregnancy results in the termination of the employment contract and expulsion from the country. . . . There is thus a total suspension of the female worker's biological rights during her overseas employment." Aihwa Ong, "A Bio-Cartography: Maids, Neoslavery, and NGOs," in *Migration and Mobilities: Citizenship, Borders, and Gender*, ed. Seyla Benhabib and Judith Resnik (New York: New York University Press, 2009), 171. See also Pheng Cheah, "Necessary Strangers: Law's Hospitality in the Age of Transnational Migrancy," in *Law and the Stranger*, ed. Austin Sarat, Lawrence Douglas, and Martha Merrill Umphrey (Stanford, CA: Stanford University Press, 2010), 21–64.

47. Mariarosa Dalla Costa and Selma James, "Women and the Subversion of the Community," in *Materialist Feminism: A Reader in Class, Difference, and Women's Lives*, ed. Rosemary Hennessy and Chrys Ingraham (New York: Routledge, 1997), 40–53, 46.

48. The literature on passing has revolved around Nella Larsen's novel *Passing* (1929), which dramatized the situation of light-skinned African American women passing for white, terrified of the possibility that their children might turn out not to be white.

49. Shellee Colen, "'Like a Mother to Them': Stratified Reproduction and West Indian

Childcare Workers and Employers in New York," in Ginsburg and Rapp, eds., *Conceiving the New World Order*, 78–102, 78.

50. Foucault, *"Society Must Be Defended,"* 249.

51. Nikolas Rose, *The Politics of Life Itself: Biomedicine, Power, and Subjectivity in the Twenty-First Century* (Princeton, NJ: Princeton University Press, 2006), 13, 15.

52. Melinda Cooper and Catherine Waldby, *Clinical Labor: Tissue Donors and Research Subjects in the Global Bioeconomy* (Durham, NC: Duke University Press, in press).

53. Ann S. Anagnost, "Strange Circulations," in Clough and Willse, eds., *Beyond Biopolitics*, 213–37.

54. Nancy Scheper-Hughes, "The Global Traffic in Human Organs," *Current Anthropology* 41, no. 2 (2000): 191–211, 194.

55. Helena Ragoné, *Surrogate Motherhood: Conception in the Heart* (Boulder, CO: Westview, 1994).

56. David L. Eng, *The Feeling of Kinship: Queer Liberalism and the Racialization of Intimacy* (Durham, NC: Duke University Press, 2010).

57. The literature on transnational adoption is extensive. See, e.g., Sara K. Dorow, *Transnational Adoption: A Cultural Economy of Race, Gender and Kinship* (New York: New York University Press, 2006); Diana Marre and Laura Briggs, eds., *International Adoption: Global Inequalities and the Circulation of Children* (New York: New York University Press, 2009); and Michele Bratcher Goodwin, ed., *Baby Markets: Money and the New Politics of Creating Families* (Cambridge: Cambridge University Press, 2010).

58. Eng, *The Feeling of Kinship*, 105.

59. Amrita Pande, "Commercial Surrogacy in India: Manufacturing a Perfect Mother-Worker," *Signs: Journal of Women in Culture and Society* 35, no. 4 (2010): 969–92.

60. Amrita Pande, "'It May Be Her Eggs but It's My Blood': Surrogates and Everyday Forms of Kinship in India," *Qualitative Sociology* 32, no. 4 (2009): 379–97.

61. At the end of Rebecca Haimowitz and Vaishali Sinha's *Made in India* (2010), a documentary about the global surrogacy industry, the Indian American businessman who mediates a surrogacy transaction announces that the market for surrogacy is expanding into Ukraine and Lithuania.

62. Shulamith Firestone, *The Dialectic of Sex: The Case for Feminist Revolution* (New York: Bantam, 1970), 238.

63. Sarah Franklin, "Postmodern Procreation: A Cultural Account of Assisted Reproduction," in Ginsburg and Rapp, eds., *Conceiving the New World Order*, 323–45, 325.

64. For a review of the extensive and complex feminist debate surrounding Firestone's fantasy (which itself has a convoluted literary history that can be traced back to Charlotte Perkins Gilman's *Herland* [1915]), see Mandy Merck and Stella Sandford, eds., *Further Adventures of* The Dialectic of Sex: *Critical Essays on Shulamith Firestone* (New York: Palgrave, 2010).

65. Judith Butler, "Reply from Judith Butler to Mills and Jenkins," *differences: A Journal of Feminist Cultural Studies* 18, no. 2 (2007): 180–95, 186.

66. See Ziarek, "Bare Life on Strike."

67. The cinematic archive offers a number of other forms of resistance. The female character in Stephen Frears's *Dirty Pretty Things* (2002), a Turkish asylum seeker in London, who is forced to perform fellatio on the sweatshop owner who threatens to report her to immigration, bites his penis. It is an act borrowed from the tradition of slavery, in line with the secret at the heart of Gayl Jones's neoslavery novel *Corregidora* (1975). In both Moodysson's *Lilja 4-Ever* (2000) and the Dardenne brothers' *Lorna's Silence* (2008),

we are faced with the most extreme act: an actual or symbolic suicide, which renders the trafficking machine inoperative.

68. Patterson, *Slavery and Social Death*, 6.

69. Tornatore quoted in Ulmer, "The Unknown Man."

70. On the heterogeneity of violence, see Étienne Balibar, "Violence and Civility: On the Limits of Political Anthropology," *differences: A Journal of Feminist Cultural Studies* 20, nos. 2–3 (2009): 9–35.

71. The relation between the national and the global has been theorized most productively in relation to the concept of security. See, e.g., Claudia Aradau, "Securing Life: Human Trafficking, Biopolitics, and the Sovereign Pardon," in *Accumulating Insecurity: Violence and Dispossession in the Making of Everyday Life*, ed. Shelley Feldman, Charles Geisler, and Gayatri A. Menon (Athens: University of Georgia Press, 2011), 166–84.

72. On the corporatization of border control, see Ginette Verstraete, "Technological Frontiers and the Politics of Mobility in the European Union," in *Uprootings/Regroundings: Questions of Home and Migration*, ed. Sara Ahmed, Claudia Castañeda, Anne-Marie Fortier, and Mimi Sheller (Oxford: Berg, 2003), 225–49, 241. On the corporatization of the refugee camp, see Nina Bernstein, "Companies Use Immigration Crackdown to Turn a Profit," *New York Times*, September 28, 2011.

73. On NGOs, see Jean Comaroff and John Comaroff, eds., *Law and Disorder in the Postcolony* (Chicago: University of Chicago Press, 2006).

74. On this notion of biopolitics, see Roberto Esposito, *Bios: Biopolitics and Philosophy*, trans. Timothy Campbell (Minneapolis: University of Minnesota Press, 2008). One of the examples of an affirmative notion of life that Esposito offers is that of the love of a mother for a child born out of ethnic rape.

75. Anne McClintock, "Sex Workers and Sex Work: Introduction," *Social Text* 11, no. 4 (1993): 1–10; Kempadoo, "From Moral Panic to Global Justice."

76. Hesford, "Kairos," 148.

77. Martin Rubin writes: "Thrillers characteristically feature a remarkable degree of passivity on the part of the heroes with whom we as spectators identify. These heroes are often acted upon more than they act; they are swept up in a rush of events over which they have little control." Marin Rubin, *Thrillers* (Cambridge: Cambridge University Press, 1999), 7.

78. Agamben, *Homo Sacer*, 115.

Chapter 4

1. EU jargon often retools political concepts for narrow bureaucratic ends. The EU slogan "an area of freedom, security and justice" translates as follows: "Freedom refers to free movement across internal borders; security, to protection against cross-border crime; and justice, mainly to judicial cooperation in civil as well as criminal matters." John Pinder and Simon Usherwood, *The European Union: A Very Short Introduction* (Oxford: Oxford University Press, 2007), 107.

2. Rey Chow, "The Politics of Admittance: Female Sexual Agency, Miscegenation, and the Formation of Community in Franz Fanon," in *Franz Fanon: Critical Perspectives*, ed. Anthony C. Alessandrini (London: Routledge, 1999), 35–56.

3. Jane Caplan and John Torpey, introduction to *Documenting Individual Identity: The Development of State Practices in the Modern World*, ed. Jane Caplan and John Torpey (Princeton, NJ: Princeton University Press, 2001), 1–12, 2.

4. John Torpey, *The Invention of the Passport: Surveillance, Citizenship and the State* (Cambridge: Cambridge University Press, 1999), 4.

5. Valentin Groebner, "Describing the Person, Reading the Signs in Late Medieval and Renaissance Europe: Identity Papers, Vested Figures, and the Limits of Identification, 1400–1600," in Caplan and Torpey, eds., *Documenting Individual Identity*, 15–27, 19.

6. Caren Kaplan, *Questions of Travel: Postmodern Discourses of Displacement* (Durham, NC: Duke University Press, 1996), 52.

7. Leo Lucassen writes: "Some categories of aliens suffered discrimination, such as the Chinese in the United States and the Poles in Germany, while traveling groups (often indiscriminately referred to a 'gypsies') and the migrant poor in general were regarded with suspicion, increasingly hindered in their movements, and often expelled." Leo Lucassen, "A Many-Headed Monster: The Evolution of the Passport System in the Netherlands and Germany in the Long Nineteenth Century," in Caplan and Torpey, eds., *Documenting Individual Identity*, 235–55, 236.

8. Paul Fussell, *Abroad: British Literary Traveling between the Wars* (Oxford: Oxford University Press, 1980). Kaplan reads Fussell's study critically to show that it reproduces a modernist ideology of experimental exile for which ultimately "the only passport needed to cross the border into the *Weltgeist* is an ability to make the 'distinctive aesthetic voyage.'" Kaplan, *Questions of Travel*, 30.

9. John Torpey, "The Great War and the Birth of the Modern Passport System," in Caplan and Torpey, eds., *Documenting Individual Identity*, 256–70, 257.

10. *Invisible State* is the title of Aisling Walsh's contribution to *Visions of Europe* (2004), a project that commissioned a short from one filmmaker in each EU country.

11. Lucassen, "A Many-Headed Monster," 236.

12. Caplan and Torpey, introduction to *Documenting Individual Identity*, 8.

13. Giorgio Agamben, "Bodies without Words: Against the Biopolitical Tatoo," *German Law Journal* 5, no. 5 (2004): 168–69, 169.

14. Pal Ahluwalia describes his experience as a Kenya-born Indian switching from a Kenyan passport to a Canadian one: "I remember traveling to the UK and France with my parents a couple of years later and realizing that as a Kenyan citizen my passport was a barrier to the places to which I could not travel without a plethora of visas and questions about my intent. It seemed that everyone was worried that I was a threat, that I would overstay my welcome. . . . Having a Canadian passport meant that I was no longer forced to obtain visas in most of the Western world, but at every border I was constantly reminded that I was not a 'normal' Canadian. Wherever I traveled, immigration officials were, and are, particularly keen to examine closely my passport—fearing, I suspect, that it may be forged." Pal Ahluwalia, "Death and Politics: Empire and the 'New' Politics of Resistance," in *The Postcolonial and the Global*, ed. Revathi Krishnaswamy and John C. Hawley (Minneapolis: University of Minnesota Press, 2008), 166–77, 167.

15. Lucassen, "A Many-Headed Monster," 243.

16. On the expulsion of the poor as one precursor to contemporary deportation, see William Walters, "Deportation, Expulsion, and the International Police of Aliens," in *The Deportation Regime: Sovereignty, Space, and the Freedom of Movement*, ed. Nicholas de Genova and Nathalie Peutz (Durham, NC: Duke University Press, 2010), 69–100.

17. Saskia Witteborn, "Constructing the Forced Migrant and the Politics of Space and Place-Making," *Journal of Communication* 61 (2011): 1142–60, 1142.

18. Benedict Anderson, "Exodus," *Critical Inquiry* 20, no. 2 (1994): 314–27, 323–24.

19. Umberto Eco, "An Uncertain Europe between Rebirth and Decline," in *Old*

Europe, New Europe, Core Europe: Transatlantic Relations After the Iraq War, ed. Daniel Levy, Max Pensky, and John Torpey (London: Verso, 2005), 14–20, 20.

20. Charles Piot has offered a thick description of visa lottery practices, including ensuing kinship alliances, in Togo, a study that bears comparison with some East/West European realities. See Charles Piot, *Nostalgia for the Future: West Africa after the Cold War* (Chicago: University of Chicago Press, 2010).

21. *EU Green Card Lottery* can be found at http://www.green-card-lottery-eu.org (accessed May 26, 2013).

22. The counterpoint to this is a "purloined letter" scenario whereby one not only does not hide one's passport but also stores it, ostentatiously, in plain sight. This is the spirit of a number of highly expensive passport wallets and similar storage devices that function as fashion statements.

23. See, e.g., Sean O'Hagan, "Moody by Name," *The Observer*, April 12, 2003.

24. Sophia Tabatadze made a short titled *Self Interview as Eastern and Western Europe* (2004) in which she challenged the deployment of gray in representations of East European architecture and East Europe more generally.

25. Andrei's monologue capitalizes on, in Bruce Robbins's words, "what every young protagonist of upward mobility feels: life at home is unlivable." Robbins continues: "The risk that this geopolitical version of initial deprivation will turn into gross, uncritical flattery of the society of destination is of course always high." Bruce Robbins, *Upward Mobility and the Common Good: Toward a Literary History of the Welfare State* (Princeton, NJ. Princeton University Press, 2009), 238.

26. On the relation between coerced sex trafficking and migration see Rutvica Andrijašević, "Problematising Trafficking for the Sex Sector: A Case of Eastern European Women in the EU," in *Women and Immigration Law: New Variations on Classical Feminist Themes*, ed. Sarah van Walsum and Thomas Spijkerboer (Oxford: Routledge-Cavendish, 2007), 86–105.

27. Another film that asks this question is Florin Şerban's *If I Want to Whistle, I Whistle* (2010).

28. *Lilja 4-Ever* assumes a silent intertextuality with a number of romantic comedies that find narrative resolution to what Debra Ann Castillo, writing about Latin American cinema, calls *American (visa) dreams*. Such dreams, whether American or European, often find narrative resolution in transnational coupling. See Debra Ann Castillo, "American (Visa) Dreams," *Pterodáctilo* 8 (2010), http://pterodactilo.com/numero8/?p=1555 (accessed May 26, 2013).

29. One of the most influential definitions of the border comes from Étienne Balibar: "[The border] mainly works as an instrument of security control, social segregation, and unequal access to the means of existence, and sometimes as an institutional distribution of survival and death: it becomes a cornerstone of institutional violence." Étienne Balibar, *We, the People of Europe? Reflections on Transnational Citizenship*, trans. James Swenson (Princeton, NJ: Princeton University Press, 2004), 117.

30. This is a concern expressed in Judith Butler, *Precarious Life: The Powers of Mourning and Violence* (London: Verso, 2006).

31. The history of the word *passport* includes its use in the Christian Orthodox tradition to mean "a ticket to the beyond."

32. Lauren Berlant, "Nearly Utopian, Nearly Normal: Post-Fordist Affect in *La Promesse* and *Rosetta*," *Public Culture* 19, no. 2 (2007): 273–301, 282.

33. Lauren Berlant, *Cruel Optimism* (Durham, NC: Duke University Press, 2011), 172.

34. Saskia Sassen is voicing, very carefully, a similar temptation when she writes: "I see an epochal shift that is producing structural approximations in the position of, on one hand, minority immigrants, both legal and irregular, and on the other, a growing share of citizens, not only the minoritized but also the sons and daughters of once robust middle classes who are rapidly losing economic ground. . . . Yes, there are sharp differentiations in life chances and privileges among these diverse groups, but most of them are facing variable degrees of impoverishment and loss of entitlements. This structural approximation coexists with heightened nationalisms and virulent anti-immigration sentiment." Saskia Sassen, "Borders, Walls, and Crumbling Sovereignty," *Political Theory* 40, no. 1 (2012): 116–22, 121. While I agree that borders lose some of their weight in an age of waning state sovereignty, leading to the cohabitation of various disenfranchised groups, I believe that a focus on state-issued passports yields a heightened sense of skepticism vis-à-vis the "structural approximation" of impoverishment that Sassen invokes.

35. Bert Cardullo, "The Cinema of Resistance: An Interview with Jean-Pierre and Luc Dardenne," *Studies in European Cinema* 7, no. 3 (2010): 177–92, 189.

36. On the difficulty of distinguishing between interested and authentic love, see Denise Brennan, "Love Work in a Tourist Town: Dominican Sex Workers and Resort Workers Perform at Love," in *Love and Globalization: Transformations of Intimacy in the Contemporary World*, ed. Mark B. Padilla, Jennifer S. Hirsch, Miguel Muñoz-Laboy, Robert E. Sember, and Richard G. Parker (Nashville: Vanderbilt University Press, 2007), 203–25, 206.

37. David L. Eng, *The Feeling of Kinship: Queer Liberalism and the Racialization of Intimacy* (Durham, NC: Duke University Press, 2010), 6.

38. Caroline H. Bledsoe and Papa Sow, "Family Reunification Ideals and the Practice of Transnational Reproductive Life among Africans in Europe," in *Reproduction, Globalization, and the State: New Theoretical and Ethnographic Perspectives*, ed. Carole H. Browner and Carolyn F. Sargent (Durham, NC: Duke University Press, 2011), 175–91, 182–83.

39. Robbins, *Upward Mobility and the Common Good*, xv.

40. Ibid., 4.

41. Jean-Pierre Dardenne declared in an interview: "As in all our work, we tend to augment the physical aspects, to add gestures when we shoot and reduce dialogue. And the actors bring something of themselves to it; the shoot is organic and changes with the circumstances." Cardullo, "The Cinema of Resistance," 189.

42. Joseph Mai, *Jean-Pierre and Luc Dardenne* (Urbana: University of Illinois Press, 2010), 53.

43. Ostojić describes the project: "In August 2000 I started the 'Looking for a Husband with EU Passport' project. I exchanged over 500 letters with numerous applicants from around the world. After a correspondence of six months with a German man Klemens G. I arranged our first meeting as a public performance in the field in front of the Museum of Contemporary Art in Belgrade, 2001. One month later we officially married in New Belgrade. With the international marriage certificate and other required documents I applied for a visa. . . . In spring 2005 my three-year permit expired, and instead of granting me a permanent residence permit, the authorities granted me only a two-year visa. . . . K. G. and I got divorced, and on the occasion of my 'Integration Project Office' installation opening in Gallery 35 in Berlin (July 1, 2005), I organized the 'Divorce Party.'" See http://www.brooklynmuseum.org/eascfa/feminist_art_base/gallery/tanja_ostojic.php?i=1360 (accessed May 26, 2013). See also Éric Fassin and Judith

Surkis, "Introduction: Transgressing Boundaries," *Public Culture* 22, no. 3 (2010): 487–505, 502.

44. Another artwork in this virtual exhibition would be Ghazel's *Wanted (Urgent)*, a marriage ad that the Iranian-born artist issued when she was asked to leave France. Ghazel's ad includes a black-and-white bust photograph of herself as well as the following text: "URGENT, Woman, 30, artist of Middle Eastern origin and WP (without permit) seeks a husband, from EU, preferably France, contact email. . . ." http://artefact.mi2.hr/_a01/lang_en/art_ghazel_en.htm (accessed May 26, 2013).

45. *Lorna's Silence* offers a helpful corrective to Torpey's statement: "Still, if passports were intended purely for purposes of state control, they would hardly command such a high price on many of the world's black markets." Torpey, *The Invention of the Passport*, 164. What Lorna and Sokol want is access to the privileges and constraints of EU citizenship; paradoxically, their problem, as Hannah Arendt puts it, is "not that they are oppressed but that nobody wants even to oppress them." Hannah Arendt, *The Origins of Totalitarianism* (New York: Harcourt, 1973), 295–96. Berlant argues in a similar vein that being controlled by the Belgian state is the object of utopia in the Dardennes' films. See Berlant, "Nearly Utopian, Nearly Normal."

46. Dina Iordanova draws attention to the fact that it is often not clear why one would agree to the surrender of one's ID or passport: "The other visual trope—surrendering one's passport on arrival in the foreign country (seen in *Balalayka, Lilja 4-Ever, Sex Traffic, Fuse*, and elsewhere)—appears as a consensual move." Dina Iordanova, "Making Traffic Visible, Adjusting the Narrative," in *Moving People, Moving Images: Cinema and Trafficking in the New Europe*, ed. William Brown, Dina Iordanova, and Leshu Torchin (St. Andrews: St. Andrews Film Studies, 2010), 84–117. *Lorna's Silence* helps answer this dilemma: in most cases, one is already effectively not the owner of an ID or a passport that bears one's (real or false) name.

47. On carnality, see Vivian Sobchack, *Carnal Thoughts: Embodiment and Moving Image Culture* (Berkeley and Los Angeles: University of California Press, 2004).

48. Berlant, "Nearly Utopian, Nearly Normal," 274.

49. Ibid., 291. Berlant revised this formulation, too, to say that "mobility is a dream and a nightmare." Berlant, *Cruel Optimism*, 179.

50. Zygmunt Bauman, *Globalization: The Human Consequences* (New York: Columbia University Press, 1998), 78.

51. The entire quote reads: "Residency papers for everyone means in the first place that all should have the full rights of citizenship in the country where they live and work. This is not a utopian or unrealistic political demand. The demand is simply that the juridical status of the population be reformed in step with the real economic transformations in recent years. . . . If in a first moment the multitude demands that each state recognize juridically the migrations that are necessary to capital, in a second moment it must demand control over the movements themselves. The multitude must be able to decide if, when, and where it moves. It must also have the right to stay still and enjoy one place rather than being forced constantly to be on the move. *The general right to control its own movement is the multitude's ultimate demand for global citizenship.*" Michael Hardt and Antonio Negri, *Empire* (Cambridge, MA: Harvard University Press, 2000), 400.

52. Chandra Mohanty calls for feminist transnational solidarity while acknowledging the structural limit performed by various borders. The risk inherent in the celebratory dimension of feminism without borders is that the figure of the feminist is imagined as

a cosmopolitan traveler. See Chandra Talpade Mohanty, *Feminism without Borders: Decolonizing Theory, Practicing Solidarity* (Durham, NC: Duke University Press, 2003).

53. Seyla Benhabib, *Another Cosmopolitanism* (Oxford: Oxford University Press, 2006), 175–76.

Chapter 5

1. Elizabeth Cowie, "Woman as Sign" (1978), in *The Woman in Question*, ed. Parveen Adams and Elizabeth Cowie (Cambridge, MA: MIT Press, 1990), 117–33, 121 (emphasis added).

2. On the coexistence of realism and modernism in contemporary art cinema, see Rosalind Galt and Karl Schoonover, eds., *Global Art Cinema: New Theories and Histories* (Oxford: Oxford University Press, 2010). On the threshold between wakefulness and sleep, see Mladen Dolar, "The Burrow of Sound," *differences: A Journal of Feminist Cultural Studies* 22, nos. 2–3 (2011): 112–39.

3. David Fleming, "Das Fräulein," *Cineaste* 32, no. 3 (2007): 64.

4. On the cinematic strategy of choosing to critically accentuate stereotypes, see Hamid Naficy, *An Accented Cinema: Exilic and Diasporic Filmmaking* (Princeton, NJ: Princeton University Press, 2001), 284.

5. The irony is that, in the wake of the collapse of the Cold War and its polar distinctions between gray and colorful, instead of the world having taken on the colorful tints claimed by the victors, it seems to have turned gray instead, with postindustrial, wasteland architecture (postsocialist indistinguishable from post-Fordist) as its signpost. In *Das Fräulein*, color returns to Ruža's life through revived memories of East Europe.

6. For a distinction between exilic and diasporic cinema, see Naficy, *An Accented Cinema*.

7. The counterpoint to Štaka's take on the Yugoslav diaspora is offered by Jasmin Dizdar's film *Beautiful People* (1999), which has a Croat and a Serb who run into each other in a London bus chase each other for the rest of the film. By the end, they seem to have given up the project of killing each other, but one can hardly imagine the two contemplating their common diasporic prospects.

8. Hannah Arendt, "We Refugees," in *Hitler's Exiles: Personal Stories of the Flight from Nazi Germany to America*, ed. Mark M. Anderson (New York: New Press, 1998), 253–62, 253–254.

9. On *Former West*, see n. 12 of the introduction.

10. Émile Benveniste, "Gift and Exchange in the Indo-European Vocabulary," in *The Logic of the Gift: Toward an Ethic of Generosity*, ed. Alan D. Schrift (New York: Routledge, 1997), 33–44, 38. Julian Pitt-Rivers draws attention to the specific kind of reciprocity involved in hospitality: "Host and guest can at no point *within the context of a single occasion* be allowed to be equal, since equality invites rivalry. Therefore their reciprocity resides, not in identity, but in an alternation of roles. . . . The reciprocity between host and guest is thus transposed to a temporal sequence and a spatial alternation in which the roles are reversed." Julian Pitt-Rivers, "The Stranger, the Guest and the Hostile Host: Introduction to the Study of the Laws of Hospitality," in *Contributions to Mediterranean Sociology: Mediterranean Rural Communities and Social Change*, ed. J.-G. Péristiany (Paris: Mouton, 1968), 13–30, 21, 27

11. See, e.g., Didier Fassin, Alain Morice, and Catherine Quiminal, eds., *Les lois de l'inhospitalité: Les politiques de l'immigration à l'épreuve des sans-papiers* (Paris: La Découverte, 1997); and Mireille Rosello, *Postcolonial Hospitality: The Immigrant as Guest*

(Stanford, CA: Stanford University Press, 2001). On the religious element in hospitality, see Tracy McNulty, *The Hostess: Hospitality, Femininity, and the Expropriation of Identity* (Minneapolis: University of Minnesota Press, 2007).

12. On the patron-host, see Pitt-Rivers, "The Stranger, the Guest and the Hostile Host."

13. J. Hillis Miller traces the history of the word *parasite* (beside the grain) from "something positive, a fellow guest, someone sharing the food with you, there with you beside the grain," to "a professional dinner guest, someone expert in cadging invitations without ever giving dinners in return," to "a person who habitually takes advantage of the generosity of others without making any useful return." J. Hillis Miller, "The Critic as Host," in *Deconstruction and Criticism*, by Harold Bloom, Paul de Man, Jacques Derrida, Geoffrey Hartman, and J. Hillis Miller (New York: Continuum, 1979), 217–53, 220. See also Michel Serres, *The Parasite*, trans. Lawrence R. Schehr (Baltimore: Johns Hopkins University Press, 1982).

14. Jacques Derrida, *On Cosmopolitanism and Forgiveness*, trans. Mark Dooley and Michael Hughes (London: Routledge, 2001), 16–17.

15. Immanuel Kant, *Perpetual Peace and Other Essays*, trans. Ted Humphrey (Indianapolis: Hackett, 1983), 118.

16. Miller, "The Critic as Host," 220–21.

17. It is helpful to remember here one of the most famous scenes of hospitality. Howard Zinn writes: "When Columbus and his sailors came ashore, carrying swords, speaking oddly, the Arawaks ran to greet them, brought them food, water, gifts. He later wrote of this in his log: '. . . They willingly traded everything they owned . . . They would make fine servants . . . With fifty men we could subjugate them all and make them do whatever we want.'" Howard Zinn, *A People's History of the United States: 1492–Present* (New York: Harper, 2001), 1.

18. Pitt-Rivers contends that the hostility of the guest is "socialized" through hospitality as a way of keeping it "in abeyance." Pitt-Rivers, "The Stranger, the Guest and the Hostile Host," 20, 25.

19. Miller, "The Critic as Host," 221.

20. How radical can the otherness of the guest be? Judith Still quotes Jacques Derrida, "Hostipitality," *Angelaki: Journal of the Theoretical Humanities* 5, no. 3 (2000): 3–18: "Is hospitality reserved, confined to man, to the universal brother? . . . Hospitality, therefore—if there is any—must, would have to, open itself to an other that is not mine, my hôte, my other, not even my neighbor or my brother, perhaps an 'animal.'" Judith Still, *Derrida and Hospitality: Theory and Practice* (Edinburgh: Edinburgh University Press, 2010), 229.

21. On calculation, see Pheng Cheah, "Necessary Strangers: Law's Hospitality in the Age of Transnational Migrancy," in *Law and the Stranger*, ed. Austin Sarat, Lawrence Douglas, and Martha Merrill Umphrey (Stanford, CA: Stanford University Press, 2010), 21–64.

22. On this architectural conundrum, see Marcus Waithe, *William Morris's Utopia of Strangers: Victorian Medievalism and the Ideal of Hospitality* (Cambridge: D. S. Brewer, 2006).

23. Jacques Derrida, "Quand j'ai entendu l'expression 'délit d'hospitalité' . . . ," *Plein droit* 34 (April 1997): 3–8.

24. Still, *Derrida and Hospitality*, 29. This elsewhere of hospitality is both space and time determined. Not only other places but also other (earlier) times are invoked as

sites of abundant hospitality. The Victorians famously idealized medieval forms of hospitality. See Waithe, *William Morris's Utopia of Strangers*.

25. Tahar Ben Jelloun, *French Hospitality*, trans. Barbara Bray (New York: Columbia University Press, 1999).

26. Benveniste, "Gift and Exchange in the Indo-European Vocabulary," 39, 40–41.

27. Pitt-Rivers maintains that the hospitality relation translates into "kinsmen or blood-brothers." Pitt-Rivers, "The Stranger, the Guest and the Hostile Host," 26.

28. Jacques Derrida, "Step of Hospitality/No Hospitality," in *Of Hospitality: Anne Dufourmantelle Invites Jacques Derrida to Respond*, trans. Rachel Bowlby (Stanford, CA: Stanford University Press, 2000), 75–156, 155.

29. Felicity Heal draws attention to the historical conflation of *keeping house* and *keeping hospitality*. Felicity Heal, *Hospitality in Early Modern England* (Oxford: Oxford University Press, 1990), 6. It is on account of the labor extracted from the women of the house in the service of hospitality that the housewife is often figured as inhospitable, "not wanting dirt to be brought into her nice, clean house," as Still puts it. Still, *Derrida and Hospitality*, 195.

30. We need to unpack the class-determined, often racialized plural *women of the house*. Think, e.g., of the famous dinner scene in Virginia Woolf's *To the Lighthouse* that has Mrs. Ramsey triumph as a hostess and an expert in the art of commensality, a triumph the reader is eager to celebrate, forgetting the labor of invisible female servants that compensates for Mrs. Ramsey's emancipation from the physical labors of hospitality. In the world of contemporary migration, female guests are often put to work in the kitchen and the laundry room—in private households and in the hospitality industry.

31. Derrida declared in an interview: "It is always in the name of pure and hyperbolic hospitality that it is necessary, in order to render it as effective as possible, to invent the best arrangements [*dispositions*], the least bad conditions, the most just legislation. This is necessary to avoid the perverse effects of an unlimited hospitality whose risks I tried to define." Jacques Derrida, "The Principle of Hospitality," *parallax* 11, no. 1 (2005): 6–9, 6.

32. Maurice Blanchot, "The Main Impropriety," *Yale French Studies* 39, "Literature and Revolution" (1967): 50–63.

33. Drawing on Émile Benveniste's work on the Indo-European roots of hospitality, McNulty writes: "The one who offers hospitality must be the master *chez lui*; the 'I am in my place' [*je suis chez moi*] is part of the condition of offering. But as this etymology makes clear, this 'place' or *chez soi* is not just a dwelling place—the house in which the master makes the law—but the fact of residing within an identity, the *chez soi* of ipseity in which the master gathers together and disposes of what is proper to him. The master who is eminently himself offers hospitality from the place where he is 'at home,' from a position of ipseity as self-identity." McNulty, *The Hostess*, x.

34. Pierre Klossowski, *Roberte ce soir* and *The Revocation of the Edict of Nantes*, trans. Austryn Wainhouse (Chicago: Dalkey Archive, 2002), 115, 12, 9, 13.

35. Ibid., 11.

36. Studying an actual photograph of one such surprise, Octave sees something the human eye misses at the moment of opening the door. This is where photography—and cinema—come in to supplement the human eye. Photography, however, also renders this scene ever more complex. First, it is not clear whether Roberte poses and thus manufactures her surprise for the camera that she knows to be present. Second, Octave is not a realist photographer as he is known for "making his prints according to his whims." Ibid., 43.

37. Pitt-Rivers complicates this view: "To attempt to sleep with the host's wife or

to refuse to do so may either of them be infractions of a code of hospitality, the host's will, like the precedence which he cedes. His wife's favors are always his to dispose of as he wishes. To demand or take what is not offered is always an usurpation of the role of host." Pitt-Rivers, "The Stranger, the Guest and the Hostile Host," 28.

38. Klossowski, *Roberte ce soir*, 16, 12.

39. Ibid., 14, 12.

40. McNulty, *The Hostess*, 135.

41. Gayle Rubin, "The Traffic in Women: Notes on the 'Political Economy' of Sex," in *Toward an Anthropology of Women*, ed. Rayna R. Reiter (New York: Monthly Review Press, 1975), 157–210, 180, 183, 179.

42. Monique Wittig, *The Straight Mind and Other Essays* (Boston: Beacon, 1992), xiii.

43. Ibid., xv, 32.

44. Teresa de Lauretis, "When Lesbians Were Not Women," in *On Monique Wittig: Theoretical, Political, and Literary Essays*, ed. Namascar Shaktini (Urbana: University of Illinois Press, 2005), 54–55.

45. Monique Wittig, *The Lesbian Body*, trans. David Le Vay (London: Peter Owen, 1975).

46. Asked about the lesbian relationship in an interview, Akin responded: "Why two women? Because everything else felt like a cliché. A young, dark-haired Turk comes to Hamburg, where he falls in love with an innocent blonde? No, that's too much like King Kong and the white woman. The story only became sexy once two women were involved." "Interview with Director Fatih Akin: From Istanbul to New York," *Spiegel Online*, September 28, 2007, http://www.spiegel.de/international/zeitgeist/0,1518,508521,00.html (accessed May 26, 2013).

47. For a review of this tension, see Astrid Henry, *Not My Mother's Sister: Generational Conflict and Third-Wave Feminism* (Bloomington: Indiana University Press, 2004).

48. Lee Edelman, *No Future: Queer Theory and the Death Drive* (Durham, NC: Duke University Press, 2004).

49. Shulamith Firestone, *The Dialectic of Sex: The Case for Feminist Revolution* (New York: Bantam, 1970), 239.

50. Alexandra Kollontai, *Selected Writings of Alexandra Kollontai*, trans. Alix Holt (London: Allison & Busby, 1977), 263.

51. A film that frames Switzerland's European vocation in relation to the debate on immigration is Xavier Koller's *Journey of Hope* (1990). See Yosefa Loshitzky, "Journeys of Hope to Fortress Europe," *Third Text* 20, no. 6 (2006): 745–54.

52. Jacques Derrida, "Foreigner Question," in *Of Hospitality*, 3–74, 73.

53. Kollontai, *Selected Writings*, 291.

54. McNulty, *The Hostess*, 100.

55. This is a variation on Barbara Ehrenreich and Arlie Russell Hochschild's statement: "To an extent then, the globalization of child care and housework brings the ambitious and independent women of the world together: the career-oriented upper-middle-class woman of an affluent nation and the striving woman from a crumbling Third World or postcommunist economy. Only it does not bring them together in the way that second-wave feminists in affluent countries once liked to imagine—as sisters and allies struggling to achieve common goals. Instead, they come together as mistress and maid, employer and employee, across a great divide of privilege and opportunity." Barbara Ehrenreich and Arlie Russell Hochschild, introduction to *Global Woman: Nannies, Maids, and Sex Workers in the New Economy*, ed. Barbara Ehrenreich and Arlie Russell Hochschild (New York: Metropolitan, 2002), 1–14, 11.

56. This notion of sacrifice needs to be rigorously distinguished from nineteenth-century accounts of generous, self-sacrificing women. See Anca Parvulescu, "To Die Laughing and to Laugh at Dying: Revisiting *The Awakening*," *New Literary History* 36, no. 3 (2005): 477–95. In this scenario, it is important to repeat, Ana does not necessarily have to die. Her motto very much remains "I am alive!"

57. The phrase was coined by Lenin in 1922 and subsequently took a life of its own to refer to film as a politicized art form. See Mira Liehm and Antonín J. Liehm, *The Most Important Art: Eastern European Film After 1945* (Berkeley and Los Angeles: University of California Press, 1977).

Index